SPECIAL FORCES
AT WAR

AN ILLUSTRATED HISTORY, SOUTHEAST ASIA 1957-1975

BY SHELBY L. STANTON

WITH A FOREWORD BY MAJOR GENERAL MICHAEL D.F. HEALY, U.S. ARMY (RET.)

HOWELL PRESS

Above: A Special Forces trooper shouts the orders to charge during an all-out counterattack to regain one of Camp Ha Thanh's hilltop outposts that was overrun by North Vietnamese infantrymen on August 23, 1968. *(AP via Robert Olds)* **Page 2**: Special Forces leaders of the 2d Battalion, 3d Mobile Strike Force Command, pause during Operation Bull Run II in the Apache area of operations of War Zone D near Rang Rang. They are Sgt. Robert Anderson, Sgt. First Class Ernest Fant, Staff Sgt. Steven Francis, Capt. James P. Grey, Master Sgt. John Heilman, Sgt. First Class Joseph McCloskey, and Sgt. First Class Pablo Olivarez. This small band of courageous Special Forces troopers typified the elite teams that led hundreds of native irregulars against secret enemy base areas throughout the Vietnam conflict. *(Lee Mize)* **Pages 4-5**: The western Special Forces surveillance outpost of A Shau was situated along the border of northern South Vietnam and Laos. Camp A Shau typified the early style of mountain fort construction that occurred before the introduction of military engineer battalions, heavy earth-moving equipment, and pre-fabricated metal components. The solid structure of this strongly fortified camp was built using materials indigenous to the local area and manual labor provided by the garrison personnel. *(DOD)* **Pages 6-7**: Special Forces border-raiding patrol members, led by Sgt. First Class Howard Stevens, demonstrate the unconventional warfare style of living off the land. They dine on fish seized from a Viet Cong infiltration base in the western Central Highlands during 1963. *(Howard Stevens)* **Page 10**: Col. George C. Morton. *(Author's Collection)*

Designed by Marilyn F. Appleby.
Edited by Kathleen D. Valenzi.
Design and editorial assistance provided by Christopher D. Daly and Karina Ivanetich.
Copyright © 1990 Shelby L. Stanton. All rights reserved.

All material appearing in this book with wartime restriction stampings has been declassified in accordance with routine Group 4 twelve-year declassification schedules, or cleared by the Department of Defense for open publication.

The author and publisher have made a thorough effort to locate all persons having any rights or interests in the material presented in this book and to secure all necessary reprint permissions. If any required acknowledgments have been omitted inadvertently or any rights overlooked, we regret the error and will correct the oversight in future editions of the book.

Library of Congress Catalog Card Number 90-81633
ISBN 0-943231-28-0

Printed and bound in Japan by Dai Nippon.
Published by Howell Press, Inc., 700 Harris Street, Suite B, Charlottesville, Virginia 22901. Telephone (804) 977-4006.

First printing.

HOWELL PRESS

CONTENTS

Dedicated to Colonel George Clyde Morton
1914-1988

Col. George C. Morton, who began his military career in 1938 after graduating from the Citadel Military College of South Carolina, served with infantry units in Europe and the Philippines during World War II and with the 4th Cavalry in the Korean war. His extensive special-operations service spanned assignments with the Philippine Scouts; the Royal Hellenic Raiding Forces in Greece; commander of the first Special Forces group in Southeast Asia, U.S. Army Special Forces, Vietnam (Provisional); and chief of operations for the Laotian paramilitary forces until 1973. His professional leadership was instrumental in the creation of wartime Special Forces and the shaping of modern U.S. unconventional warfare doctrine.

FOREWORD

It was with humility and gratitude that I accepted Shelby L. Stanton's invitation to associate myself with his book. Stanton was a wartime Special Forces officer in Vietnam, and even the most casual readers will recognize the staggering enormity of his undertaking. For some, this pictorial history of the Special Forces in Southeast Asia will be an introduction to one of the most dramatic, albeit confounding, conflicts in U.S. Army history. For Special Forces veterans, it will revivify their finest hours.

The officers and men of the U.S. Army Special Forces exemplified the best of American soldiery. They lived with the people they marched among, six to twelve in a team, fulfilling their assigned tasks in a remote, alien habitat, with people they came to cherish, trust with their lives, and respect as brothers-in-arms. Not infrequently, their concern invoked total commitment and self sacrifice.

These intrepid, learn-as-you-go explorers of counter-terrorism, drug interdiction, and nation building wrote the first "how to" procedures manuals with their heroic exploits. They did not simply endure; they innovated, improvised, and overcame seemingly insurmountable obstacles. Their steadfastness to the early Special Forces became the *cause célèbre* within the Army they served and in the government of the land they loved. Long before joining Special Forces became the vehicle to a successful career, these early Special Forces soldiers harkened to their President's challenge to ask what they could do for their country by choosing to walk an unexplored pathway that enabled others to help themselves.

There were never more than 4,000 Special Forces soldiers committed in Vietnam at any one time. Yet these young Americans led upwards of 69,000 indigenous fighting soldiers, from a multitude of diverse backgrounds, throughout the length and breadth of Vietnam.

As I personally look back at my nearly 40-year association with Special Forces, my heart swells with pride. Who among us, who had the honor of marching alongside Colonel George Morton, the man to whom this book is dedicated, could ever forget his magnificent, personally exemplified leadership, courage, and loyalty. In 1962, together with Captain (later Colonel) Ronald Shackleton, the first A-Detachment commander in Vietnam, Morton drafted the blueprints that laid the foundation for the Special Forces structure in Vietnam.

Over the years others refined the blueprints, adding their own meaningful contributions in response to the ever-changing challenges facing them in Vietnam. The innovative and creative Captain (later Colonel) Bill Richardson, first commander of the Special Forces Delta Detachment, was one such contributor.

In December 1963 the first Special Forces-led indigenous reaction force, trained by Lieutenant (later Colonel) Hal Guarino, was committed to combat under my command. Colonel Ted Leonard, the commander of Special Forces in Vietnam at that time, had christened the group "Mike Force."

Our first operation took place in Vietnam's Central Highlands, and a brave young officer, Captain Herbert Hardy, commander of the Plei Do Lim CIDG Camp, was killed in action. When we evacuated his body, I fell heir to Captain Hardy's poncho-liner-blanket, which I used in Vietnam and at home for many years.

In January 1971 I was a colonel commanding the Special Forces in Vietnam, when one of my units became engaged in an operation in the vicinity of Seven Mountains IV Corps Vietnam. The unit was commanded by Major Paul Leary, with whom I had previously served and who, in 1963, had been Captain Hardy's executive officer at Camp Plei Do Lim. While trying desperately to rescue one of his surrounded units, Major Leary was killed in action. When I evacuated his body from the battle scene, I covered him with the same poncho-liner that had once belonged to Captain Hardy. It seemed to me that we had come full circle. Just two months later I returned the Special Forces Group and colors to their home at Fort Bragg, North Carolina.

Thank you Shelby Stanton for allowing me to be a part of this magnificent recorded history of our noble effort in Vietnam. And thanks especially to the officers and men of Special Forces and to their families, who suffered and sacrificed the long absences of loved ones who were valiantly answering the call emblazoned on their coat of arms, "De Oppresso Liber!"

Michael D.F. Healy
Major General, U.S. Army (Retired)

An Army Special Forces sergeant takes careful aim with his M16 rifle during a team readiness exercise at the John F. Kennedy Center for Special Warfare (Airborne) at Fort Bragg, North Carolina, preparatory to deployment to Southeast Asia. *(Paul Waring/USA)*

SPECIAL FORCES PREPARES FOR WAR

The origins of Army Special Forces began officially during World War II when the First Special Service Force, a combined United States-Canadian commando brigade led by the legendary Major General Robert T. Frederick, was formed to conduct sabotage and special strike missions behind enemy lines. On February 26, 1942, the U.S. Secretary of War authorized the soldiers to wear a crossed-arrow badge, symbolic of the famous U.S. Indian Scouts. This elite brigade assured the Allied advance in Italy by smashing through the German mountain bastion of Monte le Difensia in a six-day winter battle that allegedly earned it the enemy appellation, "The Devil's Brigade." The modern Special Forces derives much of its regular heritage and its distinctive crossed-arrows insignia from the First Special Service Force.

The roots of Special Forces unconventional warfare can be traced directly to the U.S. Office of Strategic Services (OSS) formed during World War II by Colonel William O. "Wild Bill" Donovan. The OSS was a secret government organization that infiltrated well-trained volunteers into enemy-occupied countries where they organized and assisted resistance groups. For example, small teams of OSS Jedburgh agents regularly parachuted into northern Europe. These teams, consisting of two liaison officers with an enlisted radio operator, linked up with underground resistance fighters to provide equipment and technical expertise for guerrilla tasks. The OSS also operated successfully in southern Asia.

The U.S. Army Special Forces also tracks its lineage to Col. Frank D. Merrill's renowned "Merrill's Marauders," a rugged jungle-warfare contingent officially known as the 5307th Composite Unit (Provisional). The Marauders fought throughout northern Burma, where its 3,000 soldiers engaged the Japanese in five major battles and 17 other actions. The most famous Marauder epic was the completion of a wide-sweeping movement, virtually unsupported except by air, that placed them several hundred miles behind enemy front lines and led to the capture of the vital Myitkyina airfield.

When the Army Special Forces was first organized, it also acquired the heritage and honors of the six ranger battalions of World War II and the 15 ranger companies of the Korean conflict. These units derived from the first American rangers, which were raised from militia volunteers during the French and Indian Wars. Led by the notable Major Robert Rogers, the rangers operated with stealth and daring against hostile Native American tribes, and the colonists later used these same tactics against the British during the Revolutionary War.

The modern U.S. Army Special Forces was steeped in this rich legacy when its initial 10th Special Forces Group was activated on June 20, 1952, at the height of the Korean War. The Army recalled Colonel Aaron Bank, a former Jedburgh commander, from Korea to North Carolina to activate this guerilla operations group in case of a Soviet invasion of western Europe. Colonel Bank's small nucleus of troops trained intensively in parachuting and basic unconventional warfare methods at Fort Bragg and Camp MacKall in North Carolina, and they completed advanced courses in mountain glacier, rock-escarpment, and cold weather operations at Camp Carson, Colorado. Within nine months of formation, the 10th Special Forces Group contained 1,000 hand-picked troops, many of them combat veterans of the rangers or OSS.

The first U.S. Army Special Forces was raised primarily to organize resistance movements within enemy-dominated regions during a full-scale war. At the conclusion of the Korean war, the chances of all-out war diminished, but the Special Forces gained a new place in the forefront of U.S. counterinsurgency efforts. This military task was necessitated by continuing international tensions. Small but highly skilled Special Forces teams were found perfectly tailored for a multitude of low-intensity crises. The detachments could execute important scouting or rescue missions at the highest national level, and they could also deploy overseas routinely for a multitude of training and nation-building activities.

On November 11, 1953, the basic 10th Special Forces Group

was directed to relocate to Bad Tolz, Germany, where operations could be launched close to or behind the communist "Iron Curtain" over eastern Europe. The group split in half to fulfill this requirement. On September 25, 1953, the Special Forces troops remaining at Fort Bragg were reformed into the 77th Special Forces Group. The new group, responsible for all areas of the world, except Europe, adopted the motto of its first commander, Colonel Jack T. Shannon: "Anything, Anytime, Anyplace, Anyhow!"

Meanwhile, in Germany, the 10th Special Forces Group became well established in its field of European responsibility and began wearing green berets. Berets were used occasionally, even during field maneuvers at Fort Bragg, but they became part of a wide assortment of unusual headgear worn by Special Forces troops while training in the field. These distinguishing items, worn both for comfort and for identity, quickly became associated with Special Forces commando tactics. During 1954 Colonel William Ekman of the 10th Special Forces Group approved wear of the green beret in Europe, and within a year every Special Forces trooper considered it a treasured part of his uniform.

Colonel Edson D. Raff, commander of the Army Psychological Warfare Center at Fort Bragg (the home of the 77th Special Forces Group), made the first persistent effort to get the green beret approved on an Army-wide basis. Although Raff's steadfast attempts to gain recognition for this unique headgear were repeatedly rebuffed by higher Army authorities, the Special Forces community kept up a heated struggle to gain official sanction for the green beret.

While the green beret debate was raging, the Special Forces was awarded its own shoulder-sleeve insignia. In 1956 Captain John W. Frye designed the arrowhead-shaped patch containing an upturned dagger crossed by three lightning bolts. The arrowhead symbolized the Native American hunting prowess inherited by the Special Forces. The dagger characterized the World War II-era First Special Service Force. The three lightning bolts represented the ability of Special Forces to infiltrate by air (parachuting), sea (rubber boats or underwater scuba), or land

(overland infiltration). The patch was teal blue, a color used traditionally for Army personnel not belonging to any particular branch and symbolizing the fact that Special Forces embraced personnel from all Army branches. Finally, the black and gold Airborne tab was added above the insignia to highlight the Special Forces parachute capability.

Also in 1956, the Psychological Warfare Center was enlarged and retitled as the Army Special Warfare Center and School. The center served as an institute of higher learning for the refinement of counterinsurgency operations, and it offered specialized instruction in all phases of special conflict. The training enabled Special Forces teams to survive and operate successfully for extended periods, either in isolation or among the native populace, in enemy-dominated territory.

The Special Forces operational Detachment A, commonly known as the A-Team, comprised ten enlisted troops led by a detachment commander who was a captain and his lieutenant executive officer. As one recruiting brochure of the period stated, these "twelve men were tough enough to take on fifty and trained enough to teach fifteen hundred." The specialists on each team represented a pair in each of five fields: operations and intelligence, communications, weapons, demolitions, and medicine. In addition, each specialist was trained in another field specialty in case of emergency. Every team member also possessed paratrooper and general Special Forces proficiency, and he had a working knowledge of one other language besides English.

The A-Team was authorized two senior noncommissioned officers: one Master Sergeant, who doubled as the operations and team sergeant, and a Sergeant First Class, who was the intelligence sergeant. They combined years of military experience with exceptional backgrounds in tactics, interrogation techniques, photography, and detective work. Their wide scope of knowledge was critical, because detachment commanders and executive officers, having less time in service (being captains and lieutenants), often depended greatly on these sergeants.

The team communication expertise was represented by a radio

operator supervisor and a chief radio operator. The senior radio operator, a Sergeant First Class, had many years of experience, and the junior radioman, a Sergeant, had completed 16 weeks of signal school. Both were highly skilled in the mechanics of key or voice transmitting-and-receiving equipment, antennas, generators, and cryptography.

The team contained a heavy weapons leader and a light weapons leader, both Sergeants First Class. These weapons specialists (commonly known as Weapons NCOs) were masters of at least 30 American and foreign weapons, from rifles to light mortars. Both sergeants had a thorough technical knowledge of individual weapon strengths and weaknesses, as well as how such weapons could be employed for team purposes.

The team also had a demolitions-qualified Staff Sergeant, usually known as the team engineer sergeant, and a combat demolitions specialist normally called the Demo Sergeant. Both were experts at procuring and preparing explosives, whether using regular charges or making their own incendiaries from materials at hand. They were trained to destroy everything from a foot bridge to a railroad yard, but they could also dig wells, build roads, and construct dwellings in underdeveloped lands.

Medical expertise was essential to any detachment, especially one operating far from sophisticated treatment facilities. The team medic was a medical specialist authorized in the grade of Sergeant First Class (or Specialist 7th Class). The assistant medical specialist or junior medic was a Staff Sergeant. They took care of sick or injured combatants until exfiltration, gave treatment to area natives, and taught hygiene improvement and disease prevention. Medics commenced their intensive medical training at Brooke Army Hospital in Fort Sam Houston, underwent further training at another Army hospital, and then completed advanced medical training at Fort Bragg, the U.S. Special Forces home base.

The Special Forces continued to grow and field more detachments. In April 1956 a small number of hand-picked officers and sergeants from the 77th Special Forces Group, led by Colonel Shannon, were chosen to start a Far East contingent.

This element relocated to Japan and became the 8321st Army Unit (Special Operations Detachment). On June 24, 1957, this detachment became the basis of the 1st Special Forces Group that was moved to the nearby island of Okinawa.

Special Forces operations were always global in scope, as highlighted by common alerts and operational responses mandated by the Berlin crisis and emergencies in the Congo and Caribbean. The 1st Special Forces Group on Okinawa was relatively distant from any Euro-American-African flash point of danger. But this group was destined to play a key role in Special Forces combat development. By 1959 large numbers of Special Forces troops were being sent as military advisors from Okinawa to simmering battlefronts in Laos and Vietnam.

In September 1960 the Special Forces organization was radically altered by the U.S. Department of the Army, which activated the 1st Special Forces as the parent regiment for all Special Forces groups. The 1st and 10th Special Forces Groups became part of the 1st Special Forces (Regiment). The 77th at Fort Bragg was redesignated as the 7th Special Forces Group. The 5th Special Forces Group was raised to provide rapid response teams for contingencies in Pacific Asia.

President John F. Kennedy expressed his keen faith in special warfare as a crucial military tool in U.S. foreign policy. His elite counterinsurgency warriors provided combat advice and support in numerous regions. During October 1961 Kennedy seconded the Special Warfare Center commandant, Brigadier General William P. Yarborough, in recommending the green beret as the official Special Forces headgear. On December 10 the Army formally sanctioned the green beret as part of the Special Forces uniform.

When the U.S. advisory role in Asia flared into open war, Special Forces troops entered battle as volunteers ready to tackle the most dangerous assignments and accept the most demanding circumstances. During the next decade of incessant conflict extending from the mountains of Laos to the tropics of Vietnam, the Special Forces maintained its uniquely elite fighting spirit.

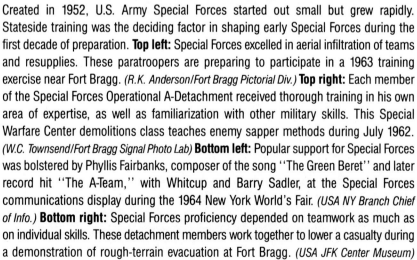

Created in 1952, U.S. Army Special Forces started out small but grew rapidly. Stateside training was the deciding factor in shaping early Special Forces during the first decade of preparation. **Top left:** Special Forces excelled in aerial infiltration of teams and resupplies. These paratroopers are preparing to participate in a 1963 training exercise near Fort Bragg. *(R.K. Anderson/Fort Bragg Pictorial Div.)* **Top right:** Each member of the Special Forces Operational A-Detachment received thorough training in his own area of expertise, as well as familiarization with other military skills. This Special Warfare Center demolitions class teaches enemy sapper methods during July 1962. *(W.C. Townsend/Fort Bragg Signal Photo Lab)* **Bottom left:** Popular support for Special Forces was bolstered by Phyllis Fairbanks, composer of the song "The Green Beret" and later record hit "The A-Team," with Whitcup and Barry Sadler, at the Special Forces communications display during the 1964 New York World's Fair. *(USA NY Branch Chief of Info.)* **Bottom right:** Special Forces proficiency depended on teamwork as much as on individual skills. These detachment members work together to lower a casualty during a demonstration of rough-terrain evacuation at Fort Bragg. *(USA JFK Center Museum)*

Okinawa was the most important Special Forces operational base for Far East activities, and the 1st Special Forces Group was responsible for most early deployments into Thailand, Laos, and Vietnam. **Top:** The 1st Special Forces Group's "Kennedy Rifles" Honor Guard, commanded by Capt. William P. Radtke, dedicates the Matsuda Training Area on Okinawa as Camp Hardy on December 21, 1964. *(William Radtke)* **Bottom:** Special Forces teams depended on unusual infiltration methods and special-issue gear. These 1962 Special Forces troops standing around a rubber boat at Matsuda Range, Okinawa, wear clothing and equipment typical of the early Vietnam period. (Left to right) Master Sgt. Davis with full rucksack, Capt. Bruschette holding carbine, Sgt. Newell wearing test-pattern tropical hat, Master Sgt. Henderson in scuba outfit, Sgt. Johnson with medical pack, and Sp4 Peterson using radio. *(Author's Collection)*

The highly proficient 1st Special Forces Group continually rehearsed infiltration methods and combatant skills such as underwater operations and jungle fighting. **Top left:** Advanced training on Okinawa included High-Altitude, Low-Opening (HALO) parachuting. *(Robert Lafoon/USA Pacific Photo Det.)* **Top right:** Special Forces scuba reconnaissance troops conduct an amphibious exercise off Sand Island, Okinawa. This training heralded later clandestine missions against the Vietnamese coast, often performed in conjunction with Navy SEALs. *(Robert Lafoon/USA Pacific Photo Det.)* **Bottom:** The 1st Special Forces Group actively trained cadres of U.S. regional allies throughout East Asia for unconventional warfare forces. Here, Capt. Nyfeler briefs Japanese Defense Minister Gen. Hayashi during Okinawa exercises in 1963. *(Author's Collection)*

Mobile training teams from the 1st Special Forces Group deployed continually to upgrade the special warfare units of Korea, the Philippines, South Vietnam, Taiwan, and Thailand. **Top:** Working in close harmony with this program, the Chinese established four exceptionally elite special warfare groups on Taiwan. One of the toughest parachute courses was conducted at the Taiwan-based Special Terrain Parachute School. Here, instructor Master Sgt. Ed Miller briefs Special Forces paratroopers of both countries. They wear helmets with face masks and protective padding for tree landings in the forested mountain ranges. *(Clayton Scott)* **Bottom:** Even ''going to the movies'' meant hard work for Special Forces. During 1961 a large contingent from the 1st Special Forces Group provided technical advice and served as soldiers for Samuel Fuller's production of *Merrill's Marauders*, filmed near Clark Field in the Philippines. *(Clyde J. Sincere Jr.)*

Barefooted Laotian recruits learn to master the techniques of mortar firing under close supervision from Special Forces White Star Mobile Training Team members in the fog-shrouded mountain jungle of Laos. *(David Paulsrud)*

SPECIAL FORCES IN LAOS

SPECIAL FORCES IN LAOS

At the conclusion of the First Indochina War, Laos existed as a former administrative entity of the French empire, lacking real national unity. The country, sandwiched between North Vietnam and Thailand, was inhabited by various racial and tribal groups scattered across the numerous mountains, plateaus, and river valleys in largely isolated and sometimes hostile communities. Laotian instability was further undermined by the struggle for national control between three warring factions: the communist-oriented Prince Souphanouvong, backed up by the Pathet Lao and supported by North Vietnamese forces; a neutralist group led by Prince Souvanna Phouma; and the conservative Prince Buoum Oum and his chief general, Phoumi Nosavan, both supported by Laotian King Savang.

The United States sent increasing amounts of military and economic aid to guarantee the Royal Laotian government's domination over Laos. France retained exclusive authority to maintain military personnel and bases in Laos in accordance with the 1954 Geneva Agreements. As a result, American aid was channeled through the French, and the U.S. Programs Evaluation Office was established to monitor equipment requirements and use.

During 1959, in response to the worsening Laotian crisis, both France and the United States reached an agreement to conduct joint training for the *Forces Armées de Laos.* Responsibility for this task was divided between technical training, under American control, and tactical training, under French control. The Army Special Forces was chosen to conduct most U.S. advisory operations in Laos because of the ideal size and remote-area skills of its small detachments.

Prohibitions within the Geneva Agreements mandated that these Special Forces teams be fielded secretly, instead of deploying them openly under the regular control of a military advisory group. In July a dozen Special Forces Field Training Teams (FTTs) were deployed to different areas of Laos on six months' temporary duty. Each team contained eight Special Forces troops

disguised as unarmed civilians. They were stationed at regional training centers together with soldiers of the French Military Mission. The Special Forces taught basic weapons maintenance and proficiency courses and gave specialized training in other fields, such as radio handling.

This limited Special Forces training effort was interrupted on August 9, 1960, when Laotian Captain Kong Le's battalion of paratroopers seized the capital of Vientiane in a sudden coup and declared a new independent Neutralist government. Opposing forces under General Phoumi Nosavan withdrew to the lower Mekong River town of Savannakhet and set up a pro-Western resistance front. These forces, actively assisted by Special Forces with the secret blessing of U.S. authorities, were molded into an offensive army to retake the capital.

After the Kong Le coup and in response to the U.S. decision to support the anti-communist faction of General Phoumi Nosavan, the French formally withdrew their military forces from Laos. The Special Forces rapidly filled the void left by departing French advisors, and troops were assigned directly to combatant units of the *Forces Armées de Laos.* For the first time, Special Forces advisors were employed in a frontline combat capacity, and Vientiane was recaptured in December 1960.

During February 1961 the Special Forces added nine more teams. The reinforcement permitted the Special Forces to place advisors with each of the 21 existing or newly activated Laotian battalions. In March the Special Forces was reorganized, and each team was filled to a normal A-Detachment, 12-member authorization level. Special Forces spread its resources further by splitting many detachments into six-member Field Training Teams, a concept that allowed more coverage of the fluid battle zone without cancelling training-site presence. B-detachments were introduced as control elements in each military region. The 1st and 7th Special Forces Groups formed Teams BA, BB, BC, and BD for the Kha tribal program at Saravane, the northern I and II Military Regions at Luang Prabang, the central III Military Region at Savannakhet, and the southern IV Military Region at Pakse, respectively. The main Special Forces Control Detachment was headquartered at Vientiane.

Special Forces involvement now encompassed such a large scale that the confidentiality of its assignment was largely compromised. Accordingly, on April 19 the Programs Evaluations Office was redesignated as Military Assistance Advisory Group, Laos, and all pretense of secrecy was dropped. Special Forces teams were retitled as White Star Mobile Training Teams.

The most important Special Forces task involved shaping the *Forces Armées de Laos* into an army capable of protecting the government and the Laotian heartland. Much of this work depended on the instruction offered by Special Forces teams assigned to the Noncommissioned Officers School in each military zone, the National Aspirant (officer candidate) School at Dong Hene in central Laos, technical schools, the Artillery and Armor schools, and the Combined Arms Center. The Special Forces also emphasized upgrading the Airborne Center at Fort Seno, because its three parachute battalions were envisioned as the basis for an elite, centralized response force.

Laotian battlefront defenses were improved by locating Special Forces split A-Teams with combat battalions. In this capacity the Special Forces rendered valuable advice and support, coordinated aerial resupply, and performed critical observation and intelligence-gathering missions. Each team also participated in energetic civic-action and medical-treatment projects that upgraded local living conditions and encouraged village allegiance to the central government. Special Forces duty ranged from teaching foreign soldiers infantry tactics to building schools and healing the sick, and these ''Green Berets'' soon earned the respect of the regular Army advisory group, the Central Intelligence Agency, and other government agencies.

Special Forces also undertook two major unconventional programs in Laos. Both programs concentrated on training minority tribal groups as irregular forces capable of conducting guerrilla warfare across rugged terrain or behind enemy lines. The Meo Program was conducted among the Meo nomadic mountain people of northeast Laos. Incessant combat in the Meo homeland

region had created thousands of refugees, and these provided the early basis for several *Auto Défense de Choc* companies, which exhibited considerable mountaineering skills and bravery.

During the spring of 1962, Special Forces installed its Meo training center at Site 20 on the fortified mountain of Phou Bia. The Meos were given advanced instruction in leadership, communications, demolitions, weapons, and combat at the individual, squad, and platoon levels. Despite problems occasioned by no Meo written language, inter-agency difficulties, and lack of consistent U.S. policy, the Special Forces molded the Meo warriors into formidable and loyal allies.

The Kha program, the second unconventional training activity, was designed by Special Forces to use the various Kha tribes in harassing and raiding enemy rear bases and installations, especially along the Ho Chi Minh Trail—the primary overland North Vietnamese resupply route across Laos into South Vietnam and Cambodia. The Kha were receptive to Special Forces plans, because they were mistreated by both Laotians and Vietnamese.

On December 23, 1961, the major Kha effort was initiated among the southern tribes in the *Plateau des Bolovens.* Coded Operation Pincushion, the Kha training scheme included quick-fire ranges, ambush and counterambush courses, and night marksmanship. Individual fighting skills were taught and refined. The Special Forces intended to train Kha tribesmen on an area control basis. This concept would allow the natives to protect their villages and patrol the jungle, while conducting their usual hunting and farming occupations. The Special Forces also wanted a system of forward patrol bases in the Kha area that could be stockpiled with ammunition resupplies and other necessities.

Each Kha training cycle took five weeks, and 11 Special Forces teams were detailed to this duty by mid-April 1962. Unfortunately, higher authorities refused to adopt Special Forces suggestions for the newly created guerrilla movements, depending instead on the poorly organized and uncoordinated efforts of Laotian military zone commanders. The Laotians, lacking proper communications and forward intelligence, were unable to strike swiftly in classic guerrilla actions, and the Meo and Kha programs never realized their potential.

Political circumstances remained chaotic while the Special Forces continued its multi-faceted White Star program. A token cease-fire had become effective May 3, 1961, but no side observed this unsatisfactory arrangement. The communists violated the cease-fire repeatedly and made several advances, but the *Forces Armées du Royaume* (renamed on September 15 from the *Forces Armées de Laos*) were unable to regain territory through aggressive maneuvering. Despite several sharp clashes, the Royal Laotians were increasingly driven on the defensive in a war dominated by small-unit skirmishing and prolonged periods of inaction. During May 1962 General Phoumi was decisively defeated at Nam Tha after he disregarded Special Forces advice and lost many of his troops and much equipment in a series of stunning Pathet Lao onslaughts that broke the Mekong Valley line.

By the summer of 1962, Special Forces activities in Laos—begun in August 1959 as a limited training mission—had evolved into a major field advisory role with responsibility for an entire national army engaged on the battlefield. Special Forces advisors and forward logisticians were concentrated in 48 Field Training Teams from the 1st and 7th Special Forces Groups, 18 of which were devoted to the counterinsurgency arm composed of Meo and Kha tribesmen. President John F. Kennedy approved raising the authorized level of Special Forces in Laos to 500 troops, but the peak strength of 430 Special Forces troops in Laos was never surpassed.

In June 1962 the United States realized that Phoumi's losses at Nam Tha had compromised all hope of a favorable settlement. The following month a cabinet headed by the neutralist Souvanna Phouma was agreed upon by all three Laotian princes, and a ''Declaration on the Neutrality of Laos'' was signed July 23. The agreement specified the withdrawal of all foreign military personnel within 75 days. The number of Special Forces diminished until all advisory personnel left Laos on October 6, 1962.

During 1963, in the wake of continued North Vietnamese in-cursions into neighboring Laos, the Special Forces renewed its military assistance support to the Meo tribal groups as part of a clandestine Central Intelligence Agency program to strengthen irregular forces. During the following year Pathet Lao and North Vietnamese forces began to improve their positions in central Laos. Special Forces patrols countered by reconnoitering the enemy stronghold of Tchepone, an important staging area on the Ho Chi Minh Trail.

In the midst of these planning activities, Premier Souvanna Phouma was ousted by a successful rightist coup on April 19. Afterwards, the communists renewed their offensive, and the United States was forced to dispatch Thai artillery and Special Forces advisors to defend several areas. By late summer, however, the military situation was stabilized.

The stalemated war in Laos taught Special Forces a multitude of valuable lessons. When training teams lived in the field as part of the units they supported, they often gained the confidence and cooperation of their counterparts and maintained a close working relationship. Knowledge of Lao and other native languages gave Special Forces greater efficiency over regular advisors who relied on interpreters. Special Forces also confirmed that prime physical conditioning, skillful experience, and mature judgment were absolute requirements for successful advisory assignments. Special Forces also gained the chance to test weapons, radios, and operating methods within the tropical combat environment of Southeast Asia.

The lasting Special Forces legacy of Laos, however, was its great achievement in demonstrating the flexibility and inherent expertise of the special warfare establishment as a prime instrument of national policy. Special Forces performed a sensitive military assignment of great significance at minimum cost, and it proved fully deserving of equal partnership with other U.S. Army branches. The dedication of the Special Forces and White Star Field Training Team members sent to Laos eventually culminated in the establishment of Special Forces as a separate Army branch more than 25 years later in 1987.

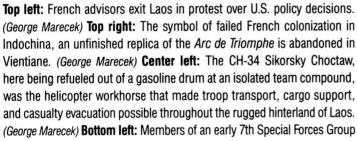

Top left: French advisors exit Laos in protest over U.S. policy decisions. *(George Marecek)* **Top right:** The symbol of failed French colonization in Indochina, an unfinished replica of the *Arc de Triomphe* is abandoned in Vientiane. *(George Marecek)* **Center left:** The CH-34 Sikorsky Choctaw, here being refueled out of a gasoline drum at an isolated team compound, was the helicopter workhorse that made troop transport, cargo support, and casualty evacuation possible throughout the rugged hinterland of Laos. *(George Marecek)* **Bottom left:** Members of an early 7th Special Forces Group

Field Training Team at Ban Houei Sai, a Mekong River bastion in the northern "Golden Triangle," wear wide-brimmed bush hats and field caps instead of conspicuous green berets. *(Donald Valentine)* **Bottom right:** During the joint phase of U.S.-French training, Special Forces instructors taught Laotian soldiers how to stack arms in French fashion. This small difference belied larger problems of coordination between France and the United States that prevented a unified approach toward Laotian military improvement. *(David Paulsrud)*

Top: The political turmoil in Laos overshadowed the U.S. military training effort and was destined to have a crucial impact on future Special Forces development. On August 9, 1960, Capt. Kong Le used his elite *2d Bataillon de Parachutiste* to stage a *coup d'état* in the Laotian capital of Vientiane. This episode created an international crisis, which resulted in a precipitous French military withdrawal. Special Forces, directed to fill the gap with combat advisors, successfully demonstrated its versatility in reacting to conventional emergency situations outside the special-warfare arena. *(Samuel Skemp)* **Bottom:** Special Forces established a "rump" or rebel assistance group at Savannakhet that reformed the Laotian army and recaptured Vientiane in December 1960. During April 1961 the United States established a Military Assistance Advisory Group for Laos, and Special Forces assumed an open operational role with its White Star Mobile Training Teams. Here Lt. Col. Aito Keravuori, the White Star commander, coordinates with Field Training Team captains George Buck (FTT-21) and Prewitt (FTT-28) at Fort Seno. *(George Marecek)*

Top: Most Special Forces White Star locations in Laos were composed of a simple dirt airstrip and a small military compound in the midst of rugged jungle wilderness. Battalion garrisons were scattered to control important valley passes and other key terrain features, because vast overland distances prohibited the maintenance of a regular battle line. The Special Forces, trained in remote-area survival, excelled in successfully defending such localities—even if totally surrounded by enemy forces. *(Samuel Skemp)* **Bottom left:** The Laotian combat zone was typified by long periods of static warfare punctuated by sharp skirmishes. A standard hallmark of many remotely situated teams was a pet monkey, here held by FTT-15 commander Lt. Shelton. *(George Marecek)* **Bottom right:** The most treasured item of the Special Forces Field Training Team inventory was a home-made alfresco ''hot shower unit.'' This mobile shower, constructed in the mountain ranges north of Luang Prabang, comprised a 55-gallon drum, a water heater, and jerry-rigged plumbing. *(George Marecek)*

Top left: In northern Laos, Master Sgt. Edmundson checks a native dwelling during a Special Forces patrol through the opium-rich ''Golden Triangle'' near Burma and Thailand. Special Forces interdiction of area drug-smuggling routes was the precursor of larger operations against South American drug traffic during the 1990s. *(Donald Valentine)* **Top right:** In southern Laos during January 1962, the 3d Kha Marquis Company was raised as part of a Special Forces guerrilla warfare program to secure the *Plateau des Bolovens*. *(Donald Blackburn)* **Center left:** Sgt. Lucas prepares his meal at Thakhek, underscoring the common quip that the lack of kitchen facilities mandated local cooking as a new team specialty. *(George Marecek)* **Center:** Master Sgt. Fewske, unhampered by the lack of electric power, types an operations order on a manual typewriter at the Team BD Pakse headquarters. *(George Marecek)* **Center right:** White Star teams often depended on parachuted supplies, and the Special Forces padded fragile items, like radios and ammunition rounds, in empty drums for protection during airdrops. The teams used the barrels for water storage and field-expedient showers. *(George Marecek)* **Bottom:** A forward Special Forces advisory team quarters in a typical upland Laotian infantry-battalion post. *(Samuel Skemp)*

Top left: The White Star Mobile Training Team command post in the capital of Vientiane was linked by air with its far-flung subordinate detachments throughout Laos. *(George Marecek)* **Top right:** Unmarked aircraft brought the first clandestine Special Forces teams into Laos. Team members wore civilian clothing and carried no visible identification or weapons. *(Samuel Skemp)* **Center left:** The White Star commander, left, frequently visited the forward training sites by air because normal communications were either unreliable or subject to interception. In this instance, he personally reviews Laotian squad tactics with commanders Capt. Buck (FTT-21) and Lt. Harrison (FTT-27) in central Laos. *(George Marecek)* **Center right:** The key airfield and central Special Forces base of Savannakhet was located in the Laotian plain along the Mekong River. (George Marecek) **Bottom:** Much of upper Laos was secured by the crucial airfield at Luang Prabang, capable of delivering prompt air support to beleaguered Special Forces-advised outposts in the northern mountains. *(David Paulsrud)*

Top left: Most White Star Mobile Training Team activity, which included raiding, limited counterattacks, and bitter fighting over certain localities, transpired during the prolonged cease-fire negotiations, as the armies maneuvered for positional advantage on the battlefield. A Special Forces range sergeant, standing center, instructs infantrymen south of Luang Prabang during a temporary lull in combat. *(David Paulsrud)* **Center right:** In accordance with high-level instructions, sensitive documents were routinely destroyed, erasing the record of many Special Forces Laotian operations. Master Sgt. Weeks, Control Detachment BC intelligence NCO, burns classified material behind the Savannahket headquarters. *(George Marecek)* **Bottom left:** The Laotion peace negotiations were held at this building in Vientiane. On June 12, 1962, the Laotian princes agreed on a coalition government, and the White Star program ended several months later. *(George Marecek)* **Bottom right:** Captains Hinds and Mogle dry out clothing and ponchos along a jungle-road bivouac near the forward supply base of Thakhek. *(David Paulsrud)*

Top: Special Forces duty in Laos was marked by unique military improvisation with materials at hand, combined with sensitivity to the cultural welfare of the indigenous population. Success with Meo tribal warriors depended on excellent native relations. The closeness of this affinity is demonstrated by FTT-22 commander Lt. Marecek, right, who was honored with the request to be god-father of a Meo soldier's baby at Kiou Cha Chan. *(George Marecek)* **Bottom left:** Laotian mountain warfare produced several Special Forces tactical innovations. Sgt. First Class Dean, standing third from left, transformed the 75mm recoilless rifle into a weapon capable of indirect fire by mounting it on a heavy machine gun tripod. *(Jimmy Dean)* **Bottom right:** Special Forces knowledge of animal husbandry was important in the Laotian hill country. Site 20 commander Maj. Faistenhammer made good use of native transportation during security checks of outlying villages near Xieng Khouang. *(Ludwig Faistenhammer Jr./Adam Dintenfass Collection)*

Top left: Special Forces training in Laos covered almost every facet of military ground operations. Here, Laotian soldiers learn weapons disassembly at Savannahket. *(William Craig)* **Top middle:** Laotian paratrooper recruits practice formation drill. *(George Marecek)* **Top right:** Laotian paratrooper trainees use the mock-door exit structure in front of the 34-foot tower at Seno. Such rickety platforms never met Army safety standards, but they were effective. *(George Marecek)* **Center left:** The Meo irregular warfare program training staff assembles for a group picture at Site 20. *(Ludwig Faistenhammer Jr. / Adam Dintenfass Collection)* **Center right:** Maj. Gen. Reuben Tucker, Chief of MAAG Laos, visits a Special Forces training base. *(George Marecek)* **Bottom left:** Sp4 Deveraux and Sgt. Newton instruct Laotian soldiers in bore-sighting a 57mm recoilless rifle. *(George Marecek)* **Bottom right:** Sp4 Osborne teaches Laotian soldiers how to use explosives to clear a jungle landing zone at Xieng Sone. *(George Marecek)*

Top: Frontline infantry battalions, nestled in tented positions behind a few strands of barbed wire, guarded the main western population centers and road arteries in Laos. Special Forces split A-Teams, composed of only six men each, were located with these battalions and shared the same dangers as their Laotian comrades. *(Samuel Skemp)* **Bottom left:** Special Forces fought several rearguard actions against major Pathet Lao offensives, and their solitary courage was often instrumental in preventing a total enemy breakthrough when Royal Laotian defenses disintegrated. Sp4 ''Tex'' Simmons occupies a foxhole position on the edge of the Ban Houei Sai airfield during the May 1962 battle of Nam Tha. *(Donald Valentine)* **Bottom right:** Laotian casualties from the Nam Beng valley campaign are treated at a temporary Special Forces medical aid station. *(Julius Wyngant)*

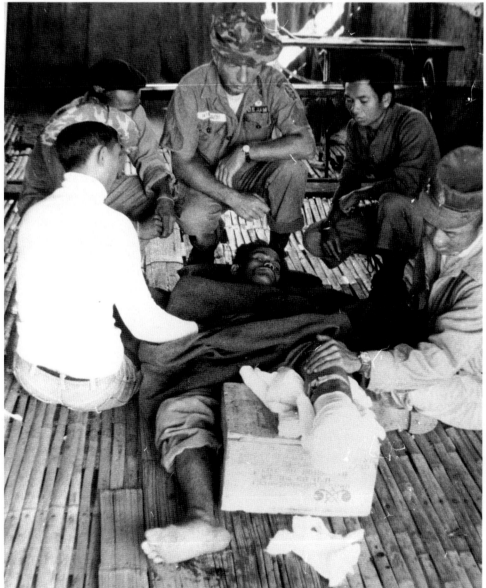

Top: Special Forces involvement in Laos continued on a clandestine basis in response to communist aggression, long after the Geneva Peace Accords were signed in mid-1962. Col. George Morton, the former commander of U.S. Army Special Forces, Vietnam, was summoned to Laos, where he raised a secret Special Forces-advised irregular army for the Central Intelligence Agency. Col. Morton, right, oversees a 1965 allied counterattack near the *Plaine des Jarres* with Air Force Col. Al Blizzard. *(Author's Collection)*
Bottom: Laotian Col. Nu Phet, commander of *Groupement Mobile 18*, poses with Special Forces enlisted advisors (left to right) Jimmy Dean, Richard La Hue, Lupe Rodriguez, and J.O. Wells during a raiding operation from Pak Song across the *Plateau des Bolovens. (Jimmy Dean)*

SPECIAL FORCES ENTERS VIETNAM, 1960-1964

When the 1st Special Forces Group was activated on Okinawa in June 1957, it was designated as the principle unconventional warfare organization responsible for the Pacific area. The group sent mobile training teams throughout the Far East to train allied personnel in Special Forces techniques and operations. During the same year, the first Special Forces team arrived in the Republic of Vietnam. This team taught commando tactics to the South Vietnamese counterespionage-specialized 1st Observation Group at the coastal port of Nha Trang. Three years later, the small Vietnamese cadre became the basis of the Vietnamese Special Purpose Forces—the *Lực-Lượng Dặc-Biệt* (LLDB)—when it was redesignated as the 77th LLDB Group in 1960.

In the meantime, the insurgent Viet Cong communists organized a well-coordinated campaign against the South Vietnamese regime of President Diem, and by 1959 guerrilla warfare had spread throughout much of the countryside. During May 1960 the United States expanded its assistance to South Vietnam by sending a contingent from the 7th Special Forces Group to teach counterguerrilla tactics at the ranger training centers of Da Nang, Nha Trang, and Song Mao. In November Diem survived a coup attempt, and the United States developed a comprehensive plan for Vietnamese military development under the regular Army supervision of the Military Assistance Advisory Group, Vietnam. Special Forces training and assistance of conventional units, common in Laos, was not duplicated in Vietnam.

Throughout 1961 communist guerrilla activity—financed and largely directed by North Vietnamese authorities acting in concert with Sino-Soviet suppliers—escalated to alarming levels. The United States sent additional military and economic aid to bolster the sagging South Vietnamese defenses. Fearful of Viet Cong success among Montagnard tribal groups and mindful of Special Forces success with the Kha and Meo tribes of Laos, the Central Intelligence Agency (CIA) developed plans for Special Forces organization of ethnic and religious minorities inside Vietnam.

The Montagnards comprised more than a hundred nomadic tribes, and their culture and language differed among each group and often between villages of the same tribe. Village-oriented people, the Montagnards relied on slash-and-burn agriculture and hunting for their livelihood. Shared Montagnard traits included a deep hostility toward the Vietnamese, who regarded the Montagnards contemptuously as inferior savages, and an equally intense desire to be left alone. However, the CIA realized that several Montagnard tribes had fought for the French in the First Indochina War, because the French had protected their lands from Vietnamese encroachment. It decided to build on this favorable experience in seeking Montagnard allegiance to the allied cause. The Special Forces were chosen to execute the CIA's delicate task, because the tribes only accepted advisors who understood their native culture and were willing to share their primitive lifestyle.

In October 1961 exploratory talks were held with Rhade tribal leaders in the Vietnamese Central Highlands, and permission was granted for Special Forces to form a village self-defense area development program in Darlac Province. During the following month, the Special Forces also initiated a Mountain Commando paramilitary program under CIA guidance that was later retitled as the Montagnard Mountain Scouts. In December, 40 additional Rhade villages agreed to join the Darlac Province development project, and Special Forces began training village defenders and strike forces at Buon Enao. Early development work was extremely demanding. Because recruits often had to be wheddled from local village leaders, a large amount of time was devoted to screening for Viet Cong, and training was delayed by the need to nourish the natives.

At the beginning of 1962, Special Forces was engaged in operations to help rural civic-action cadre, district volunteers, ranger units, mountain commandos, and selected village tribal defenders. Much of the instruction outside Darlac Province was concentrated at the Hoa Cam Training Center outside Da Nang. Other programs were introduced at the insistence of

A Special Forces-led Montagnard commando team of U.S. Army Special Forces, Vietnam (Provisional), mountain scouts, equipped with carbines and Browning automatic rifles, pushes through dense tropical foliage in pursuit of Viet Cong guerrillas near Ba To, Vietnam, during January 1963. *(Henry Backes Jr./USA)*

President Diem. These consisted of a bizarre mix of Catholic parish priest forces led by ''Fighting Fathers,'' a teenage combat organization known as the ''Catholic Youth,'' and paramilitary political-action contingents called either *Force Populaire* or Republican Youth.

During February General Paul D. Harkins became commander of the newly established U.S. Military Assistance Command, Vietnam (MACV). This command included an operations staff that contained a Special Warfare Section headed by Colonel George C. Morton. He closely coordinated the growing Special Forces commitment within South Vietnam and insured the foundation of a solid unconventional warfare presence in that combat theater. The first full A-Team was assigned to the Darlac Province Rhade experiment and flown into Buon Enao. Within three months, both MACV and the CIA responded to the resounding success of the Rhade enterprise by formulating a Special Forces mission that became its mainstay: the Civilian Irregular Defense Group (CIDG) program.

The CIDG program was designed to establish area-development centers in regions of minimal government control, where Viet Cong presence was often a factor. The area-development centers were envisioned as bases of operations where Special Forces, working through the Vietnamese *Lực-Lượng Dặc-Biệt,* could establish village defensive systems and train irregular strike forces to carry out counterguerrilla operations. Once the Special Forces extended government control into an area-development center, the complex was scheduled for turnover to sole Vietnamese control.

Special Forces responsibilities continued to grow as the CIDG program took shape. In June the CIA directed Special Forces to start a border-reconnoitering Trailwatcher project. This was followed closely by the mid-year formation of the Office of Rural Affairs at the U.S. Operations Mission, which extended major assistance to Special Forces provincial civic-action and domestic-improvement plans. By August, in Darlac Province alone, the scope of Special Forces action included more than 200 villages and 60,000 natives under five A-Detachments. At this time 16 Special Forces teams were stationed in various Vietnam training and area-development centers. The Department of Defense agreed to take over the CIDG program from the CIA within a year, permitting complete Special Forces control.

This situation expedited the urgent requirement for a permanent Special Forces Command headquarters. In September the U.S. Army Special Forces, Vietnam (Provisional), was created under Colonel Morton. He instituted a normal Special Forces chain of command that streamlined control through three intermediate B-Detachments to the 26 scattered field A-Detachments. Colonel Morton's provisional group assumed full operational control of the A-Detachments in a staged sequence for each of Vietnam's four Corps Tactical Zones (CTZs).

In February 1963 Colonel Morton moved his headquarters from Saigon to the port city of Nha Trang to further centralize Special Forces control and simplify logistical arrangements. Shortly after this move was completed, the Special Forces declared the Buon Enao complex fully secure and turned it over to the Darlac Province Chief for Vietnamese control. Morton's group was now expanded to include four B-Detachments controlling 37 A-Detachments. Paramilitary efforts were enhanced by the June arrival of the first complete civil-affairs, psychological-operations team. With the exception of four A-Detachments engaged in CIA cross-border surveillance, Colonel Morton exercised full jurisdiction over Special Forces programs in South Vietnam.

The Special Forces broadened the diverse composition of its forces by adding two militant religious armies. The fanatic Hoa Hao Buddhist sect of the lower Mekong River joined the Civilian Irregular Defense Program. The program also took over responsibility for the Cao Dai, an armed Buddhist splinter group that displayed strong grievances against Viet Cong intrusion on sacred religious grounds northwest of Saigon.

In December 1963 Special Forces reached another major turning point in its future development. President Diem was assassinated in a military *coup d'état* that overthrew his regime. This change in governments gave the U.S. Army an opportunity to curb many independent Special Forces activities that Diem had approved. The Vietnamese government also took immediate steps to curtail the independence of Diem's *Lực-Lượng Dặc-Biệt*.

American Army planners were primarily concerned about the flow of Viet Cong supplies and reinforcements across the border. MACV staff planners conceived of a string of fortified camps, manned by small Special Forces detachments and mercenary tribesmen, controlling the length of Vietnam's frontier. Colonel Theodore Leonard was placed in command of the Special Forces Group and directed to deemphasize area-development projects. Teams were relocated on a priority basis along the jungled mountains and swampland to screen Vietnam's border. In order to garrison the new fortresses, Special Forces was impelled to displace some tribes and dragoon unwilling Vietnamese from their home areas.

The Army insisted that Special Forces conventionalize its CIDG forces. The Special Forces hoped to use the natives in a guerrilla role, but the Army wanted all available units employed in supplementing the hard-pressed regular Vietnamese combat formations. In the midst of this redirection, the Special Forces camp at Hiep Hoa—just west of the capital of Saigon—was overrun by a surprise Viet Cong attack. The deteriorating situation in South Vietnam was further underscored in January 1964, when Major General Nguyen Khanh ousted General Minh as premier. In the Central Highlands the Viet Cong conducted a heavy assault on Camp Plei Mrong that demolished the Special Forces compound and killed most of its defenders.

During the spring of 1964, the Army further subordinated Special Forces by transferring detachment operational control in each Corps Tactical Zone to the senior MACV advisors of that zone. These officials burdened Special Forces teams with advisory and regular pacification duties in the more difficult and dangerous districts. Such additional chores placed a severe strain on the Special Forces' ability to manage the overall CIDG move to the border. In July the precarious defensive arrangements of isolated Special Forces compounds were again highlighted by Viet Cong attacks against Camps Nam Dong and Polei Krong.

During August General William C. Westmoreland became the commander of Military Assistance Command, Vietnam, and Colonel John Spears assumed command of the Vietnam-based Special Forces Group. On the battlefield the Viet Cong gained more victories against a weakened South Vietnamese army, divided by bickering senior officers in the coup-prone national government.

The Montagnards also chafed at their continued mistreatment by Vietnamese authorities. The Special Forces attempted to defuse growing Montagnard resentment, but during September a violent Montagnard revolt against the Republic of Vietnam erupted in five CIDG camps around Ban Me Thuot. This action greatly exacerbated Special Forces difficulties. The revolt was ended when a superficial compromise on native rights was reached, but the damage was lasting. The Special Forces fell almost completely out of Vietnamese favor and only slowly regained the trust of MACV. The Vietnamese eventually retaliated by closing all former rebel camps.

By the end of September 1964, Special Forces reached a strength of 950 troops organized into five B-Detachments and 44 A-Detachments that controlled nearly 20,000 native troops. The Army transferred the regular 5th Special Forces Group from Fort Bragg to Nha Trang, where it absorbed the original provisional Special Forces Group. All temporary teams were ordered to transition to a permanent change of station. This policy cancelled team rotations by introducing cyclic replacement of Special Forces personnel into permanently based team compounds on one-year combat assignments.

The Special Forces accomplishments during its first years of Vietnam service were profound. It displayed its finest attributes of tolerating hardship and deprivation in order to win over native tribes to the Civilian Irregular Defense Group program. Special Forces demonstrated its valor by its determination to safeguard large areas of Vietnam, by insuring village protection, tribal education, medical treatment, and civil assistance despite the enemy's numerical superiority. The Special Forces also proved its value as an integral part of the Army team when directed to reorient its efforts toward conventional border security.

Top: Early advisory efforts to the Republic of Vietnam were typified by the second Special Forces mission to that country. Special Forces training teams under Col. William Ewald were dispatched from the 77th Special Forces Group. They established ranger training sites at Da Nang, Song Mao, and Nha Trang from May 13 to November 17, 1960. They also provided the basis of the Vietnamese ranger program by selecting cadre and instructing them in physical conditioning, weapons techniques, and patrol tactics for anti-guerrilla company units. *(William Ewald)* **Bottom:** Capt. Raymond L. Call, Special Forces training detachment commander at Nha Trang during the 1960 mission, visits a forward ranger patrol base 20 miles inland near the village of Dong Trong. The white band around his utility Spring-up cap was a training identification emblem for Special Forces instructors during this mission. *(William Ewald)*

Top: This aerial view of the northern town of Hau Duc (Try My) shows the usual population patterns in the Vietnamese countryside where Special Forces was situated. The village is in the foreground with the district headquarters adjacent to the airfield. On a hillside across the Vang River stand the clustered houses of a Montagnard resettlement area. *(Author's Collection)* **Bottom left:** The first Special Forces mission to Vietnam in June 1957 trained commando parachutists of the 1st Observation Group at Nha Trang. *(William Ewald)* **Bottom right:** Camouflage training and patrol preparation being conducted at the Special Forces Da Nang training site in 1960. *(William Ewald)*

Top left: The United States hoped to apply the lessons of the successful British counterguerrilla effort in the nearby Federation of Malaysia against the Viet Cong insurgency in South Vietnam. Special Forces sent selected troops through the British Far East Land Forces Training Center at Kota Tinga, Malaysia, and studied contemporary British control measures such as this Malaysian peninsula road checkpoint. *(Federation of Malaysia Information Service)* **Top right:** President John F. Kennedy was instrumental in creating a strong Special Forces presence in Southeast Asia. In January 1961, during his first month of presidency, Kennedy announced a major counterinsurgency plan that formed the basis for expanded U.S. military assistance to the Republic of Vietnam. *(Fabian Bachrach/USA)* **Bottom:** Throughout the remainder of 1961, the U.S. Joint Chiefs of Staff met in crucial Pentagon sessions under the chairmanship of Gen. Lyman L. Lemnitzer (third from right, arms folded across notebook). They authorized increasing levels of advisory and Special Forces support to South Vietnam. *(Frank Hall/DOD)*

Top left: Special Forces Detachment A-113 of the 1st Special Forces Group, under the command of Capt. Ronald A. Shackleton, was the pilot team that initiated the joint CIA-Special Forces CIDG project at Buon Enao during February 1962. In this rare picture Capt. Shackleton (center) teaches Rhade volunteers to use rifles instead of crossbows. *(Sanford A. Morton)* **Top right:** The Rhade village of Buon Enao, located near Ban Me Thuot in the Vietnamese Central Highlands, was the Special Forces trial CIDG base camp. At this complex, pictured in March 1962, local Montagnards were trained to defend and patrol neighboring hamlets in Darlac Province. *(USA Command & General Staff College Military Review)* **Center left:** Gen. Maxwell D. Taylor, the Chairman-designate of the U.S. Joint Chiefs of Staff, is greeted upon his arrival at the Buon Enao center by Master Sgt. John O'Donovan. At center is Capt. Terry Cordell, the commander of A-334, who was killed just days later on October 15, 1962, while repulsing a major Viet Cong attack on the camp. *(Al Chang/USA)* **Bottom left:** Special Forces commander Col. George Morton serves as one of the pallbearers during plane-side services for Capt. Cordell, whose personal heroism and love of the Montagnard people was responsible for much of the Buon Enao success. *(Author's Collection)* **Bottom right:** Special Forces advisors at Buon Enao and other Rhade settlements transformed the tribesmen into effective security and strike forces that prevented enemy domination over Darlac Province. *(USA)*

Top left: Montagnard chieftains ruled their tribes in strict accordance with native customs that generally discouraged outside contact. Special Forces often won approval of chiefs and powerful shamans by passing rigid initiation rites to gain acceptance as Montagnard advisors. *(USIS)*
Top right: Montagnard villagers watch cautiously as a Special Forces team approaches their longhouses. *(USOM)* **Bottom:** A Special Forces detach-ment commander and his interpreter approach an unknown Montagnard village in Khanh Hoa Province. The rest of his team and a Marine observer stay at a respectful distance beside their CIA-furnished trucks. Once invited inside, the team will bring gifts and medical aid to the villagers and extend Special Forces protection in a carefully planned program aimed at cementing a permanent bond with the community. *(USOM)*

42

Top left: The simplistic Montagnards ate from the same pots and pans used to feed the animals. *(Jack Abraham)* **Top right:** Military rank did not always equate to local importance. This Rhade native private also held the exalted position of religious musician in animistic Montagnard rites to drive out evil deities. *(DOD)* **Center left:** The most sacred Montagnard rituals were reserved for their dead, and natives feared death outside tribal territory without proper ceremony—an important military concern for Special Forces. These burial grounds and urns are pictured near Camp Plei Yt. *(Author's Collection)* **Center right:** The Montagnards were skilled hunters and used poison arrows as part of their array of exotic weapons. This Montagnard finishes a crossbow near Special Forces Camp Ba To. *(DOD)* **Bottom:** Bru Montagnard women in Quang Tri Province bring firewood to their village past fortifications built under Special Forces supervision. *(Stephen Hembree)*

Top: Special Forces payment for Montagnard services often varied widely from conventional monetary reimbursement. Gold coins, silver bracelets, brass rings, glass-bead jewelry—and in this case a new fighting cock—were typical forms of reward. *(USIS)* **Center left:** Jarai Montagnards of Pleiku Province move their house to a new Special Forces camp during 1963. *(Author's Collection)* **Center right:** Special Forces took its first Central Highland census by lining up the Montagnard villagers in family units. The senior male of each family became No. 1, his wife No. 2, and the children were numbered by their ages, oldest to youngest. This photographic muster of each village could be compared quickly during unannounced visits by patrols looking for missing village members who might be Viet Cong suspects. *(George Marecek)* **Bottom left:** Many Montagnard children orphaned by war, such as this six-year-old girl at Buon Mi Ga, were adopted by Special Forces soldiers and brought home to the United States. *(Jack Abraham)* **Bottom right:** The Montagnards accepted only those who shared their life style. Seeking permission to give air support to Special Forces-led native contingents with his Skyraiders, Air Force Lt. Col. David Sparks, commander of the 20th Special Operations Squadron, participates in the traditional village ritual at Buon Ea Jong by drinking ''Nam Pie'' rice wine. *(USAF)*

Top left: Even Montagnard children sometimes participated in village defense as couriers and ammunition bearers. *(USA)* **Top right:** Friendly Montagnard relations with Special Forces inevitably resulted in Viet Cong reprisals, and villagers were occasionally grouped within protective fortifications to increase their security. These Montagnards are temporarily housed in Army tents at Camp Tan Rai in Lam Dong Province. *(Author's Collection)* **Center left:** In some cases enemy control of the countryside mandated permanent tribal resettlement close to Special Forces camps. The Montagnards were afraid of any relocation away from their native village, and Special Forces took extra care in conducting such movement. *(Clyde J. Sincere Jr.)* **Center right:** The Montagnards obeyed their sorcerers and religious leaders devoutly, and Special Forces accorded great respect to these powerful individuals. *(Paul Campbell)* **Bottom:** Punishment in Montagnard society could be brutally effective. After Rhade villagers found this girl taking rice to her banished Viet Cong boyfriend near Buon Mi Ga, she was shackled by logs in this position for more than six weeks. *(Jack Abraham)*

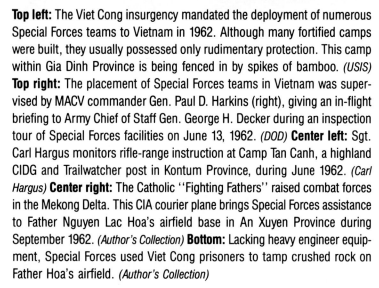

Top left: The Viet Cong insurgency mandated the deployment of numerous Special Forces teams to Vietnam in 1962. Although many fortified camps were built, they usually possessed only rudimentary protection. This camp within Gia Dinh Province is being fenced in by spikes of bamboo. *(USIS)*
Top right: The placement of Special Forces teams in Vietnam was supervised by MACV commander Gen. Paul D. Harkins (right), giving an in-flight briefing to Army Chief of Staff Gen. George H. Decker during an inspection tour of Special Forces facilities on June 13, 1962. *(DOD)* **Center left:** Sgt. Carl Hargus monitors rifle-range instruction at Camp Tan Canh, a highland CIDG and Trailwatcher post in Kontum Province, during June 1962. *(Carl Hargus)* **Center right:** The Catholic ''Fighting Fathers'' raised combat forces in the Mekong Delta. This CIA courier plane brings Special Forces assistance to Father Nguyen Lac Hoa's airfield base in An Xuyen Province during September 1962. *(Author's Collection)* **Bottom:** Lacking heavy engineer equipment, Special Forces used Viet Cong prisoners to tamp crushed rock on Father Hoa's airfield. *(Author's Collection)*

Top: Catholic Youth contingents were sponsored by President Diem, who demanded their inclusion in the CIDG program in exchange for his continued support of Special Forces efforts. During the night of October 30-31, 1962, two Viet Cong battalions nearly succeeded in overrunning Camp Long Phu, a Catholic Youth center under Special Forces protection in Chuong Thien Province. In this critical encounter Sgt. Tung of the 77th LLDB Group took advantage of aircraft-dropped flares that temporarily startled the enemy in the pre-dawn darkness. He maneuvered a Catholic Youth platoon behind the communist assault battalion and mowed down the silhouetted attackers. His action turned the tide of the battle and bolstered Special Forces confidence in Vietnamese special-purpose troops. *(Author's Collection)* **Bottom:** Sp5 James Gabriel Jr. was killed when a Vietnamese Republican Youth patrol base was overrun near Da Nang on April 4, 1962, and the Special Forces demonstration area at Fort Bragg was named in his honor. *(Jason T. Woodworth)*

Camp Ha Tien on the South China Sea was the southern anchor of the projected Special Forces border line. It was situated in the extreme southwestern tip of Vietnam's Mekong Delta, adjacent to Cambodia. Ringed by a hilltop trench line and several mortars that offered good protection for this stage of the war, the camp served as a training base for Vietnamese border-surveillance leaders. *(Author's Collection)*

Top: One of the distinguishing features of the Special Forces CIDG concept was the importance given to population support measures. Camp Ha Tien's civic-action program included medical assistance visits to insure a friendly government presence among the mixed Vietnamese-Cambodian inhabitants of this coastal frontier community. *(1st SFG PIO)* **Center left:** The dispensary at Camp Ha Tien, staffed by the Special Forces medical supervisor and a trained midwife, offered both medical and dental services. *(1st SFG PIO)* **Center right:** Animal preservation was of prime Special Forces concern, because the natives often depended on hunting as a way of life. Team mascots were not uncommon. This Asiatic Black Bear cub held by Sgt. Phil Dierks was adopted after villagers killed its mother. *(Donald Green)* **Bottom:** Special Forces marksmen shot this Bengal Tiger after it terrorized several Montagnard villages. *(Army News Features)*

Top: The Mountain Commando paramilitary organization was a Vietnamese political-action program initiated by the CIA during November 1961 and later redesignated as the Mountain Scouts. Provincial and district chiefs selected 15 to 18 men in their regions and sent these hand-picked troops through commando training at the Special Forces training centers of Hoa Cam and later Plei Yt. The trained teams returned to their home areas to function as hunter-killer groups capable of tracking Viet Cong guerrillas and providing intelligence for civil authorities. Unfortunately, the province and district chiefs used them primarily as bodyguards and hunting guides. *(Author's Collection)*
Bottom: A Mountain Commando team prepares to leave the Special Forces training center on a long-range patrol. *(Henry Backes Jr./USA)*

Top left: The Trailwatcher program was initiated in June 1962 by the CIA to take advantage of Montagnard warrior talents following regular South Vietnamese failures in patrolling border regions. The Special Forces was given the mission of training the Trailwatchers, later redesignated as Border Surveillance units, and using them to detect Viet Cong movements and eliminate enemy portage parties. The recruits were organized as company-sized units for an eight-week training session in Thua Thien Province. *(New Crawley/USA)* **Top right:** Special Forces teaches a M3 submachine gun class on a firing range at the Plei Yt Training Center. *(Henry Backes Jr./USA)* **Bottom left:** Commandos consult with a Special Forces advisor during a combat raid. *(USA)* **Bottom right:** Special Forces sergeants escort a Montagnard surveillance team in pursuit of Viet Cong troops near Ba To. *(Henry Backes Jr./USA)*

Top: Col. George C. Morton served initially as the Chief of the Special Warfare Branch on the MACV senior staff and was appointed to command all Special Forces in Vietnam on September 1, 1962. He was a renowned special-warfare expert who displayed great tenacity and leadership skill in building a solid foundation for the massive Special Forces endeavor in Southeast Asia. He is seen here (right) with Father Tung and Major Douthitt at Long Phu in the Mekong Delta, where Special Forces enabled the Diem-supported Catholic Youth defenders to survive despite repeated Viet Cong attacks. *(George Morton Family Collection)* **Center:** Col. Morton's treasured Vietnamese parachutist certificate. *(George Morton Family Collection)* **Bottom:** Col. Morton (left) stands next to Jim Garrison (center) and Vietnamese Presidential Survey Office Chief Col. Le Quang Tung (right), who was assassinated along with President Diem in the November 1963 coup. *(George Morton Family Collection)*

Top: The elite Australian Army Training Team arrived in Vietnam during 1962 and provided advisors to the South Vietnamese Army, the Montagnards, territorial forces, and local village defense units for more than ten years. The superb morale and jungle expertise of the Australians resulted in close integration with the Special Forces structure, even to the extent of commanding entire A-Detachments. Here a CIDG reaction force receives instructions from a joint Australian-American Special Forces team near Khe Sanh. *(MACV PIO)* **Center left:** Australian mastery of tropical patrolling and night ambush techniques became essential to the security of several Special Forces area projects. *(Author's Collection)* **Bottom left:** Australian Col. Frank P. Serong, commander of the Australian Army Training Team, was also a special advisor on counterinsurgency to the senior MACV staff. *(Australian Army)* **Bottom right:** Australian Captains James Burrows (left) and Jock Irvine (center) coordinate Vietnamese air support prior to a mission. They were among the first Australian Army Training Team members to join Special Forces during 1963. *(Australian Army)*

Top: Camp An Diem was typical of many early Special Forces camps. It was established west of Da Nang in Quang Nam Province during March 1963 by Detachment A-214 to convert the Katu tribe into native irregulars fighting for the Saigon regime. This detachment began training CIDG natives and initiated work on the campsite. During September the original team was replaced on normal rotation by A-213, which continued to strengthen defenses and patrol against Viet Cong lines of communication. An airstrip at An Diem was finally completed in March 1964, and A-224 relieved A-213 the following month. Hostilities in another sector of Vietnam actually determined An Diem's fate. The camp was closed on July 11, 1964, to allow A-224's relocation to Camp Nam Dong. The latter compound had been devastated by a heavy Viet Cong assault that had killed or wounded most defenders. The Special Forces command determined that it was more important to replenish the garrison at Nam Dong than to maintain An Diem. *(Author's Collection)* **Bottom:** Native carabineers sharpen their marksmanship on the Special Forces rifle range in March 1963. *(Jose Rivera/USA)*

Top: Special Forces border-screening responsibilities were a natural outgrowth of special warfare capabilities in conducting small-unit raids and surveillance operations. The Special Forces was unable to completely seal the 900-mile length of South Vietnam's rugged international boundary, but its troops detected, harassed, and interdicted Viet Cong infiltration routes parallel to or across the border-control zone in almost every area. Sgt. 1st Class Howard Stevens displays a captured communist flag while leading a victorious raiding expedition that destroyed a highland jungle way station on the Laotian frontier during 1963. *(Howard Stevens)* **Bottom:** Dead Viet Cong soldiers, lashed to poles, are carried from a river-crossing ambush site for a quick head count during Stevens' patrol. *(Howard Stevens)*

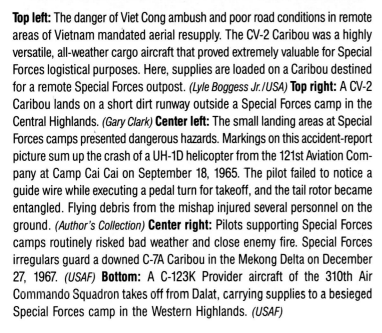

Top left: The danger of Viet Cong ambush and poor road conditions in remote areas of Vietnam mandated aerial resupply. The CV-2 Caribou was a highly versatile, all-weather cargo aircraft that proved extremely valuable for Special Forces logistical purposes. Here, supplies are loaded on a Caribou destined for a remote Special Forces outpost. *(Lyle Boggess Jr./USA)* **Top right:** A CV-2 Caribou lands on a short dirt runway outside a Special Forces camp in the Central Highlands. *(Gary Clark)* **Center left:** The small landing areas at Special Forces camps presented dangerous hazards. Markings on this accident-report picture sum up the crash of a UH-1D helicopter from the 121st Aviation Company at Camp Cai Cai on September 18, 1965. The pilot failed to notice a guide wire while executing a pedal turn for takeoff, and the tail rotor became entangled. Flying debris from the mishap injured several personnel on the ground. *(Author's Collection)* **Center right:** Pilots supporting Special Forces camps routinely risked bad weather and close enemy fire. Special Forces irregulars guard a downed C-7A Caribou in the Mekong Delta on December 27, 1967. *(USAF)* **Bottom:** A C-123K Provider aircraft of the 310th Air Commando Squadron takes off from Dalat, carrying supplies to a besieged Special Forces camp in the Western Highlands. *(USAF)*

Top: Helicopter warfare was a vital adjunct of Special Forces operations in Vietnam. This pair of CH-21 ''flying bananas'' skims over a Mekong Delta tree line as they prepare to land reinforcements on a Special Forces-held landing zone during April 1963. *(Ricardo A. Hinojosa/USA)* **Bottom left:** Two JOV-1C Mohawks of the 23d Special Warfare Aviation Detachment (Special Forces Surveillance) take off from the Tan Hiep airstrip on an aerial-observation mission over a Viet Cong stronghold during 1963. *(MACV PIO)* **Bottom right.** An O1 Bird Dog lands at Camp Ploi Mrong during a 1965 aerial-reconnaissance mission. These fragile aircraft provided vital aerial spotting, radio relay, and emergency resupply services throughout the war. Their pilots were accepted as part of the Special Forces community. *(Baker)*

Top: Border-surveillance camps were assigned to cover operational areas as the strength of their native garrisons permitted. Special Forces-advised camp strike forces increasingly used conventional tactics to block or intercept enemy infiltration. This Koho Montagnard strike force is equipped with rocket launchers for anti-bunker fighting. *(Steve Stibbens/Pacific Stars & Stripes)* **Bottom left:** Fortified camps were fixed defensive installations designed to withstand sustained Viet Cong assaults, and they provided home bases for indigenous strike forces engaged in border surveillance. The Special Forces command bunker was central to camp defense. It featured an antenna array and searchlights, as well as nearby identification panels or fire-direction arrows for day or night air support. *(DOD)* **Bottom right:** Border surveillance exacted an increasing toll on Special Forces advisors. This plane-side memorial service at Tan Son Nhut air base was held for Sgt. Robert J. Hain, killed by a Viet Cong sniper on May 6, 1963, just a month before his temporary-duty team was scheduled to return to Okinawa. *(Robert Cabral)*

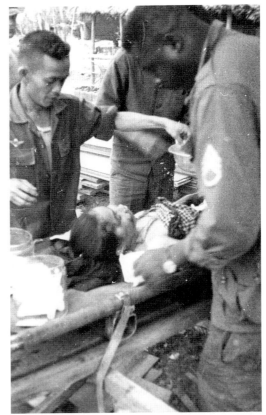

THE GREEN BRASSIERE

Put silver wings upon her stone
To let her know, she's not alone
We love the girl who's buried here,
The girl who wore the Green Brassiere

Let me tell you about this girl
She was truly a Vietnamese pearl
She wore a flower about her ear
And on her chest, a Green Brassiere

Press silver wings into her chest
Put there by America's best
She's been loved both far and near
She's the girl in the Green Brassiere

In the States a Vietnik waits
Burning cards at the White House gate
He'll just wait for about a year
While everyone else enjoys the Green Brassiere

One night on base she came 'bout eleven
She thought she'd walked right into heaven
The fighter pilots of the Third Wing
Showed the Green Brassiere a hell of a fling

A VC shell came from above
Only left one thing to remind us of
This little girl we love so dear
A slightly tattered Green Brassiere

Put silver wings upon her stone
To let her know she's not alone
We love the girl who's buried here
The girl who wore the Green Brassiere

Top left: Native quarters in the border-surveillance camps often consisted of tents and grass-matted huts among a maze of zigzag communication trenches and fighting positions near the camp wall. *(DOD)* **Top right:** The heightened tempo of conflict along the border resulted in frequent civilian casualties from enemy boobytraps, as well as allied ordnance, and Special Forces medics worked frantically to treat life-threatening cases. *(Lee Mize)* **Center left:** Christmas in a Special Forces border-surveillance camp lacked some of the traditional ornamentation but none of the spirit. *(Lee Mize)* **Center right:** Special Forces troopers (holding drinks, left to right) Howard Gradey, Fargos, Larry Schied, and Fred Fiedler temporarily relax from frontline duty in a Saigon nightclub. *(Fred Fiedler)* **Bottom:** Special Forces humorists kept the music but rewrote the words to the popular Ballad of the Green Berets, composing another version more commonly recited in Vietnam. *(Mark Berent)*

Top left: Camp Loc Ninh was established in the rubber plantations far north of Saigon to provide border surveillance near Cambodia. Here, Special Forces Staff Sgt. Arthur Fletcher helps a CIDG light-weapons team repair its .30-caliber machine gun preparatory to a field mission. *(USIS)* **Top right:** Hand grenade throwing practice for native irregulars is conducted under the watchful eye of Sgt. Lewis. *(Henry Backes/USA)* **Center left:** Loc Ninh contained a mixed Cambodian-Stieng Montagnard garrison under Special Forces supervision. *(Author's Collection)* **Center right:** Loc Ninh defenses were strengthened by this field-expedient wooden rack for a 3.5-inch multiple-rocket weapon during 1963. *(Author's Collection)* **Bottom right:** The camp wall at Loc Ninh was reinforced by a Special Forces-produced, swivel-mounted 3.5-inch rocket launcher in 1963. *(Author's Collection)*

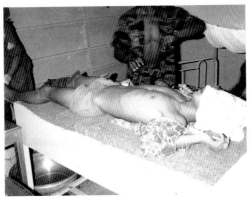

Top: Camp Chau Lang was an important border-surveillance camp in the Mekong Delta during 1963. This 7th Special Forces Group team used the site to train several camp strike-force companies and 2,000 hamlet militia. *(JFK Center Museum/Angram Collection)* **Center:** Chau Lang's area-pacification program resulted in Viet Cong targeting of the compound, as evinced by this VC recon photo on a roll of film captured during a Special Forces patrol. Note the camp watch tower at far right. *(Author's Collection)* **Bottom left:** Military supplies are parachuted to Camp Chau Lang in November 1963 after the Viet Cong cut the local road net. The marked mine fields on both sides of the airstrip were not designed to defeat an enemy ground assault but rather to channel the attackers into pre-selected "killing zones" covered by camp automatic-weapon positions. *(Author's Collection)* **Bottom right:** A strike-force soldier receives emergency treatment at Camp Chau Lang after his right foot was blown off by a mine explosion on March 8, 1964. Enemy anti-personnel devices were a continual danger to Special Forces patrols in all areas of Vietnam. *(Author's Collection)*

Top: Special Forces battle casualties rose sharply with the escalation of Vietnam hostilities in 1963. Special Forces Staff Sgt. Claude W. McBride of the 1st Special Forces Group was killed by a sniper while valiantly defending this isolated mountain landing zone near An Diem on August 23. A downed Marine helicopter marks the shattered battlefield, secured by a Special Forces patrol on the forward slope shortly after the action. *(Author's Collection)* **Bottom:** The Special Forces headquarters at Da Nang, in charge of Vietnam's northern I Corps Tactical Zone, was renamed Camp McBride in honor of Sergeant McBride's heroic Vietnam service. *(1st SFG PIO)*

Top left: Special Forces patrol leaders Sergeants First Class Robert Pronier and Bill Craig stop momentarily to eat chow and discuss their route of advance in the highland jungles near the Vietnamese border. They are accompanied by novelist Robin Moore, in background with pipe, who later wrote the best-selling novel *The Green Berets*. *(Donald Greene)* **Top right:** Patrols faced hazardous exposure while crossing mountain streams. *(Author's Collection)* **Center left:** Patrol members probe through an open bamboo thicket preparatory to attacking a Viet Cong position. *(Donald Greene)* **Center right:** Sleeping arrangements during a patrol deep in enemy territory consisted of a poncho and liner spread out in a small clearing, with weapons kept nearby and dry off the wet jungle floor. *(Donald Greene)* **Bottom:** Sgt. Charlie Webb, holding the AR-15 rifle newly issued to Special Forces advisors, sits alongside his interpreter and Bru tribal company commander while on patrol. *(Donald Greene)*

Camp Hiep Hoa was established on a canal overlooking the Viet Cong-dominated Plain of Reeds during February 1963. The Viet Cong assaulted the fort after midnight on November 24 and breached its defenses after camp defectors killed several men on guard and machine-gunned other soldiers exiting the billets. Special Forces personnel recaptured the machine gun and held their positions until wounded and overpowered. **Top left:** Lt. John R. Colby, the Special Forces detachment executive officer seen here days before the attack holding his 12-gauge shotgun, valiantly defended the camp until severely wounded. *(John Colby)* **Top right:** Sgt. First Class Isaac Comacho was captured at Hiep Hoa but escaped from his Viet Cong captors, becoming the first American prisoner in Vietnam to return. He stands between Sergeants First Class Charles Hosking Jr. and Rock Lane on the day of his return, July 13, 1965. *(Hosking Children's Collection via Ray Bows).* **Center left:** Camp Hiep Hoa interior with (1) mortar position, covered to keep out rain; (2) SF team house; (3) trucks later demolished by the Viet Cong; (4) observation tower; and (5) LLDB quarters. *(John Colby)* **Center right:** The sugar mill adjacent to Hiep Hoa was guarded by local howitzer crews who refused to fire in the camp's support. *(Author's Collection)* **Bottom:** Camp Hiep Hoa CIDG soldiers guard Viet Cong prisoners before the attack. *(John Colby)*

Top: Special Forces worked closely with two paramilitary forces responsible for internal province security. The Civil Guard, later renamed the Regional Forces, were locally recruited constabulary companies under command of the province chiefs. The Self Defense Corps, later renamed the Popular Forces, consisted of village platoons created to safeguard individual communities in the absence of regular Vietnamese Army protection. The Regional Forces/Popular Forces (RF/PF) were nicknamed ''Ruff-puffs.'' Maj. David E. Shepherd Jr., right, a U.S. Operations Mission provincial representative and former deputy commander of the Special Forces Training Group at Fort Bragg, holds a Lee Enfield Mark IV sniper rifle while accompanying the district chief and Army advisors during a 1964 ''Ruff-puff'' operation near Ben Luc in Long An Province. *(David Shepherd Jr.)* **Bottom:** Capt. Jim Morris surveys his Special Forces irregular advisory outpost from the door of a cargo aircraft as it departs Vietnam for Okinawa in June 1964. Morris later recounted his experiences as a Special Forces combat officer in his excellent post-war book *War Story. (Jim Morris)*

Top left: Countering the Viet Cong often meant endless weeks of frustrating searches that produced few tangible results. This tired CIDG boat crew returns empty-handed from a river patrol with full boxes of ammunition and weary expressions. *(Lee Mize)* **Top right:** The peaceful solitude of a Vietnamese peasant cultivating his rice fields, like this farmer outside Bien Hoa, was often deceptive and required continual Special Forces alertness for potential Viet Cong activity. *(USIS)* **Center:** When found, the Viet Cong suffered the full wrath of Special Forces vengeance. A border-surveillance patrol from Moc Hoa torches Viet Cong supply huts found in a dense swamp forest. *(Fred Fiedler)* **Bottom:** A Special Forces sergeant gingerly removes a jammed bazooka round during an engagement with entrenched Viet Cong guerrillas north of Dam Pau on January 8, 1964. Such incidents emphasized the need for experienced advisors accompanying native patrols. *(Steve Stibbens/Pacific Stars & Stripes)*

Top left: Special Forces advisory duty was extremely dangerous, and the lightly armed sergeants and officers depended greatly on personal sidearms. Sgt. John Watson, wearing the distinctive pocket patch of Detachment A-424 ''McCulloch's Airborne Tigers'' (named after team commander Capt. William Crews McCulloch) takes aim with his revolver on the range at Camp Buon Beng during 1964. *(Bill Brooks)* **Top right:** Sgt. First Class Jason T. Woodworth totes his M16 rifle on patrol outside Ben Cat. The M16's rapid fire gave Special Forces advisors a battlefield equivalent to modern automatic rifles carried by the Viet Cong, but production limitations prevented CIDG natives from obtaining them until late in the war. *(Jason T. Woodworth)* **Bottom:** Special Forces service in the multitude of camps situated to cover Vietnam's jungle valleys, highland plateaus, and delta marshlands was difficult and lonely. These sergeants at Camp Phey Srunh rest after a long patrol march through the tropical rain forest of Tuyen Duc Province during mid-January 1964. *(Steve Stibbens/Pacific Stars & Stripes)*

Top left: Several Special Forces camps experimented with balloons to lift radio antennas and increase transmission range. The signature of the system, whether flown in Vietnam's flat Mekong Delta or rugged mountains, caused no enemy action against either the balloon or its ground terminal. *(USACTIV)* **Top center:** Special Forces communications balloons were not fielded beyond the compounds, although they could be transported elsewhere by truck or helicopter if necessary. High monsoon winds made them impractical in certain seasons. *(USACTIV)* **Top right:** The main antenna at Camp Tuyen Nhon in the Mekong Delta was heightened and stabilized against the ferocity of monsoon storms by the use of empty bomb crates during June 1967. *(Author's Collection)* **Bottom left:** Radio transmission balloon hoisted by Camp Tuyen Nhon. *(Ensign/USA)* **Bottom right:** The GRC-109, a continuous-wave radio that worked well despite Vietnam's tropical terrain and atmospheric conditions, could operate from a variety of power sources, such as this hand-cranked generator. It could receive both Morse Code and voice, but the operator could only transmit using the former. *(John L. Brady/USA)*

SLANT WIRE

ANTENNA LADDER LEAD

Top left: Special Forces radiomen rigged antennas in trees to increase range across heavy jungle, as shown during this December 1964 patrol outside Plei Mrong. *(Author's Collection)* **Top right:** Special Forces radiomen tested two high-frequency radios in Vietnam from October 1964 through January 1965: the lightweight PRC-64 radio (left) and an experimental PRC-77 radio set (right). The PRC-64 performed well in the continuous-wave mode but its unreliable voice mode limited its use to trained key operators. The PRC-77 became common after mid-1968. *(Author's Collection)* **Center left:** The long-distance nature of Special Forces operations demanded field flexibility in signaling arrangements. This Special Forces slant antenna, rigged on the Loc Ninh airstrip during Mike Force operations, permitted transmissions over the jungle to Bien Hoa. *(Tom Myerchin)* **Center right:** Typical Vietnam communications included an overhead shelter of leaves, such as this one protecting PRC-64 and PRC-77 test radio sets during a 1964 rainstorm. The slant wire for control and antenna lead-in are marked on the photo. The spool near the front trooper's hand is a doublet antenna wire reel. *(Author's Collection)* **Bottom:** Sgt. Poole of Project Delta employs the commercial Hughes HC-162 radio during combat in 1965. Field-recommended power supply inclusion and dry-cell battery operation were adopted, making it the basis of the GRC-74 Special Forces portable radio. *(Donald Valentine)*

Top: Special Forces Detachment A-334, located at Camp Plei Do Lim and advised by Capt. Herbert F. Hardy Jr., employed CIDG Montagnard forces in a combat role, which caused resentment from the Vietnamese LLDB team also located at the camp. Despite these strained tensions, Capt. Hardy and Sgt. First Class William E. Edge led a company-sized Montagnard scouting expedition into the Rapan Mountains to locate Viet Cong facilities. During an assault on an enemy training base, the Montagnard company broke and ran, but the two Special Forces advisors boldly continued the attack and destroyed the enemy positions. When Capt. Hardy was killed in action while leading another patrol less than two weeks later on March 4, 1964, the compound was redesignated Camp Hardy in his memory. *(Author's Collection)* **Bottom:** Wires connecting defensive explosive charges with remote firing devices are checked along the Plei Do Lim perimeter. *(Author's Collection)*

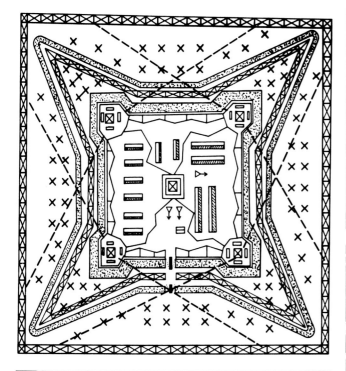

Top left: Adequate security of the Special Forces camp environment was of critical importance. The defensive layout of Camp Minh Thanh allowed broad overlapping fields of fire, as shown by the dashed lines. The camp was surrounded by mine fields (marked by Xs), several trenches with spikes (dotted areas), and multiple concertina wire fence lines (rows of Xs). Camp weapons included 57mm recoilless rifles (arrow triangles), mortars (crossed boxes), and machine gun nests (open boxes). Wavy lines within the camp trace the interior communications trench. *(5th SFG Opns Logistic Div.)* **Top right:** The camp gate at Minh Thanh, a Special Forces post that guarded important rubber-producing areas on the fringe of War Zone C. *(USASFV PIO)* **Center left:** Minh Thanh aid station contained instructional wall graphics. *(USASFV PIO)* **Center right:** The medical supervisor and staff at Minh Thanh during 1964. *(USASFV PIO)* **Bottom left:** Water storage and shower facilities. *(USASFV PIO)* **Bottom right:** Minh Thanh Special Forces quarters. *(USASFV PIO)*

Top left: Gen. William C. Westmoreland took command of MACV on June 20, 1964, and forged new Special Forces directions in Vietnam—from placing the 5th Special Forces Group in charge of MACV reconnaissance training to approving multi-purpose reaction units, called mobile strike forces, for each military zone. *(MACV PIO)* **Top right:** Gen. Harold K. Johnson, seen inspecting captured weapons at Camp Binh Thanh Thon, was appointed Army Chief of Staff in July 1964. He expressed private displeasure with many aspects of the Vietnam war, including what he saw as the stagnation of Special Forces talent in immobile campsites. *(George Marecek)* **Center right:** U.S. Secretary of Defense Robert S. McNamara derived his enthusiasm for Special Forces from President John F. Kennedy and viewed the CIDG program as agreeably cost-effective. He follows Detachment C-4 commander Lt. Col. Bob Hessinger during a Vietnam visit to Camp My Da, a low-water Mekong Delta camp with floating barrels underneath its helicopter platform. *(George Marecek)* **Bottom right:** U.S. Army Pacific commander Gen. John K. Waters inspects an Australian-American team from a Special Forces gun jeep. He welcomed more Special Forces teams in Vietnam, but not at the expense of the 1st Special Forces Group on Okinawa. *(Lee Clayman)*

Camp Polei Krong in Kontum Province was subjected to a strong Viet Cong attack in the pre-dawn hours of July 4, 1964, heralded by infiltration parties that slipped within the main compound. The main assault force, supported by enemy weapons along the edge of the airstrip (center), broke through the parapets and engaged the Special Forces and surviving camp defenders in a savage melee that ended at the ferry crossing on the river's edge (right corner). The disaster was attributed to lax defensive precautions and inside Viet Cong cooperation. The latter misfortune was verified by camp plans found on an enemy body and the murder of several sentinels and LLDB sergeants before they could reach their posts. The Vietnamese government took advantage of the tragedy at Polei Krong by hurling accusations of disorderly conduct at both U.S. and LLDB advisors, despite the individual bravery of detachment members and many Montagnard defenders. However, this defeat pointed out two great CIDG deficiencies of the time: each camp was on its own during hours of darkness, because Vietnamese reinforcement was unlikely before daylight, and Viet Cong control of many remote areas made close surprise attacks possible. *(Author's Collection)*

Top: Camp Nam Dong in the southwestern portion of Thua Thien Province was struck by a massive surprise attack before dawn on July 6, 1964, just two days after Polei Krong was hit. Because Nam Dong was scheduled to be closed out, its defenses were neglected to the point that high grass obscured most perimeter fields of fire. The Viet Cong battalion surged forward in three drives organized behind well-coordinated mortar barrages. The first enemy assault wave stormed through this gap in the camp wall, but Special Forces and Nung defenders held the inner perimeter until daybreak and prevented a complete overrun. *(DOD)* **Bottom left:** Camp

Nam Dong was defended by (left to right) Detachment A-726 Sergeants Merwin D. Woods, Thomas L. Gregg, Michael Disser, Raymond Whitsell, Terrence D. Terrin, Vernon L. Berson, and Lt. Julian Olejniczak. Missing from this photo are Capt. Roger H.C. Donlon and Sergeants Thurman R. Brown and Keith E. Daniels. *(USA)* **Bottom right:** Team Capt. Roger H.C. Donlon of the 7th Special Forces Group led the heroic defense of Nam Dong despite serious wounds. He earned the first Medal of Honor awarded in the Vietnam conflict. *(USA)*

Top left: Viet Cong weapons gathered from the Nam Dong battlefield testified to the strength of the enemy battalion attempting to destroy the Special Forces camp. *(DOD)* **Top right:** This blood-splattered mortar position was continually grenaded by Viet Cong sappers who had reached hand-throwing range of the emplacement by crawling through the tall grass and breaching the wire barrier. Capt. Donlon was wounded several times while repeatedly attempting to rescue a team comrade injured by grenade fragments at this position. *(DOD)* **Center left:** Returning to Camp Nam Dong after the battle, Capt. Donlon inspects barbed wire replaced along the perimeter. *(Gilbert Meyers/USA Pacific Photo Det.)* **Center right:** During the mass attack, the outer portion of Nam Dong was completely demolished, but the defenders managed to withdraw to the inner core of the camp and hold on with limited ammunition until daylight. *(DOD)* **Bottom:** Well-muscled Viet Cong shock troops wore red and blue swimming trunks and carried handcuffs for prisoners. The close-cropped hair and clean fingernails of many dead soldiers suggested that the enemy received cadre reinforcements just prior to the battle. *(DOD)*

Top left: An evening meal is prepared by a Special Forces interdiction patrol prior to occupying night security positions in the Western Highlands. *(Author's Collection)* **Top right:** Col. John H. Spears took over the U.S. Army Special Forces Group, Vietnam (Provisional), in August 1964, merging the command with the 5th Special Forces Group when it arrived in Vietnam that September. He commanded both organizations and is shown with Group mascot ''Bullet'' at his desk. *(John Spears/Adam Dintenfass Collection)* **Center:** One of Col. Spears' major tasks was gaining control of area segments along the international border by expanding patrols to seal enemy approach routes into Vietnam. This Plei Mrong patrol crosses a stream in the tri-border area as part of this mission. *(Author's Collection)* **Bottom:** A Special Forces-led CIDG patrol performs a long-range mission to detect infiltration routes in the mountainous border-control zone west of Kontum in December 1964. *(Author's Collection)*

Top left: A Special Forces border camp required a minimum of four border-surveillance companies in order to keep two in the field for week-long patrols. Accordingly, the 400-man garrisons of most camps were usually organized into four 100-man companies. These Montagnard irregulars attired in dapple-style camouflage move out of a company patrol base in the Central Highlands near Polei Krong. *(Author's Collection)* **Top right:** Special Forces desired greater dispersal of its patrolling resources, but the CIDG program lacked competent native leaders who could be entrusted with independent missions. This limiting factor necessitated Special Forces accompaniment since little was accomplished by patrols unescorted by American advisors. *(Author's Collection)* **Bottom:** Special Forces and their native irregulars were used to the heat, rain, and discomfort inherent in tropical warfare, and MACV planners hoped that each camp could patrol effectively within a ten-mile radius. This calculation translated into a 20-mile ideal interval between camps. However, the closest Special Forces came to this goal was in late 1964, when the building of two additional Mekong Delta camps resulted in distances averaging 27 miles between camps in western Vietnam. *(Author's Collection)*

Top: On September 19-20, 1964, the Montagnards in five camps revolted against the national government. The rebellious forces included the Ban Don native garrison, seen in this picture returning from an elephant-mounted patrol. The Jarai and Rhade Montagnards at Ban Don tied up their LLDB advisors and joined other forces participating in the uprising by marching on Ban Me Thuot. *(Author's Collection via George Morton)* **Bottom:** The Detachment A-75 airfield sign at Ban Don reflected the isolated characteristics of the westernmost Montagnard camp in Darlac Province. *(Howard Linscott)*

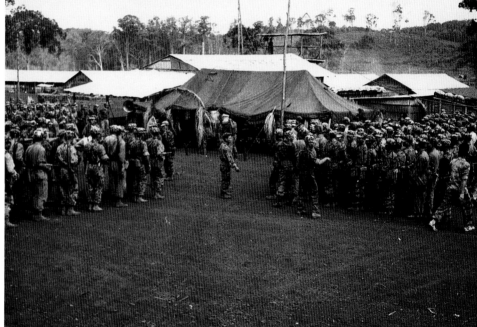

Top right: Camp Bon Sar Pa was located in the jungle hill country on the Cambodian border within the upper reaches of Quang Duc Province, southwest of Ban Me Thuot. On the night of September 19, 1964, the Mnong and Rhade Montagnards inside the camp slaughtered the camp's Vietnamese soldiers and imprisoned their Special Forces team A-311A advisors. *(Charles Darnell)* **Bottom right:** The crude stake fence enclosing Camp Bon Sar Pa offered little defense against a concentrated counter-attack, but the numerous Americans and Vietnamese held hostage by a large rebel contingent inside the compound precluded such an option. *(Charles Darnell)*

Top: The Montagnard force from Camp Bon Sar Pa presented the most dangerous threat to Vietnamese authorities during the revolt, because it marched quickly toward Ban Me Thuot and took several hundred Vietnamese hostages along the way. *(Author's Collection)* **Bottom left:** The tense Bon Sar Pa crisis was not resolved until September 28, 1964, when the Montagnards released their prisoners inside the camp and terminated the revolt. Here the camp commander Charles B. Darnell holds the II Corps Tactical Zone camp flag. *(Charles Darnell)* **Bottom right:** Discarded rebel weapons from the native garrison at Camp Bon Sar Pa are piled up at the conclusion of the Montagnard uprising *(Charles Darnell)*

Top left: The Special Forces were very concerned about the impact of the Montagnard revolt, because the camps were a vital link in wresting the border area from strong Viet Cong influence. The degree of Viet Cong hostility is reflected in this sign found by a patrol outside Buon Mi Ga demanding ''an immediate end to the U.S. Imperialists Aggressive War in South Vietnam.'' *(Jack Abraham)* **Top right:** A prisoner taken by the Montagnards awaits his fate at the hands of his captors. *(Jack Abraham)* **Center:** The Montagnards used the weapons and training received by Special Forces throughout the course of the September 1964 revolt. *(Jack Abraham)* **Bottom:** The Special Forces team house at Camp Buon Mi Ga carries identification on the tin roof for the benefit of helicopters. The Montagnards barely tolerated Vietnamese authority under the best of circumstances, and during the revolt the native Mnongs in this garrison killed ten Vietnamese advisors and completely disarmed Captain Loa's Detachment A-121A. *(Jack Abraham)*

Top left and top right: Helicopters lifted the Special Forces team out of Camp Buon Mi Ga on the day after the revolt. The armed Montagnard camp force that marched on Ban Me Thuot was concerned for the safety of their families left behind at the campsite. This factor weighed heavily in their decision to cease further resistance. *(Jack Abraham)* **Center left:** The outer perimeters of Montagnard camps were laced with punji stake pits that had to be uncovered for the safety of allied forces. *(Jack Abraham)* **Center right:** Montagnard women hulling rice at Buon Mi Ga patiently await the return of their husbands and sons encamped around the provincial capital of Ban Me Thuot in a ''show-down'' with Vietnamese authorities. *(Jack Abraham)* **Bottom:** Ritualistic animal sacrifice was a solemn Montagnard custom, often more crucial toward influencing tribal decisions than the military actions of either side. *(Jack Abraham)*

Top left: A Mnong chieftain from Buon Mi Ga prays for a peaceful resolution of the rebellion by sacrificing a chicken and drinking ''Nam Pie'' rice wine from a centuries-old jug in conformity with tribal ritual. *(Jack Abraham)* **Top right:** The Mnong Montagnards from Camp Buon Mi Ga took trucks and moved west toward Ban Me Thuot, where they maintained a roadblock. *(Jack Abraham)* **Center left:** Montagnard soldiers expressed only superficial faith in the Vietnamese government, and many were actually sympathetic to the dissident Rhade independence movement *Front Unifie Pour La Libération des Races Opprimees* or ''FULRO.'' *(Jack Abraham)* **Center right:** Camp Buon Mi Ga after being razed to the ground and abandoned as a Special Forces site following the conclusion of the Montagnard revolt. *(Jack Abraham)* **Bottom:** Special Forces advisors talk over the situation as armed Montagnards observe in the background. The Montagnards clashed briefly with Vietnamese Army units, but Capt. Loa convinced the rebels to surrender and arranged for their transport back to Buon Mi Ga. *(Jack Abraham)*

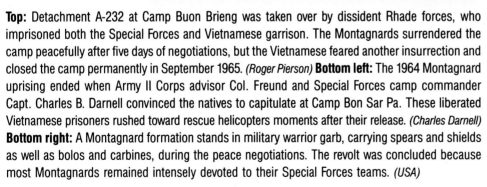

Top: Detachment A-232 at Camp Buon Brieng was taken over by dissident Rhade forces, who imprisoned both the Special Forces and Vietnamese garrison. The Montagnards surrendered the camp peacefully after five days of negotiations, but the Vietnamese feared another insurrection and closed the camp permanently in September 1965. *(Roger Pierson)* **Bottom left:** The 1964 Montagnard uprising ended when Army II Corps advisor Col. Freund and Special Forces camp commander Capt. Charles B. Darnell convinced the natives to capitulate at Camp Bon Sar Pa. These liberated Vietnamese prisoners rushed toward rescue helicopters moments after their release. *(Charles Darnell)* **Bottom right:** A Montagnard formation stands in military warrior garb, carrying spears and shields as well as bolos and carbines, during the peace negotiations. The revolt was concluded because most Montagnards remained intensely devoted to their Special Forces teams. *(USA)*

Top left: Following the 1964 Montagnard revolt, the Saigon regime and U.S. government implemented token changes, such as the naming of Montagnard commanders to certain Special Forces camps. In exchange, on January 17, 1965, various Montagnard hamlets pledged renewed loyalty to South Vietnam at Ban Me Thuot. This native honor guard for the ceremony was drawn from selected members of each rebellious camp. *(Allen K. Holm)* **Top right:** Mounted Montagnard standard bearers parade their native colors through Saigon. The South Vietnamese government invited a contingent of the Special Forces-led highland natives into the capital for the first time while commemorating the overthrow of the Diem regime on November 1, 1965, but it did not allow them to carry weapons during the parade. *(USA)* **Center:** In an exceptional display of political sensitivity following the Montagnard revolt, Vietnamese II Corps Tactical Zone commander Maj. Gen. Vinh Loc, dressed in highland finery, participates in a native ceremony by sipping rice wine as he is presented the Montagnard bracelet. *(USA)* **Bottom:** Political expediency took precedence over personal sentiments as Maj. Nguyen Dinh Vinh, the Vietnamese province chief, and his officers attended the ceremonial feast that marked the cessation of the Montagnard revolt. Later the Vietnamese closed all Special Forces camps associated with Montagnard unrest. *(Roger Pierson)*

Top: The Montagnard rebellion within the Central Highlands did not slow the pace of Special Forces commitment in other regions, and Camp Ben Cat was opened on the edge of the Viet Cong Iron Triangle base area during September 1964. The Special Forces accomplished the first persistent allied penetration of this enemy sanctuary by launching repeated sorties into the jungle redoubt. They netted prisoners who revealed an extensive labyrinth of secret tunnels and cache sites. *(Jason T. Woodworth)* **Bottom:** Special Forces senior Sergeants Bert ''Duncan Hines'' Smith (left) and ''Sak'' Sakomoto (right) coordinate with a Vietnamese CIDG leader outside Ben Cat. In addition to combat strikes, Special Forces concentrated on village improvement and agricultural civil assistance to loosen the Viet Cong strangle-hold over the population in the Iron Triangle vicinity. *(Jason T. Woodworth)*

Top: Special Forces depended closely on the growing number of Army helicopter units that ferried troops and provided aerial firepower in their support, and the Viet Cong struck back at these aviation resources by raiding Camp Holloway outside Pleiku on February 7, 1965. A combination Viet Cong sapper and mortar attack demolished scores of helicopters and killed numerous servicemen, prompting the United States to send combat units into Vietnam for greater protection of its bases. *(DOD)* **Bottom:** Henry Cabot Lodge (center), the Ambassador to Vietnam and the special presidential consultant for Vietnam after May 1964, urged the United States to send major Army units into the growing conflict. He is shown with U.S. Secretary of Defense Robert S. McNamara (right) and Gen. Maxwell D. Taylor (left), who succeeded Lodge as Ambassador to Vietnam. Following the Camp Holloway attack, their advice to President Lyndon Johnson resulted in the Joint Chiefs of Staff alerting the 173d Airborne Brigade for Vietnam duty on February 11. The arrival of large Army combat formations soon eclipsed press headlines about Special Forces involvement in Vietnam but never lessened the actual range of special warfare requirements. *(DOD)*

A Special Forces raiding party in the Mekong Delta moves out at first light and boards watercraft for a dawn river assault on Viet Cong positions south of Camp Cai Cai. The aidman, carrying a medical backpack in the foreground, prepares to follow his detachment commander, who is pointing out directions to thc Vietnamese officer in charge. *(Author's Collection)*

SPECIAL FORCES AND THE AMERICAN BUILDUP, 1965

During 1965 the Special Forces continued to develop and strengthen its Civilian Irregular Defense Group (CIDG) program in Vietnam. The program had grown quite large from its original inception as a mobile training team augmentation in one cluster of Rhade villages to a major combat-theater counterinsurgency effort. Despite its size, the program still relied on its original concept of recruiting natives from remote areas in an attempt to secure territorial control and enhance regional development.

Direction for the CIDG program in each area was accomplished by small Special Forces operational detachments fielded in campsites throughout the country. Each camp was occupied ideally by one American A-Team, its counterpart Vietnamese *Lực-Lượng Dặc-Biệt* team, and armed indigenous forces hired, clothed, fed, supplied, and paid for by Special Forces funds. Using these camps as centers of training and replenishment, Special Forces personnel advised and led camp strike forces in performing area pacification and border-surveillance operations that often combined both military and civil-assistance aspects.

The most distinguishing feature of the CIDG program was its recruitment of native volunteers as full-time paid combatants. Those who were accepted into the program were called strike-force personnel. Although cash payment for service gave a mercenary character to Special Forces efforts, it also insured that paramilitary combatants accepted into the program were actually willing to fight the Viet Cong.

Throughout the year, Special Forces was also engaged in moving CIDG forces toward the border in accordance with earlier mandates that emphasized the interdiction of Viet Cong infiltration zones as a priority mission. Planning and initiating these border operations, highlighted by the construction of new frontier camps, accounted for much Special Forces activity. The closing of many older camps, however, was necessitated as more Special Forces assets were relocated closer to the western boundary of Vietnam.

The building and maintenance of the camps became a major preoccupation of Special Forces teams, especially as CIDG program villagers were transplanted to remote and dangerous areas. The scarcity of materials for construction was a great problem, and materials used often depended on geographical location. Sturdy wooden logs became battlements in the mountainous highlands, but in the southern Mekong Delta, packed mud and dried reeds had to suffice. As a result of the 1964 Nam Dong battle, most camps added core or inner perimeters, a notion derived from medieval castle keeps, which gave a second zone of defense to each camp. Such inner strong-points proved instrumental in saving camps like Dong Xoai from total destruction.

The camp strike forces were provisional light rifle company organizations composed of patrol squads, and each camp was authorized a minimum of three camp strike-force companies. The camp provided a base for these strike forces and developed into fortified homes for the natives and their dependents. Some patrols cleared local roads and monitored villages around the camp, while other patrols, returning from longer reconnaissance missions, rested. In addition, Special Forces continued training and preparing other patrols. This cyclic pattern resulted in one-third of the strike force, or one company, continuously out of the camp on active operations; one-third, or a second company, in camp resting and performing interior guard; and the remaining one-third, the final company, training and preparing to go on combat operations.

Camp defensive precautions were intensified so that teams could withstand the intensity of enemy attacks encountered at Song Be, Dong Xoai, and Bu Dop. Special Forces team quarters and facilities were among the first targets of the Viet Cong in such an attack. Because the opening barrage concentrated on these pre-selected areas, in August 1965 orders were issued that no more than three Americans could sleep in the same building and that duplicate-skills personnel, such as senior and junior radiomen, could not be billeted together. Personnel were dispersed to take up residence among the command bunkers, communications bunkers, dispensaries, supply shacks, and expedient shelters.

At Dong Xoai and Bu Dop the first rounds of enemy shellfire were aimed at destroying the communication facilities. In response, Special Forces placed all radio equipment underground or in alternately covered positions, and hand-held radios were given to all posts. Recognizing that the Viet Cong possessed detailed knowledge about all interior camp arrangments and heavy weapons emplacements, teams began switching mortars and machine guns within their camps after nightfall. These internal corrective actions, coupled with larger measures such as the raising of mobile reaction forces to assist beleaguered camps, began to afford Special Forces greater protection throughout Vietnam.

The Viet Cong were not content to harass Special Forces outposts. They also successfully challenged South Vietnamese units on the open battlefield. The manifest superiority of these main force Viet Cong units over Vietnamese government forces during the year forced Military Assistance Command, Vietnam (MACV), lacking other reserves, to use Special Forces as an emergency substitute. The Special Forces were directed to perform such conventional missions as defending critical airfields, guarding highway passes, and securing military complexes until larger Army and Marine units could reach Vietnam from the United States.

Camp strike forces performed these missions at great human cost and with varying degrees of success, because they were not designed as regular combat elements. Special Forces paramilitary components were organized into companies primarily for administrative control convenience. Native training was restricted to rudimentary patrolling and discouragement of local communist guerrillas. Reaction drills were limited to defending nearby hamlets in case of Viet Cong trouble. Special Forces instruction included only basic weapons handling, scouting and raiding probes, bivouac preparation, elementary first

aid, and health and sanitation. Some border-surveillance camp companies were taught advanced patrolling in order to intercept infiltrating Viet Cong, but even these companies were incapable of normal operations requiring coordinated movement or artillery fire.

Montagnard allegiance to Special Forces leaders and their natural bravery in battle led to overall MACV satisfaction with their performance, but conventional assignments miscalculated irregular capabilities. The unsuitability of native paramilitary contingents for sustained offensive actions became apparent in the February struggle for retention of the critical Mang Yang and An Khe mountain passes. Special Forces-led camp strike forces suffered heavy losses while trying to dislodge Viet Cong forces holding this key terrain.

Four factors regarding Special Forces CIDG operations became apparent during the year's fighting. First, the camps, which were isolated in areas often controlled by the Viet Cong, were too far apart for mutual support and were unlikely to receive reinforcements in case of attack before dawn. Second, in operations away from native home districts, the effectiveness of camp strike-force personnel diminished. The irregulars, not obligated to remain at their posts, could turn in their weapons and return to their villages whenever they chose, and they did so on many occasions. Third, the camp strike forces were lightly equipped partisans, lacking the training and discipline of regular troops, and they were short on competent junior leaders. Finally, the Viet Cong continued to operate at will because of poor government intelligence collection. Villager information on Viet Cong presence and movement could not be relied on, whereas Viet Cong intelligence and counterintelligence measures were excellent and resulted in surprise attacks against camps and patrols.

In the arena of military advisory assistance, Special Forces control and field detachments were increasingly ordered into unsecured areas to stake out an American presence. The Special Forces fulfilled these perilous assignments, which often detracted from special-warfare tasks and placed some teams in extremely hazardous locations. One B-Detachment sent on a provincial advisory basis to Song Be was virtually annihilated in the resulting battle of May 11, 1965.

Colonel William A. McKean assumed command of the 5th Special Forces Group on July 16, just as the Special Forces role in the countryside was irrevocably altered by regular Army forces arriving in Vietnam. The latter proved both a help and a hindrance to Special Forces.

Army units offered a degree of security for Special Forces camps undreamed of several months earlier. The potential of this assistance was graphically revealed in the October battle of Camp Plei Me, when the 1st Cavalry Division became largely responsible for breaking the major North Vietnamese siege around the critical highlands post. Other support ranged from artillery firebases established near favorite Viet Cong targets, like Camp Bu Dop, which had sustained a heavy assault July 20, to paratrooper alerts in support of Vietnamese relief attempts, typified by Camp Duc Co, besieged for two months in the summer.

Unfortunately, the sudden influx of regular formations was often accompanied by hasty deployment decisions that closed down long-established Special Forces sites and interrupted successful area-development programs. Conventional divisional and brigade commanders sometimes misjudged or misunderstood the insurgent situation in their tactical areas and refused to heed Special Forces advice. In the worst cases—illustrated by forced population resettlement from fertile valleys perceived as being ''pro-VC''—these actions cancelled years of patient Special Forces work and actually fueled the enemy resistance movement.

Project Delta, a combat force composed of Special Forces-led reconnaissance teams and airborne ranger companies for use on special missions, developed into an important response force during 1965. These reconnaissance teams were directed to find enemy target areas and then destroy them by calling in airborne ranger companies, other combat troops, or air strikes.

Project Delta's success was premised on mastery of infiltration tactics and the assignment of Special Forces advisors at the patrol level.

When Colonel McKean relinquished command of the 5th Special Forces Group, he summed up many valuable observations about the nature of Special Forces fighting in Vietnam: ''The 'special' about Special Forces is simply that the noncommissioned officers are the finest to be found anywhere in the world. Their multiple skills and individual motivation are exploited to the fullest in the combat environment of the A-Detachment in VC-dominated areas. If today's Special Forces NCO has any peer, it was probably the tough, self-reliant, combat-tested soldier who fought on the Indian frontier of our own country....Also to my surprise, I discovered that the CIDG troops are not the band of unskilled, disorganized, disgruntled peasants I had envisioned. They are, in fact, closely knit religious or ethnic minority groups with a fierce loyalty to each other and to those who will treat them with respect and consideration....The addition of airmobility has proved to be of particular value....Similarly, the engineer augmentation has greatly assisted in improving airfields and expediting camp construction.''

During 1965 the Special Forces completed its fifth year of active Vietnam combat service under very difficult circumstances created by the failure of the South Vietnamese regular Army to stem communist advances. This situation created a requirement for Special Forces to assume a conventional offensive role, along with other U.S. measures to stiffen the Saigon regime—most notably the regular Army buildup. The expanded strength of Special Forces matched its increased level of activity. At the beginning of the year, the 5th Special Forces Group in Vietnam contained about 1,500 personnel scattered among 48 camps, with a CIDG strength of about 20,000 camp strike-force personnel. By the end of the year, the Special Forces Group had expanded to almost 2,000 troops in 62 camps, controlling more than 30,000 civilian irregular defenders.

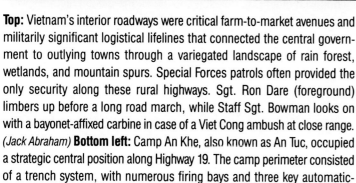

Top: Vietnam's interior roadways were critical farm-to-market avenues and militarily significant logistical lifelines that connected the central government to outlying towns through a variegated landscape of rain forest, wetlands, and mountain spurs. Special Forces patrols often provided the only security along these rural highways. Sgt. Ron Dare (foreground) limbers up before a long road march, while Staff Sgt. Bowman looks on with a bayonet-affixed carbine in case of a Viet Cong ambush at close range. *(Jack Abraham)* **Bottom left:** Camp An Khe, also known as An Tuc, occupied a strategic central position along Highway 19. The camp perimeter consisted of a trench system, with numerous firing bays and three key automatic-weapons bunkers at the main corners, entirely surrounded by barbed wire fences. The camp is shown during its most critical period of February 1965, when Viet Cong insurgents attempted to severe Highway 19, which is seen running diagonally through the picture. *(Author's Collection)* **Bottom right:** This view, taken at a slightly different angle in frame sequence just to the east of Camp An Khe, shows the two bridges of Highway 19 that spanned the swift Song Ba. The camp was situated between two rugged mountain passes and assigned to defend the winding roadway defiles that were subject to enemy ambush. *(Author's Collection)*

Top: The Viet Cong attempted to sever Highway 19 near Camp An Khe on February 20, 1965. The ensuing battle to clear the Viet Cong from around Mang Yang Pass resulted in high casualties to Special Forces-led troops. Some of the heaviest fighting occurred on this field, still strewn with wreckage, after helicopters landed a reinforcing ''Eagle Flight'' platoon from Pleiku. *(Author's Collection)* **Center:** In pursuit of their plan to sever Highway 19 in this area near Mang Yang Pass, the Viet Cong destroyed or besieged Special Forces outposts and ambushed several convoys. Special Forces reaction teams from Camps An Khe and Soui Doi were sent into battle from both directions to clear the roadway. *(Gerald W. Foy)* **Bottom:** Highway 19 connected Pleiku, shown here, and the interior Central Highlands with the Vietnamese coast. Gen. Westmoreland was afraid that Viet Cong success in severing the route would effectively cut the country in half. *(Author's Collection)*

Top left: Dao Phu Quoc, a Vietnamese island located south of Cambodia, was in perennial danger of being conquered by pirates or insurgents. The government was primarily interested in its suitability as an isolated prison site capable of replacing those on the mainland. The struggle to pacify this rugged tropical island constituted one of the hardest and most frustrating Special Forces assignments. Lack of water-crossing equipment led to field-expedient substitutes during this Special Forces coastal raid. *(Author's Collection)* **Top right:** Phu Quoc defensive improvements depended on laborious Special Forces and indigenous ''self-help'' projects, such as the construction of this munitions bunker. *(Author's Collection)* **Bottom:** The Special Forces subdued Dao Phu Quoc and enabled the construction of a new central prisoner-of-war facility on the monsoon-swept island by 1968. The Australian ambassador congratulates members of Detachments B-44 and A-441 on their progress during a typical rainstorm on July 31, 1967. *(Author's Collection)*

Top left: The main responsibility of Special Forces in Vietnam was to impart combat skills to indigenous leaders, such as these native commanders, who are checking final coordination of an assault element just before battle. *(Jack Abraham)* **Top right:** The interior of each Special Forces camp contained a unique mix of Army construction and native dwellings that housed garrisons of Montagnard mercenaries, Vietnamese soldiers, American troops, Nung bodyguards, combat interpreters, civilian contractors, post exchange girls, and native families—all speaking between five and eight languages. While Special Forces camps were governed by regulations, the set of rules was only as effective as the camp commander's ability to enforce them. *(Jack Abraham)* **Center left:** LLDB Capt. Y-Quat and

Sgt. First Class Gaydosik pose after a combat raid that rescued a Montagnard girl from two years of Viet Cong captivity. Camp commanders were responsible for allocating resources among competing demands for Special Forces assistance. *(Jack Abraham)* **Bottom left:** A facetious camp entrance sign reflects the isolation and independence of Special Forces teams in Vietnam. *(Jack Abraham)* **Bottom right:** Responsibility for the camp's success or failure usually rested on the shoulders of young captains like Jack Abraham at Camp Buon Mi Ga, who was injured while pulling a Rhade woman and her three children out of a burning longhouse. *(Jack Abraham)*

Camp Buon Ea Yang provided security along the main overland supply route to Ban Me Thuot. It was located on a 50-meter hilltop in a marshy valley about 15 miles from the Vietnamese coast. When completed, three double-apron barbed wire fences and a trench with firing bays and nine machine gun bunkers encircled the camp. The bunkers were situated at each of the camp's five corners and at the center of each trench line. The camp contained two light howitzers that covered the main avenue of approach from the southwest, six light mortar positions, a main barracks building surrounded by a log parapet with another machine gun position, and a zigzag trench leading to the upper trench system with four heavy mortars and the main bunker. *(Author's Collection)*

Top left: The shift of Special Forces toward the border was expedited in 1965, as its conventional border-control mission gained new importance because of elevated rates of enemy infiltration. Arriving Army units took over old camp areas, but uprooting Montagnard tribes from their traditional grounds was a difficult undertaking that diminished morale and effectiveness. This Caribou aircraft lands at a native collecting point to provide aerial transport for one camp's move. *(Jack Abraham)* **Top right:** Useful materials were salvaged from the old camp-site and loaded aboard aircraft for transport to new sites. The most valuable bulk materiel was barbed wire and corrugated tin sheets. *(Jack Abraham)* **Center right:** Carrying all of their worldly possessions, tribal families crowd into aircraft taking them to a new destination. *(Jack Abraham)* **Bottom:** The flight was stressful for natives afraid of leaving the ground in an airplane, but staunch communal bonds ensured that everyone followed the chiefs and sorcerers if spiritual conditions seemed favorable for a return to earth. *(Jack Abraham)*

Top: Camp survival depended on strong fixed defensive positions in contested areas, and early Special Forces became masters at field engineering when Navy Seabee or Army construction teams were unavailable. Fortifications were built out of whatever materials were available, and camp designs varied widely from site to site, but an extensive network of fighting positions linked by angular firing trenches was standard. *(Jack Abraham)* **Bottom:** Camp bunkers like this double-Browning automatic rifle embrasure at Buon Ea Yang were built to withstand potentially devastating mortar barrages and featured sandbagged heavy logs for overhead protection against shellfire. Positions had to be well built and strenuously maintained, however, because unsound earthen log bunkers and sandbagged revetments hastily assembled in the dry season deteriorated rapidly in the monsoon rains, especially if camps were poorly drained. *(Jack Abraham)*

Top left: Effective camp defense depended greatly on an early warning system assured by night security outposts and offensive patrols to ward off enemy probes, but invariably casualties were incurred on this picket duty. Sgt. First Class Gaydosik was wounded in a clearing operation outside Buon Ea Yang. *(Jack Abraham)* **Top right:** Special Forces learned they could not expect reinforcement before daylight, because camps were isolated and located in difficult terrain. Until the advent of the Fighting Camp concept, introduced later in the war, the basic criterion for camp protec-tion hinged on enabling the garrison to hold out unaided until dawn. Ammunition bunkers were kept stockpiled within easy access of crew-served weapons. *(Jack Abraham)* **Bottom:** The perimeter abatis at Buon Ea Yang was interspersed with concertina wire entanglements, mines, razor-edged punji spikes, trip holes, and sharpened nail-embedded tree stakes. These were implanted not to stop attacks, but to slow down assaulting enemy soldiers and divert them into defensive fields of fire. *(Jack Abraham)*

Top: Special Forces Detachment B-34 was stationed at Song Be in the MACV Advisory Team 94 compound during the Viet Cong attack of May 11-12, 1965. The compound (center, enclosed by fence) was not designed as a combat position. It had such amenities as separate officer and enlisted billets (twin buildings), tennis courts (below buildings), and a mess hall (left of billets) with a modern kitchen and barbecue patio. At the right end of the mess hall an emergency aid station was set up in the dining room, and five Americans were killed in this area. Just to the right of the billets is the ammunition trench defended by several Special Forces sergeants throughout the battle. At the top end of the trench is Sgt. First Class Charles D. Crockett's mortar pit. Between this ditch and the upper right fence corner was the machine gun nest valiantly defended by Sergeants Richard S. Bartlett and Horace M. Young. *(Author's Collection)* **Bottom left:** There was room-to-room fighting with numerous casualties in the mess hall as the Viet Cong overran the makeshift aid station inside. Capt. Lynch shot through this door to kill several Viet Cong. *(Author's Collection)* **Bottom right:** Song Be's defensive parapets overlooked misting jungle hills that concealed two reinforced Viet Cong regiments. *(Louis T. Dorogi)*

Top: The Viet Cong attack on the Detachment B-34 compound at Song Be was launched from the wooded slope in the middle of the picture. The Special Forces occupied the MACV team post located in the center, between the province chief's home to the right and the Vietnamese motor pool on the left. A corner of the barracks was blasted apart by mortar shells in the opening stages of the Viet Cong attack, wounding several Special Forces troops before they could reach their positions. The defenders repulsed attacks across the open ground, but the Viet Cong overran the motor pool and entered the American complex by blasting through the fence separating the two compounds. *(Author's Collection)* **Bottom:** The road leading to Song Be passed through a thick rubber forest that contained Viet Cong ambush forces. The South Vietnamese relief force wisely avoided this road, but their wide overland march toward Song Be delayed allied reoccupation of the town. In the meantime, the valiant defense by the Special Forces of its individual compound denied the enemy total victory. *(Louis T. Dorogi)*

Top: Vietnamese infantry and ranger response forces were mauled by a series of Viet Cong ambushes before they reached the beleaguered garrison. Airmobile and tracked reinforcements arrived too late to save this column of South Vietnamese armored personnel vehicles from annihilation while approaching Dong Xoai along Highway 14. *(Author's Collection)* **Bottom:** Special Forces Detachment A-342, sent to Dong Xoai on May 25, 1965, built a camp with Navy Seabee assistance on the outskirts of the district capital near War Zone D. Two Viet Cong infantry regiments led by flamethrowers and demolitions teams assaulted the unfinished compound on June 9 and pressed the defenders into a last-ditch stand within the interior strongpoint. Special Forces Lt. Charles Q. Williams, severely wounded, and Navy Seaman Third Class Marvin Shields, mortally wounded, succeeded in breaking up the final Viet Cong charges with rocket fire and were awarded Medals of Honor in recognition of their valor. *(Author's Collection)*

Top: Camp Dan Thang was a Mekong Delta border-surveillance camp situated to cover the Cambodian frontier from the western side of Ap An Nong mountain, which was incorporated into the greater defensive perimeter. The camp raised border-control companies, organized boat companies, trained local ''Ruff-puff'' contingents in mortars and rocket launchers, and conducted area-development missions. *(Author's Collection)* **Bottom:** In January 1965 Detachment A-331 at Camp Dan Thang was selected as one of the first Special Forces teams to be assigned the additional MACV role of sub-sector advisory duty. It became responsible for advising the Tinh Bien district chief in all aspects of military and civic-action missions. Capt. Charles J. Mendoza (back row, third from right) and his team, attired in tiger-stripe camouflage field uniforms, pose with their mascots at Dan Thang on April 10, 1965. *(Author's Collection)*

Top: Camp Plei Djereng was a Central Highlands border-surveillance camp covering the western tri-border zone and enemy-infiltration routes toward Pleiku. The camp, located in a broad rolling valley south of the junction between the Grai and San Rivers, fielded long-range Special Forces patrols into the densely forested mountain ranges to the east and west. *(Charles Darnell)* **Center:** A log palisade enclosed the triangular-shaped compound and contained fortified bunkers at each apex. Within the camp were six mortar positions and another log wall enclosing the main structures, seen under construction during August 1965. *(Baker)* **Bottom left:** Montagnard Jarai and Rhade irregulars receive English-language instruction at Plei Djereng. The complete or marginal illiteracy of Montagnards was a great problem in Special Forces training. *(Author's Collection)* **Bottom right:** Radio instruments, like other military equipment, were designed for persons who comprehended such concepts as numbers, time, and distance, and who understood the conventional symbols expressing such concepts. Montagnards were ignorant of these values and had to absorb them slowly. These Plei Djereng camp force personnel learn basic radio transmissions between combat missions. *(Author's Collection)*

Top: Camp Plei Mrong was located northeast of Plei Djereng and occupied a marshy, rice-cultivated valley region along the vital Central Highlands line of communications from Pleiku to Kontum Province. Defensive positions were sandbagged to absorb shell blasts, and they were connected by wire-barricaded interior battlements elevated above ammunition bunkers that housed native dependents in case of attack. Camp defenses also included four mortar emplacements *(Baker)* **Bottom left:** Plei Mrong Special Forces and indigenous communications personnel gather at the base of their newly erected bamboo signal-relay tower during 1965. *(Baker)* **Bottom right:** Aidman trainees at Camp Plei Mrong are introduced to the fundamentals of military drill by learning how to stand at attention while motionless, a strange military mystery for any Montagnard. *(Baker)*

Camp Bu Dop, garrisoned by Detachment A-341, was located on the Cambodian border and deliberately situated astride a major Viet Cong infiltration route into a guerilla base area northeast of Saigon known as War Zone D. The camp's location endangered the Viet Cong logistical corridor and prompted a major enemy attempt to wipe out the garrison. On the night of July 20-21, 1965, two reinforced Viet Cong battalions conducted an all-out attack that nearly overran the compound. Enemy shock troops crossed over the moat on bamboo ladders under fire, disregarding heavy losses, and breached the camp lines in several places. *(Author's Collection)*

Top right: The Viet Cong bridged the moats in front of the north and west walls of Camp Bu Dop under a barrage of supporting mortar fire. They concentrated their main effort against the northwest corner bunker, shown here before the battle. The enemy used recoilless rifles to batter down this position, killed the defenders in hand-to-hand combat, and stormed into the main camp. *(Author's Collection)* **Bottom right:** The defense of Bu Dop rested on the shoulders of youthful troops like Special Forces Sp4 Lynden R. Steele, who recalled in a post-war veterans newspaper article that ''the degree of trauma, the significance of a situation, the individual tendency to internalize or reject experiences throughout a Vietnam tour, all had a major affect on us...then as now.'' *(Lynn Steele)*

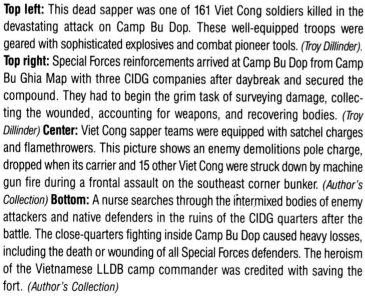

Top left: This dead sapper was one of 161 Viet Cong soldiers killed in the devastating attack on Camp Bu Dop. These well-equipped troops were geared with sophisticated explosives and combat pioneer tools. *(Troy Dillinder).*
Top right: Special Forces reinforcements arrived at Camp Bu Dop from Camp Bu Ghia Map with three CIDG companies after daybreak and secured the compound. They had to begin the grim task of surveying damage, collecting the wounded, accounting for weapons, and recovering bodies. *(Troy Dillinder)* **Center:** Viet Cong sapper teams were equipped with satchel charges and flamethrowers. This picture shows an enemy demolitions pole charge, dropped when its carrier and 15 other Viet Cong were struck down by machine gun fire during a frontal assault on the southeast corner bunker. *(Author's Collection)* **Bottom:** A nurse searches through the intermixed bodies of enemy attackers and native defenders in the ruins of the CIDG quarters after the battle. The close-quarters fighting inside Camp Bu Dop caused heavy losses, including the death or wounding of all Special Forces defenders. The heroism of the Vietnamese LLDB camp commander was credited with saving the fort. *(Author's Collection)*

Top: Camp Cai Cai, also known as Dan Chu, was established during April 1965 in Kien Phong Province close to the Cambodian border. The camp's garrison, advised by Detachment A-412, defeated incessant Viet Cong attempts to overrun this important border surveillance site during the course of the war. The boggy conditions of this swamp site are apparent both in the nearby village and around the raised berm connecting the camp with the aircraft landing pad, at right center, on which a Chinook helicopter has landed. *(Author's Collection)* **Bottom:** Camp Cai Cai was attacked by more than a hundred Viet Cong troops on July 26, 1965. Four months later, at the end of November, the camp was hit by a close infantry assault that followed a blistering mortar and recoilless-rifle barrage. This view shows the critical bunker at the apex of the camp overlooking the Rach Cai Cai toward Cambodia. *(Author's Collection)*

Top left: Camp Duc Co, a significant border-surveillance camp west of Pleiku near the Cambodian boundary, was besieged by enemy forces from the end of June until mid-August 1965. The strain of continual combat is reflected on the faces of these Montagnard defenders during the battle. *(Richard Johnson/USA)* **Top right:** In response to the deepening Vietnam crisis, U.S. Defense Secretary Robert McNamara (center) heads the critical Pentagon meeting of the Joint Chiefs of Staff on April 5, 1965. On the following day President Lyndon Johnson authorized the use of regular Army and Marine combat units for offensive operations in South Vietnam. *(DOD)* **Bottom:** During the Duc Co siege, a large Army unit—the 173d Airborne Brigade—was placed on standby to assist a Special Forces camp for the first time in the war. However, South Vietnamese troops finally broke through after 48 days. This aerial view of Camp Duc Co after the siege reveals its relocation from the original, destroyed triangular post. *(Author's Collection)*

Top left: Regular Army formations entering Vietnam in 1965 were preceded by legions of engineers needed for base construction. When the jungle was cleared around An Khe for the arriving 1st Cavalry Division, Sgt. First Class Louis LePage and Sgt.-Maj. Bill White watched incredulously from the Special Forces compound on the other side of Highway 19. *(Gerald W. Foy)* **Top right:** Heavy earth-moving equipment scraped out enough acres of helipad and billeting space near An Khe to house a 20,000-strong airmobile division, not far from the minuscule 12-member Special Forces campsite. *(Author's Collection)* **Bottom:** During September 1965 the 1st Cavalry Division finished moving into An Khe and renamed their massive base Camp Radcliff. Gen. Westmoreland directed the newly arrived division to assume the former Special Forces mission of safeguarding Highway 19's central mountain passes. *(Gilbert Meyers/USA)*

Top: A concerted North Vietnamese drive to capture the Central Highlands during October 1965 was thwarted by Camp Plei Me. The commitment of the 1st Cavalry Division to assist the Special Forces resulted in the first major Army battle of the Vietnam war. This aerial reconnaissance photograph taken on August 23, 1965, shows the defensive arrangements at Camp Plei Me a few weeks before the enemy attack. *(Author's Collection)* **Bottom:** NVA artillery spotters occupied the critical mountain of Chu Don overlooking Plei Me throughout the battle and directed extremely accurate rocket and mortar barrages against the Special Forces installation. One of the first allied objectives following the lifting of the Plei Me siege was the recapture of this hilltop, and these Montagnard strike-force personnel secured the summit. *(Nick Walsh)*

Top left: A Special Forces counterattack outside Plei Me hustles back prisoners under fire. The Special Forces garrison was reinforced during the siege by a reconnaissance patrol of Project Delta, led by Maj. Charlie Beckwith, that infiltrated through North Vietnamese lines. *(Nick Walsh)*
Top right: The North Vietnamese sustained heavy losses in repeated attacks on the camp, but they always attempted to retrieve casualties. A Special Forces patrol later found in the jungle around the camp carefully prepared NVA graves, ceremoniously guarded by carved wooden soldiers. *(Nick Walsh)*
Bottom left: The Plei Me defensive perimeter, looking toward Cambodia, before the battle. Enemy sappers armed with satchel charges and bangalore torpedoes led a mass charge across this wire barrier on the night of October 20-21, 1965. *(Nick Walsh)* **Bottom right:** Special Forces weapons leader Ron Maddox, in leopard-spotted fatigues, and demolitions expert Nicholas Walsh, in tiger-stripe uniform, express joyful gratitude for the arriving 1st Cavalry Division troops that forced the North Vietnamese Army withdrawal. *(Nick Walsh)*

Top: Tactical air strikes delivered by high-performance aircraft, like this F-100 Supersabre of the 3d Tactical Fighter Wing over War Zone C, gave Special Forces a great battlefield advantage that outweighed many of the deficiencies of its local troops. *(USAF)* **Bottom:** Four Air Force Supersabre pilots who flew on behalf of Special Forces gather on the runway after a Vietnam mission. They are (left to right) Capt. Daniel Taylor Jr., Maj. Swart Nelson, Capt. Mark E. Berent, and Capt. Robert Putney. The close relationship between the Special Forces and the Air Force was exemplified by Capt. Berent, who patrolled with Mike Forces to gain insight into ground tactical considerations. He later wrote about this experience in his classic book *Rolling Thunder*. *(USAF)*

Top left: Special Forces received some of its most accurate air support from versatile Douglas A-1 Skyraiders of the 633d Special Operations Squadron, typified by this Skyraider banking into a dive over the Central Highlands during a Special Forces fire fight. *(USAF)* **Top right and center right:** On-ground Air Force fighter pilots assisted Special Forces Lt. Spinaio and Capt. Klys, while B-42 Forward Operating Base personnel at Ba Chuc directed Skyraider strikes against the Viet Cong mountain bastion of Nui Giai in December 1966. *(Author's Collection)* **Bottom:** A C-7 Caribou lands at Pleiku after parachuting cargo to a besieged Special Forces highland camp, as a damaged A-1 Skyraider awaits repairs in the midst of the Tet offensive. The Air Force performed brilliantly in this hard-fought campaign, even to the point of giving aerial assistance to threatened Special Forces camps while warding off enemy rocket attacks against its own airfields. *(USAF)*

Top left: During the Vietnam conflict, Special Forces field camps received 85 percent of their supplies by aerial transport. Cattle bound for a forward campsite are loaded onto a C-123 transport of the 315th Special Operations Wing at Phan Rang. Their rumps are painted with their destination. *(USAF)*
Top right: Not all cargo was strictly military, but it always consisted of items important to outpost welfare. Special Forces Air Movements Officer CW3 Miller stands next to a pallet of beer headed for a border-surveillance post during 1965. *(Baker)* **Center left:** The Air Force proved a tremendous morale booster when delivering Christmas gifts to secluded camps. Santa Claus is greeted by Detachment B-23 commander Lt. Col. Maurice C. Williams at Camp Nhon Co in December 1968. *(USAF)* **Center right:** The holiday bedecked ''Santa-bou,'' an Air Force C-7A Caribou of the 483d Tactical Airlift Wing, brought gifts and refreshments to 50 remote Special Forces camps during the Christmas season in 1968. *(Carl Leach)* **Bottom:** Special Forces Lt. Col. Wadie J. Rountree, B-Detachment commander at Ban Me Thuot, checks off a load of Okinawa-procured squid and fish rations for the Montagnards with 458th Tactical Airlift Squadron boss Lt. Col. George Rawlings in September 1968. *(USAF)*

Top: This C-130 Hercules releases its Low-Altitude Pallet-Extraction System (LAPES) load while skimming over the airstrip at Camp Thien Ngon in October 1968. *(USAF)* **Center left:** C-7 Caribous, lined up at the Pleiku airfield, await parachute-equipped cargo sleds destined for outlying Special Forces camps during June 1969. *(USAF)* **Center right:** Crated livestock were airdropped by cargo parachutes to ensure that distant camps had fresh meat. *(Author's Collection)* **Bottom left:** C-7 Caribou Air Force flight engineer Technical Sgt. Armand Lara helps Sgt. First Class Joe H. Vargas don a parachute preparatory to a fuel resupply para-drop over Camp Ha Thanh in September 1969. *(USAF)* **Bottom right:** A LAPES-delivered truck is driven off the runway by Staff Sgt. Howard F. Cranford at Camp Thien Ngon in late 1968. *(USAF)*

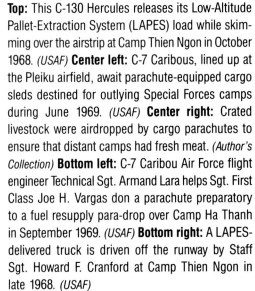

Top: Special Forces psychological operations in Vietnam were designed to gain and hold the loyalty of the people and to enlist their cooperation in defeating the insurgency. Psychological operations also attempted to influence enemy troops and their supporters among the VC-sympathetic peasantry in remote areas. A C-47 Skytrain of the 9th Special Operations Squadron drops Special Forces propaganda leaflets over hostile Katu mountain tribes near Laos. *(USAF)* **Bottom left:** Special Forces Sgt. Stephen L. Wheeler checks mission data as boxes of psychological warfare leaflets are loaded onto a C-47 Skytrain of the 5th Air Commando Squadron at Binh Thuy airfield. *(USAF)* **Bottom right:** Special Forces psychological warfare was fully integrated with other civic-action programs and benefited from a genuine understanding of native languages, customs, and beliefs. When successful, these measures could lead to local disclosures of enemy target areas for military action. An A-1 Skyraider from the 633d Special Operations Squadron unleashes its ordnance in support of an engaged Special Forces unit in the Central Highlands. *(USAF)*

Top left: The Special Forces employed helicopter operations on a wide scale in Vietnam, but it possessed no special warfare aviation resources past 1963. Different Army helicopter units rendered airmobile support ''as required and as available.'' Expedient medical evacuation was perhaps the greatest Special Forces requirement, as demonstrated by this specialized UH-1D medical ambulance helicopter hoisting a wounded patrol member out of the tropical jungle. *(USA)* **Top right:** A Special Forces-directed helicopter uses public-address loudspeakers in an attempt to induce the Viet Cong to surrender by offering a reward for turning in weapons during November 1965. *(James Pickerell)* **Center:** Relatively inaccessible Special Forces mountain garrisons depended almost entirely on airmobile logistical support. This UH-1B helicopter airlifts drums of fresh water to Detachment A-324 atop Nui Ba Den during 1964. *(USIS)* **Bottom:** The Special Forces depended greatly on airmobility to deliver its mobile reaction forces within striking range of threatened camps. *(Baker)*

Top: Camp Bong Son was established in the midst of a pro-Viet Cong agricultural region during May 1965 as part of the Special Forces emergency defense of coastal Binh Dinh Province, but it suffered heavy losses guarding Phu Cu Pass that September. *(Author's Collection)* **Center left:** The sacred temple of the Cao Dai religious army led by Special Forces was located at Tay Ninh. When that locality became a base of the 25th Infantry Division, Cao Dai CIDG troops were redirected to provide security patrols for Army soldiers in the region. *(Waters/USA)* **Center right:** To make room for 1st Infantry Division elements deploying into Phuoc Vinh, Detachment A-312 was relocated from the military installation, upper right, to the nearby ranger compound at Cao Vinh, center, during January 1965. *(USA)* **Bottom:** The first Army units arrived in Vietnam confident of success against the enemy, but they were introduced quickly to the harsh realities of Vietnam combat. These 173d Airborne Brigade paratroopers make radio contact with Special Forces-led native troops moving to protect the American positions from flank attack during a jungle battle. *(James Newlin/USA)*

Top left: For Special Forces, one of the most sought-after advantages of the regular Army buildup in Vietnam was the opportunity to secure greater camp protection from artillery firepower. These howitzers of the 1st Infantry Division were stationed temporarily at a fire-support base near Bu Dop. *(121st Signal Bn.)* **Top right:** Army conventional infantry units were responsible for preserving several Special Forces camps from enemy destruction during 1965. These 173d Airborne Brigade paratroopers cross a stream during a sweep operation to protect Special Forces installations at Bion Hoa and Long Thanh. *(Mike Mealey/Pacific Stars & Stripes)* **Bottom:** Army formations that failed to coordinate their activities with Special Forces sometimes undermined years of patient area-development work. The forced evacuation of cattle and people from this valley in Quang Ngai Province by the 101st Airborne Division led to increased Viet Cong trouble around Camp Tra Bong. *(DOD)*

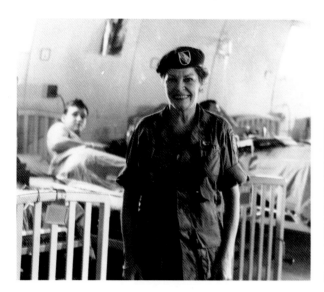

Top left: Among the most beloved Special Forces personalities was Martha Raye, whose vibrant enthusiasm and professional nursing skill greatly improved the morale of team members suffering from wounds, patrol injuries, or tropical fevers in Vietnam hospital wards. *(George Hardiman)* **Top right:** Entertainer Bob Hope and his entourage staged popular events welcomed by the troops. His helicopter is shown near the Da Nang Special Forces compound during the December 1968 Vietnam tour. *(USAF)* **Center left:** Actor and director John Wayne remained steadfast in his personal admiration and support of Special Forces and produced the only wartime Hollywood movie of their exploits, *The Green Berets. (Homer House)* **Center right:** Special Forces doctors (left to right) Capt. Short, Lt. Walker, and Capt. Waterbury relax from the strain of battlefront surgery as they enjoy the Bob Hope show at Pleiku in December 1964. *(Edward Short)* **Bottom:** MACV commander Gen. William Westmoreland, center, and U.S. Defense Secretary Robert McNamara, to the right shaking hands, visit the group headquarters at Nha Trang to approve expanding Special Forces operational responsibilities on July 19, 1965. *(Baker)*

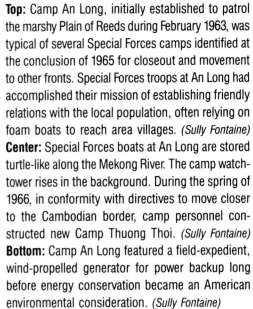

Top: Camp An Long, initially established to patrol the marshy Plain of Reeds during February 1963, was typical of several Special Forces camps identified at the conclusion of 1965 for closeout and movement to other fronts. Special Forces troops at An Long had accomplished their mission of establishing friendly relations with the local population, often relying on foam boats to reach area villages. *(Sully Fontaine)*

Center: Special Forces boats at An Long are stored turtle-like along the Mekong River. The camp watchtower rises in the background. During the spring of 1966, in conformity with directives to move closer to the Cambodian border, camp personnel constructed new Camp Thuong Thoi. *(Sully Fontaine)*

Bottom: Camp An Long featured a field-expedient, wind-propelled generator for power backup long before energy conservation became an American environmental consideration. *(Sully Fontaine)*

Top left: The Army of the Republic of Vietnam looked impressive but was largely impotent in many regions of the country. The Special Forces-advised CIDG program precluded enemy takeover of this territory through default. *(RVN PIO)* **Top right:** One overriding limitation of CIDG personnel was their diminished utility beyond home regions. The death of CIDG troops while on extended operations became a sensitive issue, provoking outrage among the native forces if the bodies were not returned for proper burial according to their religious practices—Buddhist, Catholic, or animistic—near their own villages. These fallen troops were returned for internment to Camp Dak To. *(Roger Pierson)* **Bottom left:** The intense loyalty of the Montagnards

to Special Forces was responsible for CIDG program effectiveness. This Montagnard irregular, who was taken prisoner during the battles of Tet-68 and later escaped, pointed out the location of a Viet Cong camp containing missing Americans to Lt. Thomas A. Ross at Nha Trang that August. *(DOD)* **Bottom right:** The Vietnamese *Lực-Lượng Dặc-Biệt* teams in actual command of the camps and co-located with Special Forces varied in quality, but they obtained excellent results when staffed by members like counterintelligence Sgt. Luu Van Tuowi at Song Be in 1969. *(Author's Collection)*

COST COMPARISON: CIDG vs US

INITIAL ISSUE

$ 61.06	EQUIPMENT	$ 94.05
124.00	WEAPON	124.00
$185.06	TOTAL	$ 218.05

COST PER DAY

$ .55	BASE PAY	$ 5.17
.29	JUMP PAY	1.83
.29	COMBAT PAY	2.16
.38	COST OF LIVING	—
—	FOREIGN DUTY PAY	.30
1.30	RATIONS (PATROL)	3.90
$ 2.81	TOTAL	$ 13.36

Top: The CIDG program was composed of natives hired on a contract basis who were trained, supplied, and led by Special Forces but who remained technically under Vietnamese LLDB control. This typical camp strike force from Camp Suoi Da dressed in mixed garb holds a variety of rifles and grease guns. *(USA)* **Bottom left:** The U.S. high command viewed the CIDG program as a cost-effective ancillary to regular forces in Vietnam. This wartime 5th Special Forces Group briefing chart was prepared for MACV in order to secure funding for standardized modern weapons during 1968. *(Author's Collection)* **Bottom right:** The professional limitations of the CIDG program are vividly depicted by this hill tribe camp defender. The Special Forces were acutely aware of native strengths—intimate knowledge of local terrain and operational ability to live off the land—as well as their weaknesses—a loss of motivation on extended missions and no understanding of military concepts like fire discipline or communications. *(USIS)*

Top left: The quintessential Viet Cong guerrilla crouched in a tunnel typified the combative but elusive adversaries of Special Forces in Vietnam. "Viet Cong" was a derogatory term for the insurgent communist National Liberation Front seeking to overthrow the pro-western government of the Republic of Vietnam. *(USA Military History Institute)* **Top right:** Enemy sappers, who could slip through wire obstacles and open up approach lanes for attacking infantry, jeopardized Special Forces camp survival. *(USA Military History Institute)* **Bottom:** Hooded and bound Viet Cong prisoners taken by Special Forces await transportation to a camp interrogation center. The Special Forces valued prisoners for intelligence purposes and sought to convert them to the allied cause, a goal that normally precluded mistreatment. *(Clayton Scott)*

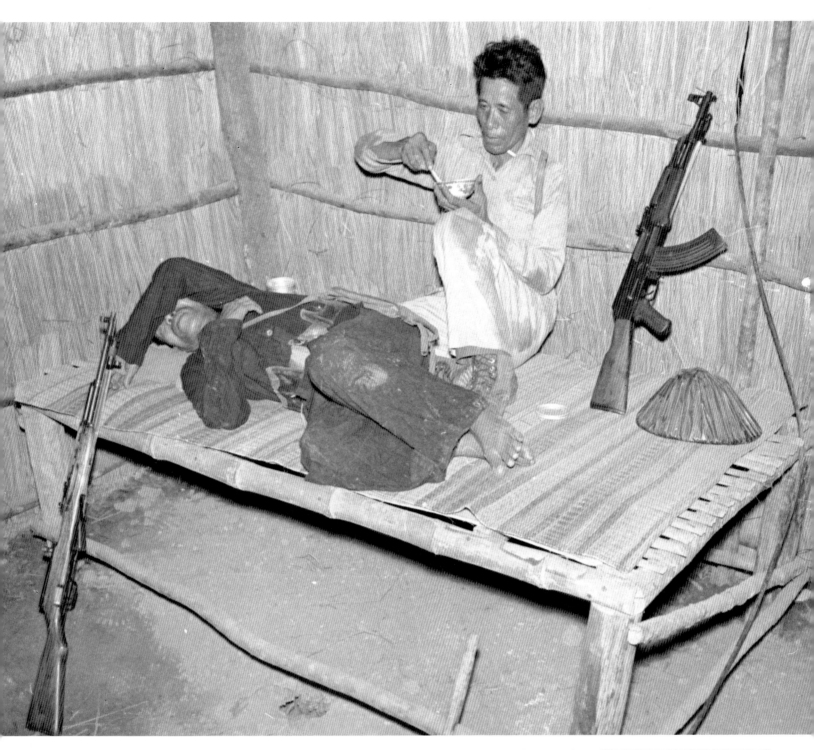

Top: Throughout the duration of the Vietnam conflict, Viet Cong units received cadre and replacements from the regular People's Army of Vietnam, referred to as the North Vietnamese Army during the war by U.S. officials. The intermixing of these forces led to the common allied designation NVA/VC to distinguish their actual composition. This Viet Cong soldier, armed with a Soviet-style SKS rifle, rests in a palm-leaf jungle hut while his North Vietnamese comrade has a quick meal beside his own AK-47 assault rifle. *(USA Military History Institute)* **Bottom:** North Vietnamese troops were well-armed and dedicated soldiers whose modern Sino-Soviet weapons and knowledge of tropical warfare constituted the greatest threat to Special Forces stability operations. *(USA Military History Institute)*

Assault helicopters whirl Army troops of the 1st Infantry Division into War Zone C to reinforce Special Forces reconnaissance troops during Operation Attleboro in November 1966. The superb Regular Army and Special Forces cooperation exhibited in this first large-scale search-and-destroy mission of the war nearly annihilated the Viet Cong 9th Division, and it marked the advent of Special Forces as a valuable component of the Total Army—even on the conventional battlefield. *(1st Inf Div PIO)*

SPECIAL FORCES AND THE AREA WAR, 1966

The area war strategy that prevailed throughout 1966 was not based on conventional battle lines but depended on operations conducted across a multitude of areas within South Vietnam. These battlefields ranged from the western border to the coast, and they often included sectors not far from Saigon, the nation's capital. Military Assistance Command, Vietnam (MACV), officers considered the far-flung Special Forces camps ideally situated to play a key role in this area style of warfare. However, these camps were built as operational bases for local area-pacification tasks and were not designed as impregnable fortresses. Each campsite contained only a few crew-served weapons and several hundred native troops led by a dozen Special Forces troops and their Vietnamese counterparts. By themselves, the camps were unable to check regular North Vietnamese forces massed in overwhelmingly superior numbers without prompt and sufficient response.

The attack on Camp A Shau exemplified the problem of camp security in Vietnam's rugged western-border zone, where the North Vietnamese were willing to disregard heavy casualties in order to secure a territorial advantage. Situated in the remote tropical periphery of northwestern South Vietnam, Camp A Shau's location interfered with enemy movement along a major Laotian infiltration network extending into the A Shau-A Loui valley basin. The camp's operational patrols were continually harassed by enemy forces intent on neutralizing the camp's effectiveness.

The final North Vietnamese Army attack on this critical border camp was well rehearsed and executed with a keen appreciation of Special Forces isolation from likely Marine or regular Army reinforcement. The enemy buildup around A Shau in the beginning of 1966 was manifested by patrol information and continuous overflights that detected numerous freshly dug weapons positions. Interrogation of two North Vietnamese defectors in April confirmed that an attack was imminent. In response the 5th Special Forces Group deployed a reinforcing Mike Force company of Nungs from Nha Trang to A Shau, but their numbers proved inadequate.

The main assault against Camp A Shau commenced on the early morning of March 9, 1966. North Vietnamese forces capitalized on adverse weather conditions and their own encircling belt of anti-aircraft guns to hinder tactical air support and resupply, cut off ground access to the camp, and prevent the arrival of helicopter-carried reinforcements to help the garrison. The attack began with a heavy barrage of very accurate mortar fire that caused extensive damage, as well as a temporary loss of communications with the fort. Although the camp defenders repulsed an initial battalion ground attack directed at the southern side of the fortified wall, it became apparent that the garrison could not hold out indefinitely.

During the two-day battle of A Shau, Air Force pilots risked intense return fire and dense cloud coverage to bomb enemy troop concentrations and deliver parachute supply drops over the fog-enshrouded camp. Air strikes were directed against the camp perimeter at the request of Detachment A-102 commander Captain John D. Blair IV, and these close napalm and strafing runs dispersed several charges made on the beleaguered compound. But the end was in sight. Bunkers and strongpoints were reduced to rubble under incessant enemy automatic weapons and rocket fire. The Special Forces capability to resist the accelerated onslaught was rapidly eroded as camp positions were overrun in heavy fighting that depleted ammunition reserves and diminished defensive strength.

The exhausted defenders were ordered to evacuate the smoking camp ruins, and 16 Marine helicopters conducted a harrowing rescue mission. Unfortunately, continuous enemy ground fire and panic among the indigenous personnel prevented complete evacuation. The remaining survivors were forced to escape into the jungle and evade enemy-pursuit parties. On March 12 the last scattered Special Forces and native irregulars were found by aircraft search crews and lifted to safety.

Despite occasional setbacks typified by the loss of Camp A Shau, the Special Forces-run Civilian Irregular Defense Group (CIDG) program continued to prove its value as a stabilizing force throughout South Vietnam's remote territory. By the spring of

1966, the presence of 75,000 armed native contingents and regional-popular forces under Special Forces control was an important adjunct to the complex war effort, ensuring allied presence in many outlying provinces. Following the battle of A Shau, the enemy shied away from large-scale attacks for the duration of the year, although several camps experienced probing activity and artillery bombardments. Aggressive Special Forces patrolling—combined with rapid reaction by helicopter gunships, fighter-bombers, and flare-transports—was credited with discouraging more meaningful Viet Cong actions.

Routine saturation patrolling outside the camps inflicted considerable losses on the Viet Cong logistical system. Tons of rice, medical supplies, weapon caches, and ammunition stocks were located and destroyed with increasing frequency. Larger allied formations were present in the field, and civilian irregular defenders doubled their reconnaissance capability by cooperating as flank-screening elements and providing blocking forces for powerful combined sweep enterprises.

Viet Cong movements were monitored with great success from the Special Forces-held mountain post of Nui Ba Den. The first Special camp opened within Viet Cong territory was accomplished during late June 1966, when Camp Trai Bi was established six miles inside War Zone C and due west of Nui Ba Den. The approach march to Trai Bi involved combating a series of enemy defensive positions, and the base received heavy shelling soon after being organized, but the new camp was steadfastly maintained. In the far north Camp Khe Sanh sustained a devastating heavy 120mm mortar barrage in January, and it was ordered ''hardened'' through reinforcements and upgraded bunker construction by General Westmoreland in September to prevent the possibility of a sudden enemy overrun. Three months later the compound was turned over to a Marine regimental garrison, and the Special Forces team was moved to another border-surveillance site nearby.

Throughout Vietnam the 5th Special Forces Group continued to stress its highly successful civil-affairs and psychological-operations campaigns. These propaganda, rural construction, and medical efforts had a far-reaching impact in favorably influencing the tribal population's willingness to support the Saigon regime—a factor that enhanced the ability of allied forces to operate effectively in many districts. Civic action included such diverse projects as building or repairing schools, setting up dispensaries, drilling water wells, installing bridges, and building roads. In return for the provision of relief supplies to war refugees, the Special Forces gained friendships, useful intelligence information, and even military volunteers. Special Forces medical patrols, often accompanied by village health workers, visited patients in the countryside who lacked access to treatment facilities.

The Special Forces also took steps to improve the Montagnard's agricultural productivity and animal husbandry within detachment operating areas. Many Special Forces camps planted demonstration garden plots that were used to introduce the people to a variety of vegetables, better farming techniques, and new farming tools. Other camp instruments included tape recorders, portable loudspeakers, and mimeograph machines, and these were often just as effective as munitions in defeating enemy intentions. Timely bulletins and propaganda messages caused numerous Viet Cong defections and solidified the pro-allied sentiment of supportive hamlets.

During the latter part of 1966, Special Forces further developed its higher command combat resources by raising Projects Sigma and Omega, which gave special corps-level reconnaissance capabilities to field force commanders in II and III Corps Tactical Zones. These supplemented the Army-level long-range reconnaissance efforts of Project Delta, which was responsible for surveillance missions in all Corps Tactical Zones of Vietnam.

The Special Forces refined the Mike Force concept, an outgrowth of the earlier Eagle Flight reaction- and reconnaissance-patrol concepts. Eagle Flights were originally created as multi-purpose reserves, composed of Special Forces leaders and indigenous troops who were familiar with Viet Cong and North Vietnamese tactics. Using swift helicopter movement to perform reconnoitering missions or reinforce threatened sectors, the Eagle Flights evolved into the Mobile Strike Forces. The latter units, composed principally of Chinese Nungs and reliable Montagnards who were under direct Special Forces command, received advanced training in airmobile warfare.

The battle of Camp A Shau underscored the need to strengthen the offensive effectiveness of these Mobile Strike Forces. As a result, during the fall of 1966, selected Mobile Strike Force resources were used to form the basis for unconventional warfare mobile guerrilla task forces. The mobile guerrilla forces specialized in striking back at the Viet Cong and North Vietnamese targets, by infiltrating and operating in enemy-dominated secret base areas on either brief or extended assignments coded as ''Blackjack'' operations.

Each mobile guerrilla force unit was trained to operate as an independent unit with no reinforcement or mutual support for the duration of its mission, and it entered its assigned tactical operational areas using the most unobtrusive means available. The force combat-reconnaissance platoon usually went in advance to scout out the region, establish an initial resupply point, and set up the patrol bases. Once successfully inserted into an area, the mobile guerrilla force operated in a partisan fashion from 30 to 60 days, being resupplied periodically by air-dropped provisions. To avoid disclosing positions during these aerial deliveries, modified 500-pound napalm containers were dropped by A-1E aircraft in fake air strikes. Instead of ''dud bombs,'' however, the canisters were packed full of bundled foodstuffs, spare batteries, ammunition, and other essentials.

Mobile guerrillas operated out of their mobile bases to conduct surveillance, search out enemy forces and installations, and collect intelligence. Once found, Viet Cong bases were monitored, raided if possible, or harassed if too well defended for guerrilla penetration. Enemy communication lines were sliced by ambushes, mines, and booby traps. Detected storage complexes were often eliminated by calling in air strikes, and the mobile guerrillas ideally assessed these results on the spot.

From the standpoint of MACV, perhaps the most notable Special Forces achievement of the year was its participation in a new pattern of area warfare being field-tested in northwestern Tay Ninh Province of War Zone C, near the Cambodian frontier. General Westmoreland hoped that a multi-divisional search-and-destroy operation could eliminate North Vietnamese Army and Viet Cong forces in this base area, but he required Special Forces reconnaissance assets to pinpoint exact enemy locations for the following ''pile-on'' by infantry and artillery battalions.

The operation, designated Operation Attleboro, represented the first search-and-destroy operation, which later typified American strategy in Vietnam. The III CTZ (Bien Hoa) Mike Force battalion of 530 Chinese Nungs under Detachment A-302 commander Captain Thomas Myerchin was moved from Loc Ninh to Suoi Da on the afternoon of November 2, 1966, and alerted to locate the 9th Viet Cong Division within War Zone C. All three ''China Boy'' Companies were deployed into battle, and on the following day a violent skirmish was fought between Special Forces-led Chinese mercenaries and the Viet Cong. The Viet Cong broke off the engagement, but Special Forces sergeants skillfully called in air strikes along the enemy path of withdrawal. On the afternoon of November 4, the 3d China Boy Company was surrounded by a regiment of Viet Cong occupying a heavily fortified tunnel complex in thick jungle and nearly wiped out.

The Mike Force reconnaissance units found the enemy in strength, but disengagement proved difficult. The battle raged on through the following day until helicopters managed to extract the survivors on the evening of November 5, 1966. Captain Myerchin's valiant Chinese detected the 271st, 272d, and 273d Viet Cong main regiments, and General Westmoreland deployed elements of the 1st, 4th, and 25th Infantry Divisions, as well as the 173d Airborne Brigade and 11th Armored Cavalry, to finish the battle. While the reconnaissance venture was costly, resulting in numerous Special Forces and Chinese dead or missing, it represented a resounding success of special-warfare tactics in finding and fixing enemy targets for later destruction by larger formations. Operation Attleboro provided an excellent example of Special Forces utilization as an essential component of total Army strategy.

Top left and top right: Camp Khe Sanh, established in the remote northwestern corner of Vietnam for Trailwatch and border-surveillance purposes along the Laotian border in July 1962, was immediately subjected to pressure by the enemy, which ambushed its medical team that December. These team members, pictured less than a year later, were among the first Special Forces to serve at the precarious site. *(Nelson Smith)* **Bottom:** Camp Khe Sanh, shown here in 1963, was initially established at the old French fort overlooking Route 9. Two years later the Special Forces relocated to a new airfield constructed nearby. *(Nelson Smith)*

Top left: Camp Tra Bong, reopened in the coastal mountain ranges of northern South Vietnam's Quang Ngai Province by combined U.S.-Australian team A-107 during late August 1965, was the scene of extensive action in 1966. *(Author's Collection)* **Top right:** A fair-weather road led into Camp Tra Bong, but local Viet Cong dominion of the valley forced Tra Bong to rely primarily on air-transported supplies from Chu Lai. This team member at Tra Bong learns elephant riding. *(MACV PIO)* **Center right:** During January 1966 the garrison suffered severe casualties when an entire Special Forces-led CIDG company was decimated in the "battle of the lost patrol." Civilian war correspondent Dickey Chapelle, a heroic journalist who endured the frontline hardships and hazards of the wars she reported, is treated by a Special Forces doctor. She would later be killed while accompanying Marines patrolling the Tra Bong region. *(David Paulsrud)* **Bottom:** The North Vietnamese Army first used heavy 120mm mortars in South Vietnam to deliver a devastating barrage against Khe Sanh on January 4-5, 1966. In response, the Marines arrived to bolster area security during April and moved onto the Khe Sanh airfield permanently in October. By December 1966 Marine expansion of the Khe Sanh combat base forced the relocation of Detachment A-101 from this compound. *(Author's Collection)*

Top: Camp A Shau, located in the far western valley of Thua Thien Province, was surrounded by high mountains covered with dense rain forest. Camp forces were responsible for Laotian border surveillance and interdiction of enemy supply lines. This view of the camp's jumble of buildings, barracks, and other structures was taken from the north end of the runway in 1964. *(Edward Short)* **Center left:** Special Forces Capt. Edward A. Short inspects the mine field along the runway at A Shau during 1965. Mines rapidly deteriorated under tropical conditions, and the man-high valley elephant grass prohibited easy replacement. *(Edward Short)* **Center right:** During February 1965 Detachment A-102 became the first permanent garrison at Camp A Shau. Seen in this picture of the team house are (left to right) Sgt. First Class Hansen, Sgt. Halbrook, Australian WO Joe Gordon, and Capt. Short. *(Edward Short)* **Bottom:** Enemy forces began building up around Camp A Shau in late 1965, prompting Marine zone commander Maj. Gen. Lewis W. Walt, second from right, to check camp defenses. He coordinates with LLDB Capt. Trung Vi Diap and the camp commander on the left and Australian WO J.R. Coutts on the right. *(Edward Short)*

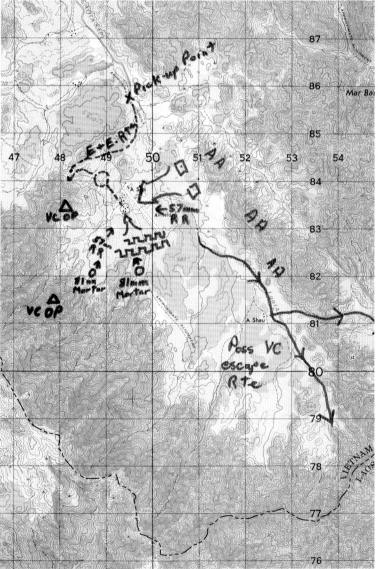

Top: Camp A Shau was overrun by a major North Vietnamese Army attack on March 9-10, 1966. Air cover was hampered by the low clouds and rolling ground fog. Initial NVA mortar barrages destroyed most of the facilities and caused a temporary loss in team communications. The main enemy assault waves struck the southern and eastern walls and smashed through the camp in fierce combat. Several gallant Special Forces-led counterattacks failed to dislodge the enemy from its newly won positions. Combat lasted several hours until the greatly outnumbered Special Forces and indigenous defenders, severely depleted by losses, retreated to make their last organized stand along the camp's northern wall. *(DOD)* **Bottom left:** The flow of the larger battle is depicted in this after-action report map. Marine helicopters attempting to retrieve the camp defenders came under intense fire from enemy anti-aircraft positions (marked by AA), forcing the camp defenders to go into the jungle and reach another extraction point (following dotted line marked F & E Rte for ''Escape and Evasion Route'') while the enemy withdrew back to Laos. *(Author's Collection)* **Bottom right:** The ruins of Camp A Shau after being overrun, looking east along the southern wall. The barracks of the 141st CIDG company, whose troops defected en masse along this wall to the North Vietnamese during combat, can be seen in the left background. *(John Erskine)*

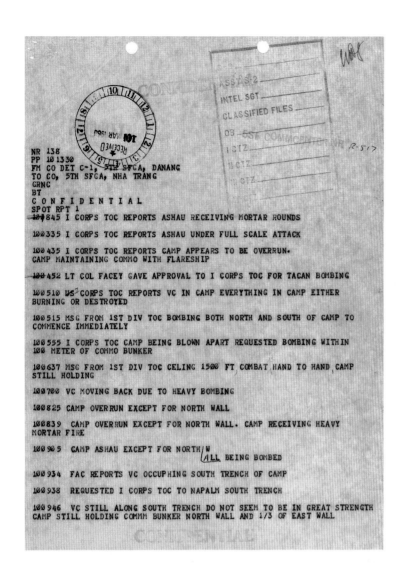

NR 138
PP 10 1330
FM CO DET C-1, 5TH SFGA, DANANG
TO CO, 5TH SFGA, NHA TRANG
GRNC
BT
C O N F I D E N T I A L
SPOT RPT 1
100845 I CORPS TOC REPORTS ASHAU RECEIVING MORTAR ROUNDS

100335 I CORPS TOC REPORTS ASHAU UNDER FULL SCALE ATTACK

100435 I CORPS TOC REPORTS CAMP APPEARS TO BE OVERRUN.
CAMP MAINTAINING COMMO WITH FLARESHIP

100452 LT COL FACEY GAVE APPROVAL TO I CORPS TOC FOR TACAN BOMBING

100510 US CORPS TOC REPORTS VC IN CAMP EVERYTHING IN CAMP EITHER
BURNING OR DESTROYED

100515 MSG FROM 1ST DIV TOC BOMBING BOTH NORTH AND SOUTH OF CAMP TO
COMMENCE IMMEDIATELY

100555 I CORPS TOC CAMP BEING BLOWN APART REQUESTED BOMBING WITHIN
100 METER OF COMMO BUNKER

100637 MSG FROM 1ST DIV TOC CELING 1500 FT COMBAT HAND TO HAND CAMP
STILL HOLDING

100700 VC MOVING BACK DUE TO HEAVY BOMBING

100825 CAMP OVERRUN EXCEPT FOR NORTH WALL

100839 CAMP OVERRUN EXCEPT FOR NORTH WALL. CAMP RECEIVING HEAVY
MORTAR FIRE

100905 CAMP ASHAU EXCEPT FOR NORTH/W
ALL BEING BOMBED

100934 FAC REPORTS VC OCCUPHING SOUTH TRENCH OF CAMP

100938 REQUESTED I CORPS TOC TO NAPALM SOUTH TRENCH

100946 VC STILL ALONG SOUTH TRENCH DO NOT SEEM TO BE IN GREAT STRENGTH
CAMP STILL HOLDING COMMM BUNKER NORTH WALL AND 1/3 OF EAST WALL

100956 U.S. PRESIDENT CALLED MACV FOR TOTAL NUMBER ON AMERICAN AT
ASHAU

101005 CEILING LIFTING IF NOT REINFORCED OR EVACUATED SOON ALL
WILL VE OVER

101021 ASHAU CALLING FOR AIRSTRIKE EAST OF RUNWAY. VC MASSING EAST
OF RUNWAY. SITATUION VERY SERIOUS

101029 MSG FROM I CORPS TOC REPORTS TAC AIR TAKING OFF FOR ASHAU
EVERY 20 MINUTES

101210 CV'2 DEPARTED TO AIR DROP with AMMO TO ASHAU CV-2 WILL FLY ALONG
AXIS OF NORTH WALL

101210 AIRCRAFT LOSSES 1 C-47, 1 F4, 2AIE, 1H-34

101210 INTENSIVE GD FIRE ON A-C

101220 CANNOT RECEIVE RESULLPLIES WITHOUT REINFORCEMENTS FIRST

101225 IS ANY HELP ARRINING ASHAU

101305 DOWN TO LAST FEW ROUNDS NO FOOD NO WATER HAVE 200 MEN OVER
HALF WIA MASSIVE AIRSTRIKE, SMOKE REUNWAY COME IN BEHIND AND GET
US OUT REQUEST FOR ARMED C-47 SUPPORT REFUSE FOR NIGHT
OPN OF 09 MAR AND REQUESTED AGAIN 100930--REFUSED AT 101200 FROM
SAIGON TACC.
C O N F I D E N T I A L
BT

NNNN

TOT 101452
TOR 101520
TOC 101525
CC R-517
BRD

Top: Control Detachment C-1, the next higher headquarters for Camp A Shau, dispatched a copy of its spot reports on the camp to the 5th Special Forces Group during the final afternoon of the battle. *(Author's Collection)* **Bottom:** These skeletal remains of a Special Forces defender killed during the fighting withdrawal to the communications bunker and northern wall were discovered during body recovery operations on March 18, 1966.

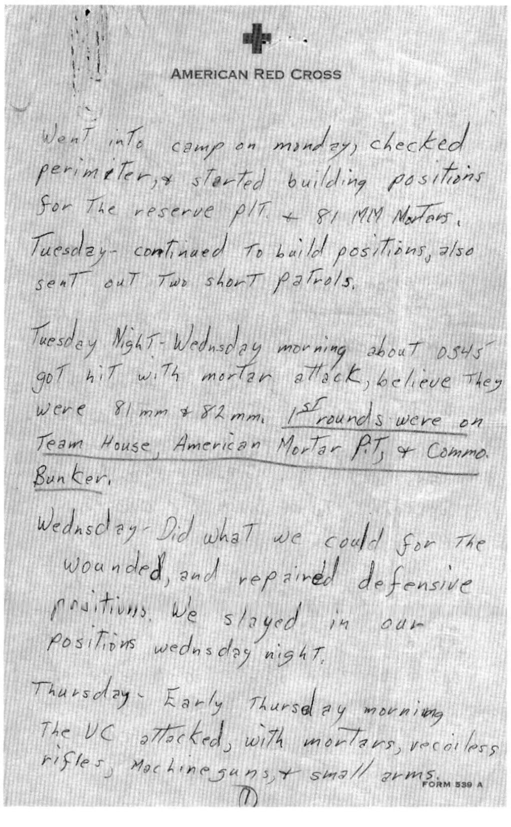

Top: A general view of Camp A Shau after the battle shows the sniper wall around the demolished LLDB quarters and the convict worker barracks in the background. The loss of A Shau was a severe blow to allied control of the frontier, and North Vietnamese Army forces later used this region as a major staging base for their sudden attack on Hue during Tet-68. Allied attempts to regain control of the A Shau valley led to several sanguinary contests later in the war, including the 1969 assault up Ap Bia Mountain or ''Hamburger Hill.'' *(John Erskine)* **Bottom:** Notes on the A Shau battle were hastily scrawled by a survivor, Capt. Tennis H. Carter, shortly after his evacuation to a medical facility. *(Author's Collection)*

Handwritten notes (left page):

AMERICAN RED CROSS

Went into camp on monday, checked perimeter, & started building positions for The reserve plt. & 81 MM Mortars.

Tuesday- continued To build positions, also sent out Two short patrols.

Tuesday Night- Wednesday morning about 0545 got hit with mortar attack, believe They were 81 mm & 82 mm. 1st rounds were on Team House, American Mortar Pit, & Commo Bunker.

Wednesday- Did whaT we could for The wounded, and repaired defensive positions. We stayed in our positions wednesday night.

Thursday- Early Thursday morning The VC attacked, with mortars, recoiless rifles, machine guns, + small arms.

FORM 539 A

Handwritten notes (right page):

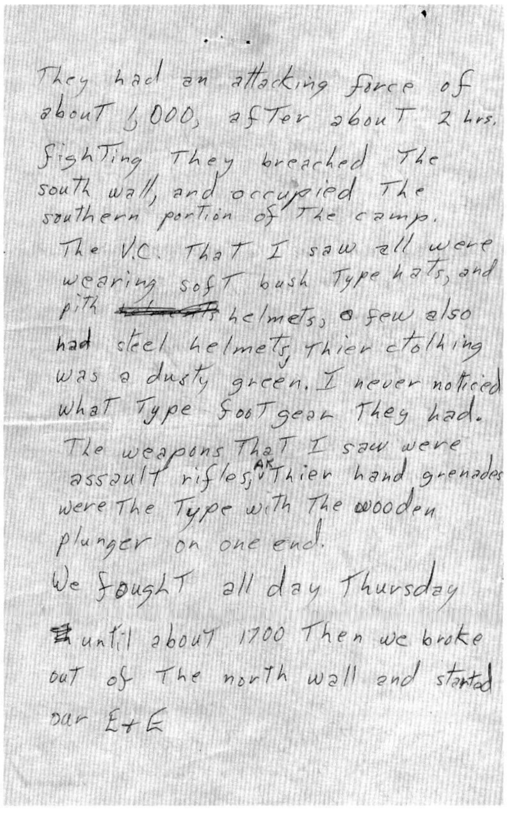

They had an attacking force of about 6,000, after about 2 hrs. fighTing They breached The south wall, and occupied The southern portion of The camp.

The V.C. ThaT I saw all were wearing soft bush Type hats, and pith helmets, a few also had steel helmets, Their clothing was a dusty green. I never noticed whaT Type footgear They had.

The weapons ThaT I saw were assault rifles, Their hand grenades were The Type with The wooden plunger on one end.

We foughT all day Thursday until about 1700 Then we broke out of The north wall and started our E+E

A SHAU

Top: Nui Ba Den ("Black Virgin Mountain"), a 3,000-foot, jungle-covered granite mountain in Tay Ninh Province, offered a superb height for continuous radio-relay throughout the III Corps Tactical Zone. A major signal installation was erected after a Special Forces camp was built on the summit during July 1964. *(Leo Raschko/USA)* **Bottom:** Nui Ba Den rose abruptly from the surrounding rice flatlands and was the sacred symbol of the Cao Dai religion. Detachment A-324 operated the radio-relay site, guarded the hilltop with Cao Dai and Vietnamese assistance, and provided local security patrols. Sgt. Willie C. Smith surveys a seemingly endless expanse of fertile rice land from atop his mountain-peak bunker. *(DOD)*

Top left: The upper path leading to the helipad on top of the mountain was first ambushed by the Viet Cong on April 5, 1966. Beginning in 1967, increased security and signal capacity on Nui Ba Den was provided by the 25th Infantry Division. Nevertheless, the Special Forces mountain post experienced its heaviest fighting during the following year. Ten Americans were killed in this one section of the path on the morning of May 14, 1968. The boulder memorialized Nui Ba Den's defenders. *(Author's Collection)* **Top right:** Special Forces Staff Sgt. Victor Kalicki and his CIDG companion enjoy a song on a Vietnamese flute during guard duty atop Nui Ba Den. *(USIS)* **Bottom:** There were no roads up Nui Ba Den, and the Viet Cong controlled the countryside around the base of the steep mountain. These factors mandated aerial resupply of the vital Special Forces radio-relay station. This CH-47 Chinook helicopter sling-loads a CONEX container and other supplies that will be used for bunker construction. *(James Ensign/USA)*

Top: Camp Suoi Da, seven miles northeast of Tay Ninh, was situated on the eastern edge of War Zone C to hamper enemy interior-infiltration routes between the Vietnamese capital of Saigon and the Cambodian border. Forces from the camp participated in extensive operations and saturation patrolling to clear Viet Cong units from the surrounding area and Nui Cau mountain. These Chinese mercenaries march into action near Suoi Da during 1966. *(Bernie Mangiboyat/USA)* **Bottom:** Detachment A-322 at Camp Suoi Da was engaged in constant camp-maintenance chores, as the camp perimeter shown here became eroded during rainy seasons. A major part of all Special Forces work in isolated campsites involved replacing sandbags, digging out drainage ditches, replacing concertina wire, and repairing airstrips. *(Author's Collection)*

140

Top left: Camp Trai Bi was the first Special Forces camp emplaced within a Viet Cong war zone. The III CTZ Mike Force began clearing a path to the new campsite, six miles inside War Zone C, on June 22, 1966. *(Thomas Myerchin)* **Top right:** This Huey helicopter of the 120th Aviation Company was downed outside Trai Bi. *(Author's Collection)* **Center left:** The Trai Bi jungle was laced with Viet Cong tunnels and fortifications, and losses were sustained during the skirmishing required to reach the site. Here, CIDG bodies are loaded on a helicopter after a fire fight. *(Thomas Myerchin)* **Center right:** A wounded Nung soldier of the III CTZ Mike Force receives treatment during the costly approach to Trai Bi. He subsequently died, because it took more than three hours to reach a clearing where a helicopter could land safely. *(Thomas Myerchin)* **Bottom:** Once established, Camp Trai Bi was successfully defended by Detachment A-323. *(Author's Collection)*

Top left: Camp Tinh Bien was a Mekong Delta border-surveillance camp located between the guerrilla-infested Seven Mountains region and Cambodia. Here, the camp's LLDB troops check out a squad-sized entrance hole capable of holding ten Viet Cong in October 1966. *(Author's Collection)*
Top right: Capt. Jerome A. Brushette's Tinh Bien camp strike force seized enemy trenches around the Viet Cong Nha Be base area during November 1966. *(Author's Collection)* **Center left:** In 1966 Detachment A-423 conducted several excursions against Viet Cong contingents in the Nha Be area and neighboring hills. This Viet Cong cave entrance was detected that October during Operation Cleansweep. *(Author's Collection)* **Bottom:** A large cavern entrance that was part of an elaborate Viet Cong base area was uncovered by Camp Tinh Bien forces in the Nha Be vicinity during October 1966. *(Author's Collection)*

Top: Despite certain Special Forces misgivings, the Special Forces goal of transferring campsites to Vietnamese control intensified from 1966, until it reached its peak under the Vietnamization crash-program declared by MACV Gen. Creighton Abrams Jr. Special Forces commander Col. Harold R. Aaron (right) and LLDB Gen. Doan Van Quang (left of speaker) register less-than-enthusiastic countenance at remarks promising Vietnamese protection during a hasty camp transfer ceremony. *(Author's Collection)* **Bottom left:** During June 1966 Col. Francis J. Kelly assumed command of the 5th Special Forces Group. He introduced mobile guerrilla-force "Blackjack" operations, strengthened the mobile reaction forces, and created a "Green Beret Navy" in the Delta. *(USA)* **Bottom right:** LLDB Capt. Chau Dien, commander of a Khmer Kampuchea Krom (KKK) Mike Force company, is awarded the coveted Green Scarf for excellence under fire at Dan Phuc during December 1966. KKK leaders controlled several ethnic Cambodian factions that fought well for Special Forces in the Mekong Delta. *(George Marecek)*

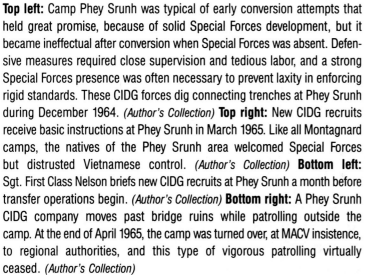

Top left: Camp Phey Srunh was typical of early conversion attempts that held great promise, because of solid Special Forces development, but it became ineffectual after conversion when Special Forces was absent. Defensive measures required close supervision and tedious labor, and a strong Special Forces presence was often necessary to prevent laxity in enforcing rigid standards. These CIDG forces dig connecting trenches at Phey Srunh during December 1964. *(Author's Collection)* **Top right:** New CIDG recruits receive basic instructions at Phey Srunh in March 1965. Like all Montagnard camps, the natives of the Phey Srunh area welcomed Special Forces but distrusted Vietnamese control. *(Author's Collection)* **Bottom left:** Sgt. First Class Nelson briefs new CIDG recruits at Phey Srunh a month before transfer operations begin. *(Author's Collection)* **Bottom right:** A Phey Srunh CIDG company moves past bridge ruins while patrolling outside the camp. At the end of April 1965, the camp was turned over, at MACV insistence, to regional authorities, and this type of vigorous patrolling virtually ceased. *(Author's Collection)*

Top left: In contrast to the Phey Srunh experience, Camp An Phu proved to be an almost model conversion success story in mid-1966. This was due, in large part, to the camp's tough Hoa Hao bandit mercenaries, who were capable of battling the Viet Cong without much outside help. Camp commander Maj. Le Van Phoi congratulates his men on April 28, 1966, as Special Forces Detachment A-424 Capt. Daniel Marvin stands nearby in right background. *(Author's Collection)* **Top right:** American and Vietnamese authorities viewed the An Phu Vietnamization project as a sign of continuing progress. The July 1966 conversion ceremony included a host of MACV dignitaries, as well as rare Vietnamese interest from top leaders such as IV Corps commander Gen. Dang Van Quang (beside microphone), a close ally of President Thieu. *(Author's Collection)* **Bottom left:** The Hoa Hao garrison of Camp An Phu defeated the Viet Cong in several encounters. Maj. Le Van Phoi gives a briefing on the victory near Khanh Binh during May 1966, while a CIDG honor guard stands with the Special Forces team. *(Author's Collection)* **Bottom right:** Hoa Hao CIDG paramilitary troops stationed at Camp An Phu receive cash bonuses and award certificates. *(Author's Collection)*

Top: Throughout 1966 Camp Cai Cai was engaged in bitter combat near the Cambodian border. The enemy mined the waterways, conducted raids, and periodically delivered intense artillery barrages, often from across the border. On April 3 Capt. Leo Donker, Detachment A-412 commander at Cai Cai, was killed by a mortar attack. Camp strike forces retaliated by engaging the Viet Cong near Ap Choi Moi during May 1966. This Special Forces advisor directs troops forward against the enemy bunker line. *(Author's Collection)* **Bottom:** Each Special Forces offensive action near Camp Cai Cai exacted an inevitable toll. Sp4 Crowder treats a CIDG native wounded in the Ap Choi Moi encounter. *(Author's Collection)*

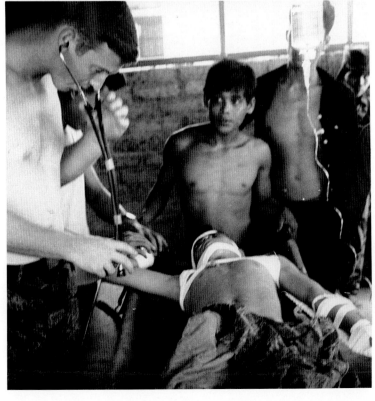

Top left: Camp Binh Thanh Thon was located in a vast swamp in northern Kien Tuong Province near the Cambodian border. Despite constant enemy ambushes along the frontier canal network, this Special Forces border post relied primarily on sampans and airboats to conduct border surveillance. During September 1966 Capt. William G. Baughn's camp strike forces penetrated a major Viet Cong swamp base. *(Author's Collection)* **Top right:** Detachment A-413 Team Sergeant leads the September combat operation deeper into Viet Cong territory. *(Author's Collection)* **Center left:** A Viet Cong fish net marked the heart of the 263d Viet Cong Battalion base. During this operation, Special Forces troops killed VC battalion commander Col. Lam Ngoc Minh. *(Author's Collection)* **Bottom:** Flood conditions enabled Camp Binh Thanh Thon assault boats to reach previously impervious Viet Cong bases during late 1966. *(Author's Collection)*

Top left: Camp Cung Son, established during January 1966 in Phu Yen Province, 20 miles west of Tuy Hoa, helped safeguard Highway 7. Its Detachment A-221 also served as a sub-sector advisory team, providing assistance to the district chief, as well as offering area protection. *(Author's Collection)*
Top right: Local natives, garbed in shirts and loincloths, practice marksmanship at Camp Cung Son. The first camp strike-force companies of selected regional natives completed training on March 26, 1966. *(Clarence McCormick)* **Center:** Special Forces sergeants, serving as company commanders within a II Corps Mike Force battalion, tensely wait for the signal to counterattack Viet Cong troops near Cung Son. Mike Forces ensured wide-ranging protection while the camp was being established. *(Gerald Foy)* **Bottom:** A Special Forces-led battalion of the II Corps Mike Force provides a screen in front of the 173d Airborne Brigade during combat operations around Camp Cung Son in 1966. *(Gerald Foy)*

Top left: Camp An Lac, located in the Mrong River valley of Darlac Province, was surrounded by bamboo forests and mountains. The Special Forces used this base to interdict Viet Cong supply routes in the lower Central Highlands. *(Author's Collection)* **Top right:** Detachment A-234 relocated to An Lac after closing Phey Srunh in early 1965. The camp force gained a significant victory against an enemy base-complex in Darlac Province in 1966, as part of a multi-company battalion fielded by several Special Forces camps. This CIDG unit returns from an operation against the Viet Cong with four prisoners and three Rhade Montagnard women, who were being used by the enemy as forced porters. *(John Shea/JFK Museum)* **Bottom:** During 1966 Special Forces patrols from Camp An Lac conducted a series of raids into the nearby mountains and liberated numerous Montagnard slaves being held by the Viet Cong. *(Gary Clark)*

CONFIDENTIAL

Camp Dak To, garrisoned by Detachment A-244, was a border-surveillance camp close to the Laotian border of Kontum Province. In this view, looking south over the airfield, the Dak Poko meanders just behind the camp (center), while the 4,500-foot-high Ngok Non range looms on the horizon. During 1966 patrols from this camp identified far-reaching North Vietnamese Army regional trail networks. A major struggle for possession of the Dak To area ensued during 1967. *(Author's Collection)*

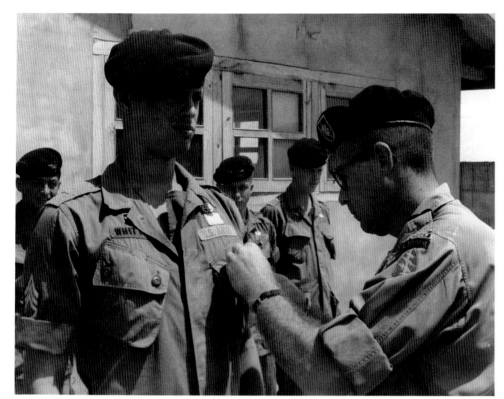

Top left: Detachment B-50, Project Omega, conducted special reconnaissance to locate enemy activities for strategic exploitation. Project Omega contained more than 70 Special Forces members and 660 irregulars, and it was oriented primarily in the Central Highlands during its Vietnam service. In addition to combat heroism, many Special Forces soldiers exhibited equal valor in saving lives. Project Omega Staff Sgt. Scott J. Whitting received the Soldier's Medal for rescuing a comrade who, weighted down with a rucksack and mortar ammunition, fell off a two-rope suspension bridge into a swift mountain stream during a September 1966 mission west of Dak To. *(Scott J. Whitting)* **Top right:** A Montagnard reconnaissance soldier of Project Omega, based in tents at the Camp Dak To forward operating base during September 1966, salutes with his rifle. *(Scott J. Whitting)* **Bottom left:** Pigs, corralled by ammunition boxes at Camp Dak To, ensured fresh food for Project Omega reconnaissance troops. *(Scott J. Whitting)* **Bottom right:** Field kitchen cooking facilities at Camp Dak To included these earthen ovens and large stew pots. *(Scott J. Whitting)*

Top: Camp Buon Blech was established in mid-1966 along the highland border of Darlac Province, near Cambodia, by Detachment A-238, with Montagnard volunteers transferred from Buon Ea Yang. The camp's mission included constructing and maintaining a forward operational base, which accomplished airfield security, and manning checkpoints along Highway 14. *(J.H. Scot Crerar/JFK Museum)* **Bottom:** During July 1966 camp forces conducted joint operations with an airmobile infantry brigade from the 1st Cavalry Division and extended patrolling into the Plei Trap valley by the end of the year. These CIDG native irregulars pass through the main gate at Camp Buon Blech. *(Gary Clark)*

Top: Special Forces mobile reaction forces were initially organized to provide zone reserve and reinforcing units for camps jeopardized by enemy buildup or under attack. Full employment of the mobile reaction force raiding, ambush, and combat-patrol capabilities was made throughout South Vietnam during 1966, when the 5th Mobile Strike Force Command saw extended action. That December the command was brought under joint Special Forces-Vietnamese LLDB control. In a typical mobile reaction mission sweeping a threatened sector, Capt. Myers questions a village chief and his deputy during late 1966. *(USA/JFK Museum)* **Bottom:** Special Forces gained great flexibility in responding to crisis situations by fielding mobile reaction forces that, unlike camp units, could deploy efficiently outside tribal areas and use swift airmobile response, usually from the 281st Aviation Company. *(Clyde Sincere Jr.)*

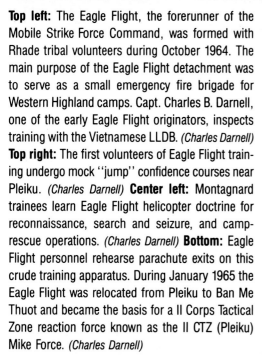

Top left: The Eagle Flight, the forerunner of the Mobile Strike Force Command, was formed with Rhade tribal volunteers during October 1964. The main purpose of the Eagle Flight detachment was to serve as a small emergency fire brigade for Western Highland camps. Capt. Charles B. Darnell, one of the early Eagle Flight originators, inspects training with the Vietnamese LLDB. *(Charles Darnell)* **Top right:** The first volunteers of Eagle Flight training undergo mock ''jump'' confidence courses near Pleiku. *(Charles Darnell)* **Center left:** Montagnard trainees learn Eagle Flight helicopter doctrine for reconnaissance, search and seizure, and camp-rescue operations. *(Charles Darnell)* **Bottom:** Eagle Flight personnel rehearse parachute exits on this crude training apparatus. During January 1965 the Eagle Flight was relocated from Pleiku to Ban Me Thuot and became the basis for a II Corps Tactical Zone reaction force known as the II CTZ (Pleiku) Mike Force. *(Charles Darnell)*

Top right: During 1966 Special Forces employed Mobile Guerrilla Forces, composed of Special Forces-led indigenous company-sized units that conducted sustained Blackjack operations against the enemy. These troops display the U.S. flag after penetrating the enemy-held Soui Kon River valley during Blackjack 23. *(Clyde Sincere Jr.)* **Top left:** A Special Forces mobile reaction patrol in a highlands jungle stream. *(Charles Darnell)* **Center right:** Camp entrance to Tran Phu, headquarters of the Control Detachment II CTZ (Pleiku) Mike Force. *(Gerald W. Foy)* **Bottom:** II CTZ Mike Force members standing (left to right) are Sergeants First Class Jones, Huff, May, and Ramsey, II CTZ Mike Force battalion commander Capt. Clyde J. Sincere Jr., and 3d Mike Force company commander Lt. Andrew Irzyk. In front (left to right) are Staff Sgt. Pall, Staff Sgt. Wyson, Sp5 McMullin, Sp4 Walker, Sgt. Panfil, and Staff Sgt. Van Poll. *(Clyde Sincere Jr.)*

Top left: Mobile Guerrilla Forces were inserted into remote regions formerly considered NVA/VC safe havens for periods of 30 to 60 days on Blackjack operations. To prevent compromise the Special Forces broke all contact with their base, including radio transmission, and were resupplied by unconventional means. Blackjack special operations were successful in penetrating isolated enemy strongholds, disrupting the enemy line of communications, attacking hidden logistical support bases, and gathering intelligence. Maj. George Marecek led Khmer Kampuchea Krom (KKK) Mobile Guerrilla Task Force 489 into the Seven Mountains region of Chau Doc Province during Blackjack 41. *(George Marecek)* **Top right:** The southern entrance to a Viet Cong mountain cave strongpoint seized by Special Forces Blackjack 41 troops. *(Author's Collection)* **Bottom:** Schematic of the Viet Cong cave complex uncovered during Blackjack 41. *(Author's Collection)*

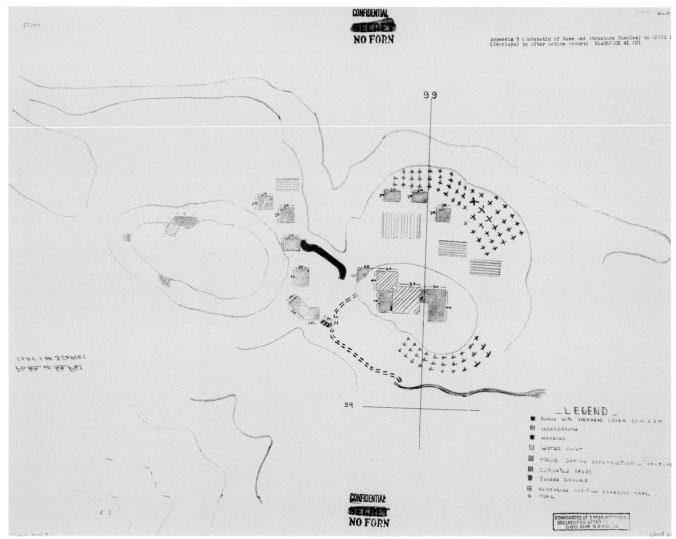

Top: From their inception in October 1966, Mobile Guerrilla Forces participated in Blackjack operations until mid-1967, when they began integrating formally with the Mike Forces to form the Mobile Strike Force, which retained the missions and capabilities of both. The 2d Battalion of Chinese Nungs from the IV CTZ Mike Force march toward Don Phuc after four months of battling on Nui Giai during Blackjack 41 in April 1967. *(George Marecek)* **Bottom left:** Victorious Mobile Guerrilla Task Force 399 members rest at the entrance to a Viet Cong headquarters captured during Blackjack 41. *(Author's Collection)* **Bottom right:** The Special Forces surprise raid on this cavern kitchen during Blackjack 41 operations caught the Viet Cong in the midst of cooking rice on their stove. *(Author's Collection)*

Operation Attleboro represented the culmination of both U.S. Army regular and Special Forces operations during 1966, because it involved the first field-testing of U.S. military strategy that would dominate the rest of the Vietnam conflict: the search and destroy pattern of area warfare. Operation Attleboro was aimed at finding and eliminating the 9th Viet Cong Division in War Zone C of the northwestern Tay Ninh Province. Special Forces Capt. Thomas Myerchin led the III CTZ (Bien Hoa) Mike Force into battle, supported by UH-1B helicopter gunships, on November 3, 1966. *(DOD)*

Top right: Aerial rocket fire explodes through the enemy-held landing zone as Tom Myerchin's three companies of ''China Boys,'' containing 530 Chinese irregulars from the III CTZ Mike Force, conduct a helicopter assault into War Zone C to find the Viet Cong in advance of larger Army formations. *(Bernie Mangiboyat/USA)* **Center right:** Special Forces Lt. Walter M. Oszozakiewicz and Sgt. Max Speers trace the expanding combat lines on their map as the III CTZ Mike Force engages the enemy on the afternoon of November 3, 1966. *(Bernie Mangiboyat/USA)* **Bottom:** Special Forces Staff Sgt. Paul Taylor wipes blood from a fallen Chinese mercenary soldier, as his indigenous medics collect the wounded on a battlefield during Operation Attleboro. *(Bernie Mangiboyat/USA)*

Top: The III CTZ Mike Force became engaged in heightened action against the 272d Viet Cong Regiment on November 4, 1966. These mortar troops fire in support of their encircled 3d China Boy Company comrades. *(Bernie Mangiboyat/USA)* **Center:** The 1st China Boy Company, temporarily stalled in a mine field while under sniper fire, awaits the signal to charge toward enemy positions in an endeavor to reach surrounded members of the 3d China Boy Company. *(Bernie Mangiboyat/USA)* **Bottom:** The III CTZ Mike Force losses, which mounted as combat increased, included a medivac helicopter that was shot down at 7:30 a.m. on November 4 while attempting to reach the 1st China Boy Company. Here, reinforcements rush to board helicopters in an effort to land more troops near the 3d China Boy Company, rendered temporarily leaderless when Sgt. First Class Finn was killed. *(Bernie Mangiboyat/USA)*

Top: Recon Platoon Leader Sgt. First Class Joe Lopez gives fresh information about Viet Cong battleground dispositions to III CTZ Mike Force Operations Sgt. First Class Asa Ballard, while the 1st and 2d China Boy Companies seek to break through to the 3d Company on November 5, 1966. Radio contact with the latter company had been broken since 7:45 that morning. *(Bernie Mangiboyat/USA)*. **Bottom:** Chinese mercenary reinforcements conduct a helicopter assault to reach the smashed lines of the 3d China Boy Company, overrun by Viet Cong attackers, during Operation Attleboro. Although Special Forces and native troops suffered considerable casualties, the III CTZ Mike Force pinpointed the location of Viet Cong bunker systems and main-force elements for larger Army formations in accordance with the MACV plan of operation. *(Bernie Mangiboyat/USA)*

Top left: 1st Infantry Division commander Maj. Gen. William E. DePuy, one of the most brilliant generals of the Vietnam war, assures Lt. Col. Newlin Happerdryt that regular Army soldiers will extract the III CTZ Mike Force if necessary. *(Bernie Mangiboyat/USA)* **Top right:** 5th Special Forces Group commander Col. Kelly presents the Green Scarf to III CTZ Mike Force heroes of Operation Attleboro at Loc Ninh. *(Thomas Myerchin)* **Bottom:** Detachment A-302 led the 3d Nung Battalion (Chinese mercenaries) of the III CTZ (Bien Hoa) Mike Force in Operation Attleboro in 1966. Standing (left to right) are Team Sgt.-Maj. Roy Matthews, Recon Platoon Leader Mike Leary, Demolitions Sgt. David Ryder Jr., Recon Platoon Leader Mike Kane; Company commander Sgt. First Class J.W. ''Silver Fox'' Edsell, and Battalion executive officer Lt. Klobe. In front (left to right) are Recon Platoon Leader Joe Lopez, Company commander Sgt. First Class George Heaps, Recon Platoon Leader Paul C. Taylor, and Battalion commander Thomas Myerchin. Not shown are Special Forces sergeants killed or wounded during the operation, including Monaghan, Garza, Heaps, Hunt, and Finn. *(Thomas Myerchin)*

Top: The 5th Special Forces Group headquarters complex at Nha Trang, located to the right of the lower runway loop and aircraft parking ramp in the middle foreground, was extensively upgraded during 1966. This aerial view of the entire Nha Trang base complex was taken in April 1966. *(USAF)* **Center:** The central landmark of Nha Trang was a huge statue of Buddha on Doi Hai Thuy that dominated the pagoda and market area of the city. The celebration of Buddha's 2,514th birthday was conducted at this site for a large gathering of American and Vietnamese Special Forces troops and their families in 1970. *(Author's Collection)* **Bottom:** The 5th Special Forces Group (Airborne) headquarters at Nha Trang, Vietnam. From this building the commander exercised command and operational control of Special Forces elements throughout all four Corps Tactical Zones and the special capital district command. *(Author's Collection)*

SPECIAL FORCES IN THE MID-WAR PERIOD, 1967

Special Forces combat actions during the mid-war period of 1967 were categorized by three basic levels. First and most common, camps experienced marginal North Vietnamese or Viet Cong interference. In these cases the enemy refrained from all-out attack and avoided the disproportionate losses that fort neutralization required. Their actions against the great majority of camps consisted of sporadic indirect-fire attacks using mortars or rockets. However, these camps still generated a high number of patrolling skirmishes beyond the compound. Secondly, of a rarer but more predictable nature, enemy action flared up whenever a Civilian Irregular Defense Group (CIDG) camp was being opened or closed. This type of activity took advantage of lessened defensive measures compared to a normally garrisoned and combat-ready camp. Finally, and most seriously, camps presenting a real nuisance against enemy main infiltration or resupply routes were more likely to be attacked directly by the enemy in great strength, and possibly even destroyed.

During 1967 Special Forces adopted what became known as "Fighting Camp" fortification arrangements to counter the latter threat, as well as to improve protective levels against other adverse situations. The Fighting Camp concept embodied several customary principles. Foremost was speed of installation—a condition mandated by both Vietnam's tropical weather conditions and the limited airlift available to Special Forces. Ideally, a Fighting Camp could be installed or remodeled within 30 days if assisted by at least one reinforced engineer platoon with specialized construction equipment. The time and amount of machinery depended primarily on camp defensive posture, size, and airfield requirements. The size of the camp was tailored so that it could be defended by one quarter of the assigned garrison strength. Once the dimensions were attained, standardized designs were employed to save time.

Austerity was another prime factor of the Fighting Camp. Construction costs were held to a minimum, and "no frills" remained a trademark of Special Forces living conditions. Local materials were used whenever possible, and most labor was provided by the garrison itself. The cost of the camp, however, depended on site location, whether there was a need to "harden" positions with concrete or overhead protection, the availability of locally skilled carpenters and other workers, and the anticipated longevity of the camp. The Special Forces planned to relocate interior camps as soon as their surrounding areas were properly pacified, but border-surveillance camps were recognized as more permanent structures.

The Fighting Camp was built for defense in depth. Secondary trench lines and interior walls were constructed to provide alternate positions. The camp was deliberately divided into sections so that enemy penetrations could be limited and sealed off. Finally, each camp had outposts and exterior picket stations to give advanced warning of enemy approach.

The exact composition and appearance of the Fighting Camps depended on the terrain, and they were classified according to types. The Subsurface Fighting Camp was built in stable ground or mountain soil with underground bunkers. The Surface Fighting Camp was erected on normal Vietnamese water-logged soil with above-ground structures. Floating Camps, assembled in the Mekong Delta to withstand flood damage, featured innovations such as rafts lashed to empty fuel drums.

Construction of New Camp Plei Djereng, occupied by Detachment A-251 in Pleiku Province, commenced on December 13, 1966, with the arrival of Special Forces Engineer Team KB-7 of the 539th Engineer Detachment. This was the first camp built under the Fighting Camp concept. The engineers on this trial effort encountered difficulties in moving construction materiel to the job site. This was a major problem in all Special Forces camp projects, because the majority could only be reached by aircraft, and the others were linked by ambush-prone roads.

During 1967 the 5th Special Forces Group command structure reflected the massive special-warfare responsibilities assigned to Special Forces in Vietnam. The five principal staff sections were engaged in assisting control and field detachments

Parachutists of the II CTZ Mike Force buckle into their parachutes on the Pleiku base airfield, preparatory to making a combat jump over the future site of Camp Bu Prang on October 5, 1967. This combat jump vividly demonstrated Special Forces proficiency in training and leading native battalions on the most hazardous combat operations. *(Ludwig Faistenhammer Jr.)*

widely dispersed throughout the country. In 1967 dollars the group budget amounted to nearly $100 million, but this figure was consumed briskly in administering, housing, clothing, and feeding more than 70,000 indigenous troops and their families. Funding increases were authorized throughout the year as Special Forces shifted more camps from relatively pacified interior areas to contested North Vietnamese infiltration corridors located on the Laotian and Cambodian borders. New construction costs, native salary increases, mercenary combat bonuses, and high ammunition expenditures soon boosted budgetary allowances to $115 million.

In January 1967 the S-1 personnel section supervised 2,745 Special Forces troops, and this number rose to 3,300 by the end of the year. The group S-2 intelligence section increased intelligence collection and productivity with augmented Army military-intelligence detachments. The group S-3 operations office coordinated planning and group objectives. The S-4 logistics section implemented the Fighting Camp concept, coordinated airlift of provisions, and performed other supply functions. The S-5 Revolutionary Development Support Activity consolidated all disaster relief; political-warfare activities; and group civil-affairs, civic-action, psychological-operations, and resettlement projects in Vietnam.

The escalation of the Vietnam conflict during 1967 involved Special Forces in greatly expanded combat operations. During the year more camps were opened in the midst of traditional Viet Cong base areas or North Vietnamese border strongholds. Camp Con Thien was constructed next to the Demilitarized Zone separating North and South Vietnam. This placement was immediately challenged by two North Vietnamese Army battalions that attempted to overrun the compound on May 8. Another ill-fated northern camp, Lang Vei, suffered a ground attack aided by inside Viet Cong infiltrators on May 4. These actions underscored the increased tempo of fighting along the northern border. By year's end several North Vietnamese divisions were located inside Quang Tri Province.

Camps Prek Klok and Tong Le Chon were established in War Zone C northwest of Saigon. Both forts came under heavy enemy attack, and Tong Le Chon was reduced to shambles by a major North Vietnamese infantry assault on August 7. Camp Loc Ninh, another War Zone C bastion, was close-assaulted several times between October 29 and November 2. During these encounters battle Detachment A-331 repulsed repeated attacks by the 9th Viet Cong Division's 272d and 273d regiments. The enemy sustained grievous casualties and failed to reach the outer parapets of the citadel.

Following this defeat, North Vietnamese and Viet Cong forces withdrew closer to the Cambodian border—within easy proximity of their main refitting and supply centers—and reconcentrated efforts against traditional border targets like Camp Bu Dop. On November 29 the enemy stormed the Bo Duc district headquarters while pinning nearby Camp Bu Dop under intense mortar and rocket barrages. In all these actions the enemy demonstrated an increased willingness to stand and fight with conventional tactics, often in spite of severe losses. Rapid reaction by Mobile Strike Forces and supporting firepower were crucial in determining the favorable outcome of the battles.

All Special Forces camps and Mobile Strike Forces were heavily engaged in extra operational duties during 1967, and they often participated in joint operations with regular Army and Marine divisions. Missions given to CIDG units included reconnaissance, search-and-destroy, flank security, blocking force, joint reaction, road and convoy escort, and special-warfare tasks. These activities, combined with ordinary offensive patrolling, caused an alarming increase in Special Forces and indigenous casualties —especially from mines and booby traps.

American formations favored using civilian irregular troops to their flanks or front, because they travelled lighter and faster than conventional units, and they could negotiate difficult jungle terrain. Because of the small stature and light equipment of indigenous troops, fewer helicopters were required to lift CIDG units into battle. Once native troops were in the field, far less logistical support was required, and fewer aircraft were needed for their employment. Their most valuable tactical advantage, however, was their intuitive grasp of area terrain, trail nets, and probable enemy ambush points and traps. Unfortunately, all irregular units were lightly armed, and their variable performance levels were contingent upon complex native interrelationships that only Special Forces advisors understood. CIDG members lacked any flexibility to cope with hurried alternate plans of action, complicated schemes of maneuver, or drastic changes occasioned by battlefield events. Another major restriction involved the sharp decline in native morale and effectiveness on any operation lasting more than 10 or 15 days.

The IV Corps Tactical Zone continued to be a Viet Cong troublespot, and it remained under primary jurisdiction of the South Vietnamese. Despite extensive flooding in the Mekong Delta during both the fall of 1966 and again in the rainy season of 1967, Special Forces responded with field-expedient watercraft and grim determination to maintain aggressive pressure against enemy swamp hideouts and border-crossing points. New camps at My Phuoc Tay, My An, and My Dien were built within enemy-dominated areas of the Plain of Reeds. In this area and along the border, there were numerous fire fights. Throughout the rest of the Mekong Delta, enemy activity was generally confined to indiscriminate shelling of district towns, small-scale attacks against lightly defended outposts, and interdiction of roads such as Highway 4 connecting Saigon to Can Tho.

In the western Central Highlands, heavy fighting erupted around Camp Dak To in Kontum Province on November 5, 1967. Camp and Mobile Strike Force reconnaissance units became embroiled in combat, and this action developed into one of the longest and hardest-fought engagements of the Second Indochina War. The camp's garrison Detachment A-244 was surrounded by the 32d and 66th North Vietnamese Army regiments entrenched in the region's towering mountains. The 4th Infantry Division and 173d Airborne Brigade fought several major battles to clear these heights. On November 15 and 16,

Camp Dak To was hit by several mortar volleys that caused serious damage and smashed three Air Force cargo planes on the runway. Another Special Forces camp, Ben Het—constructed in this same vicinity during late 1967—was subjected to daily concentrations of mortar and rocket fire.

The unique Special Forces style of native irregular warfare was highlighted during 1967 by the mass parachute assault of Operation Harvest Moon. Mike Forces conducted a combat jump to secure the landing zone at the future site of Camp Bunard and seized the objective area to prevent enemy opposition against later helicopters bringing in main construction and camp-garrison elements. Upon completion, Camp Bunard served as an important monitoring post on the northern edge of War Zone D. Another mass combat parachute jump was conducted on May 13, when Mike Force Companies were dropped over the Seven Mountains area during Blackjack 41. The third parachute assault of the year was executed by the II CTZ (Pleiku) Mike Force southwest of Ban Me Thuot on October 5, 1967, to secure the new campsite at Bu Prang.

Throughout 1967 Project Delta and other long-range reconnaissance projects penetrated deeply into significant North Vietnamese and Viet Cong secret zones, disrupting enemy lines of communication and restricting free movement. The mobile guerrilla forces were expanded so that two were available for each Corps Tactical Zone. Blackjack operational techniques were refined and developed to the point that mobile guerrillas were used for some national priority missions directed by the Pentagon Joint Chiefs of Staff.

During all these 1967 operations, Special Forces increased its capability to advise, lead, and plan a wide range of unconventional and conventional warfare operations. The mid-war period placed increased emphasis on combined operations, engineering accomplishments, staff professionalism, and small-scale conventional operations. These constituted another important step in the development of Special Forces doctrine.

Top: The Special Forces Subsurface Fighting Camp type was designed for northern and mountain regions of South Vietnam, where the soil was firm enough to allow the placement of underground main bunkers with enough reinforcing protection to survive direct mortar hits. Here, ammunition, communications, and command bunkers are being constructed below the ground inside the circular inner perimeter of Camp Mai Loc, which was built as a Subsurface Fighting Camp in Quang Tri Province during spring 1968. *(Author's Collection)* **Bottom:** In areas of Vietnam where the water table inhibited stable underground structures, but was not subject to severe flooding, the Special Forces Surface Fighting Camp style predominated. These camps contained bunkers made from either concrete, timber, or steel CONEX containers. Camp Ben Soi in Tay Ninh Province was a typical Surface Fighting Camp built by U.S. Navy Seabee Team 1104 from April to September 1965. *(USA)*

Top left: The Floating Fighting Camp style was exemplified by Camp Cai Cai in the Mekong Delta. Facilities were built either high enough to withstand complete flooding, or they were constructed on platforms secured to empty 55-gallon fuel drums that rose with the water level. On September 16, 1966, flooding caused Cai Cai's eastern wall to collapse and submerged the camp in water more than five feet deep, forcing troop quarters to be moved to the top of the barracks. *(Author's Collection)* **Top right:** This mortar repositioned on top of a bunker was a typical Floating Fighting Camp adaptation during flooding. Sampans were used to deliver ammunition during a fire mission. *(Author's Collection)* **Center left:** The floating ammunition storage rafts of Camp Cai Cai kept munitions segregated for ease of retrieval during action. Here, Special Forces sergeants swim between the rafts during the September 1966 flood. *(Author's Collection)* **Center right:** Roofed rafts lashed to empty fuel barrels kept ammunition and other vital components dry during monsoon weather. *(Author's Collection)* **Bottom:** A partially submerged Camp Cai Cai in combat-ready condition. *(Author's Collection)*

A-251   YA874459

Top: The original Plei Djereng had to be relocated because of repeated enemy attacks on the poorly situated old camp. New Plei Djereng, shown here, was rebuilt to Fighting Camp specifications by a 539th Engineer Detachment team during the period December 1966 to June 1967. The new camp, built on a low hill dominating the surrounding area, was located 15 miles east of Cambodia about two miles west of the Ia Grai River, and it was bolstered with howitzers from the 4th Infantry Division. *(Author's Collection)* **Center left:** Main gate entrance to Camp Plei Djereng, defended by Detachment A-251. During 1967 camp forces continued border surveillance and applied pressure on main North Vietnamese Army cross-border routes. *(Paradis/USA)* **Center right:** New Plei Me retained its exterior rectangular shape but featured a radically improved defensive status with the addition of underground bunkers and four light howitzers manned by CIDG crews. *(Author's Collection)*

Top left: Camp Con Thien was constructed during February 1967, only two miles south of the Demilitarized Zone separating South and North Vietnam. Special Forces engineers drill a well to insure fresh water at Camp Con Thien during early 1967. *(Author's Collection)* **Top right:** The proximity of Camp Con Thien to enemy territory subjected it to severe shelling during March and April 1967. The ridges of North Vietnam can be seen in this view of camp construction during the latter month. *(Author's Collection)* **Bottom:** The 812th NVA Regiment attempted to overrun Camp Con Thien on May 8, 1967, but Detachment A-110 and a battalion of 4th Marines repulsed the enemy attacks. Two months later, Special Forces transferred the campsite entirely to Marine jurisdiction. The conventional nature of the war around Con Thien was emphasized by this Marine M67 flamethrower tank scorching entrenched North Vietnamese Army positions outside the camp. *(William Norman/USMC)*

Top: Camp Minh Long was completed in a Hre Montagnard region of Quang Ngai Province during mid-November 1966, and Detachment A-108 commenced operations to secure its area and an overland route to the camp. Camp forces suffered heavy losses during a reaction mission on March 6. Viet Cong control of the road systems forced reliance on the camp airfield and helipad for resupply. Later MACV assigned the 11th Infantry Brigade from the Americal Division in an over-watch capacity for the camp. This view shows Camp Minh Long under construction. *(Author's Collection)* **Bottom:** Detachment A-101 relocated from Khe Sanh to Camp Lang Vei, which became fully operational on December 21, 1966. From this new location the Special Forces continued Laotian border surveillance and intelligence gathering. Enemy forces retaliated against this activity by conducting a major attack that extensively damaged the camp on May 4, 1967. Lang Vei was reconstructed by Navy Mobile Construction Battalion 11 and finished that September. *(Author's Collection)*

Top left: Camp Gia Vuc was an old French camp first occupied by Special Forces in January 1962 to secure the Hre Montagnards living in the area. By 1967 the camp defense force totalled 515 CIDG natives organized into four companies, two combat recon platoons, and one political-action team under Detachment A-103. The camp's isolation was highlighted by its location near the Song Re River, a stream too shallow for water travel in the dry season but a raging torrent during the monsoons. *(Author's Collection)* **Top right:** Camp Gia Vuc in Quang Ngai Province was the southernmost camp in I Corps Tactical Zone. Camp patrols up the Song Re valley to the north were aggressively screened by the Viet Cong because the valley was a major north-south enemy supply and infiltration corridor. *(Author's Collection)* **Center:** The camp garrison lacked artillery, but it kept several 106mm recoilless rifles positioned to ward off enemy attacks. *(Author's Collection)* **Bottom:** Fighting trenches at Camp Gia Vuc were hardened against mortar barrages and given extra support because of tropical rainstorms. *(Author's Collection)*

The II CTZ (Pleiku) Mike Force combat parachute jump was conducted over Quang Duc Province's rolling hills, interspersed with jungle and grassland, to secure the site of future Camp Bu Prang on October 5, 1967. These paratroopers descending over the drop zone, masked from enemy fire by the distant smoke screen, provided a spectacular example of the advanced tactical capability that native irregulars achieved while serving in Special Forces-led airborne mobile strike forces. *(Ludwig Faistenhammer Jr.)*

Top right: After securing the isolated drop zone from enemy control, indigenous paratroopers of the II CTZ Mike Force held the area for the safe landing of helicopters that brought CIDG forces with Detachment A-236. The latter troops, supplemented by truck convoys, actually constructed the camp. *(Ludwig Faistenhammer Jr.)* **Center right:** Once established, Camp Bu Prang became the westernmost Special Forces outpost of the southern Central Highlands, and CIDG patrols monitored a strategic enemy infiltration corridor through the surrounding grassy fields and hilly patches of jungle. *(Gary Clark)* **Bottom:** LLDB commander Lt. Col. Phong and II CTZ Mike Force commander Lt. Col. Ludwig "Blue Max" Faistenhammer Jr. hold up the battle flag just after completing the combat jump over the Bu Prang drop zone three miles from the Cambodian border. *(Ludwig Faistenhammer Jr.)*

Camp Dak To, a remote border-surveillance camp located in the towering mountains of central Kontum Province, was partially surrounded by the 24th North Vietnamese Army Regiment during May 1967. After several adverse patrol encounters, Special Forces requested assistance, and the 173d Airborne Brigade airlifted two battalions into the camp on June 17 to initiate Operation Greeley. This operation led to further clashes in the dense jungle, and more reinforcements were sent from the II CTZ Mike Force as well as the 4th Infantry Division. By late 1967 the small camp at Dak To (center boxed area left of runway) was eclipsed by the sprawl of regular Army tent concentrations, helicopter parking ramps, fuel depots, and ammo dumps. *(Author's Collection)*

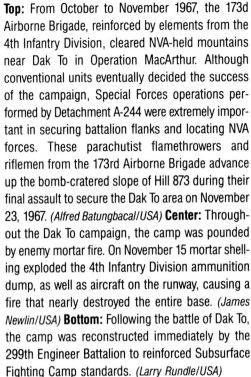

Top: From October to November 1967, the 173d Airborne Brigade, reinforced by elements from the 4th Infantry Division, cleared NVA-held mountains near Dak To in Operation MacArthur. Although conventional units eventually decided the success of the campaign, Special Forces operations performed by Detachment A-244 were extremely important in securing battalion flanks and locating NVA forces. These parachutist flamethrowers and riflemen from the 173rd Airborne Brigade advance up the bomb-cratered slope of Hill 873 during their final assault to secure the Dak To area on November 23, 1967. *(Alfred Batungbacal/USA)* **Center:** Throughout the Dak To campaign, the camp was pounded by enemy mortar fire. On November 15 mortar shelling exploded the 4th Infantry Division ammunition dump, as well as aircraft on the runway, causing a fire that nearly destroyed the entire base. *(James Newlin/USA)* **Bottom:** Following the battle of Dak To, the camp was reconstructed immediately by the 299th Engineer Battalion to reinforced Subsurface Fighting Camp standards. *(Larry Rundle/USA)*

Top: Camp Mang Buk, the northernmost interior Special Forces fort in II Corps Tactical Zone, was located in a forested mountain region 36 miles northeast of Kontum. The Detachment A-246 mission was interdicting enemy traffic across the rugged western boundary of I and II Corps zones. Tributaries of the Dak Nghe River flowing between the steep forested hills dissected the camp into four distinct compounds. *(Leo Roppo)* **Bottom left:** One of hundreds of Viet Cong bamboo stake traps encountered by Special Forces in the Mang Buk vicinity, these well-concealed deterrents were activated by trip wire and proved very effective against CIDG patrollers. *(George Marecek)* **Bottom right:** Mang Buk mustered about 450 CIDG native defenders, composed primarily of Sedang Montagnards. *(Leo Roppo)*

Top left: The prevalent log and dirt nature of original construction at Mang Buk was typified by the timbered casemate on top of the command bunker. Although Special Forces had occupied Mang Buk sporadically since May 1962, the camp was not permanently incorporated into the 5th Special Forces Group arrangement until December 1966. During June 1967 Mang Buk was rebuilt using a pre-stocked Fighting Camp package airlifted from Nha Trang. *(Leo Roppo)* **Top right:** Transition from native to CIDG warrior often included no more than a change of clothes, as these Sedang relatives demonstrate at Mang Buk. *(Leo Roppo)* **Center right:** Primitive living conditions at Mang Buk typified Special Forces service in remote regions. Here, Detachment A-246 Sp4 ''Red'' Sutherland shaves outside the team hut. *(Leo Roppo)* **Bottom:** In addition to moving all outlying villages into the Mang Buk area for protection, Special Forces personnel at Mang Buk recruited, trained, and equipped camp defense Montagnard companies. This patrol carefully crosses a Viet Cong foot bridge in enemy-controlled jungle 21 miles outside of Mang Buk. *(George Marecek)*

Top left: Camp Plateau Gi was located on a lightly forested plateau between the Ne and Pone Rivers of Kontum Province, in a region inhabited by Bahnar and Sedang tribes. Here, a member of Special Forces Detachment A-243 bathes in the Plateau Gi ''Hot Springs.'' *(Author's Collection)* **Top right:** The fire direction arrow at Camp Plateau Gi consisted of evenly spaced cans, filled with gas and sand, which signaled the direction of enemy attack for night air strikes. Arrow-illumination pots were replaced by battery-powered lights in later years. *(Author's Collection)* **Bottom:** Camp Plateau Gi featured triangular compounds with log parapets surrounded by moats. Its name derived from nearby old French fort ruins (overrun by the Viet Minh in 1954). The ''Gi'' suffix was an abbreviation of the French title for Indigenous Guard. *(Author's Collection)*

Camp Prek Klok was opened on March 20, 1967, inside War Zone C during Operation Junction City to cut a major Viet Cong resupply and infiltration route about 20 miles north of Tay Ninh. On the evening of April 14, the Viet Cong shelled Prek Klok with mortars and scored a direct hit on the ammunition dump, which demolished more than half the camp. On May 17 two Viet Cong battalions conducted a ground assault on the perimeter that was repulsed by final defensive fire and camp automatic weapons. Camp Prek Klok was hit by continual mortar and recoilless rifle bombardments throughout the year and closed in December 1967. Detachment A-322 was relocated to open Camp Katum closer to War Zone C's Cambodian border. *(Author's Collection)*

Top: Camp Tong Le Chon was opened March 24, 1967, in War Zone C near the South Vietnamese border, just south of the communist National Liberation Front headquarters in the Cambodian Fishhook. The enemy reacted to the camp's proximity to this main headquarters by executing a devastating regimental attack against the Special Forces fort on August 7, 1967. The 165th NVA Regiment almost overran the compound, but an ammunition dump fortuitously exploded in the midst of the attackers and stopped enemy momentum. A quick Special Forces counterattack by Detachment A-334 and Mike Force troops regained key positions and expelled the North Vietnamese soldiers. *(Author's Collection)*

Bottom: Dead soldiers from NVA sapper squads and wire-cutter teams lie where they fell in the forefront of the assault. Littering the foreground are lengths of explosive pipe sections, known as bangalore torpedoes, that were used to breach wire entanglements. *(Author's Collection)*

Top: Bunkers inside Camp Tong Le Chon, fabricated from reinforced steel CONEX containers, had much of their overhead timber protection and sandbagged shellburst-absorption walls blown away during the battle. Dead enemy sappers litter the ground in front of the shrapnel-riddled bunker parapets. *(Author's Collection)* **Center:** Two soldiers killed in a mutually fatal exchange of fire fell on opposite sides of an interior sandbag wall during the height of the battle for Tong Le Chon. The fallen Special Forces defender can be seen inside the walled trench, center, while his VC adversary lies at the entrance, in the left corner. *(Author's Collection)* **Bottom:** CIDG casualties are gathered by Staff Sgt. Morganfield, the Detachment A-334 medic, along the south edge of the airfield at daybreak following the battle for Camp Tong Le Chon. *(Author's Collection)*

Top: Camp Loc Ninh was located in a rubber-plantation area near Highway 13 just south of a ''Ruff-puff'' sub-sector advisory compound in the background. The latter installation was attacked by the 273d Viet Cong Regiment on October 29, 1967. When CIDG troops counterattacked to regain the compound, the Viet Cong regiment conducted two mass attacks against Camp Loc Ninh on October 31 and November 2. These ground onslaughts were pinned down in the wire barriers by a hail of defensive fire before reaching the actual camp walls. Resulting tactical air strikes caused such carnage that the enemy was routed from the battlefield. *(Author's Collection)* **Bottom:** The northeast wall at Loc Ninh, severely damaged by enemy heavy mortar and 122mm rocket blasts. *(Author's Collection)*

Top left: Special Forces-led troops counterattacked from Camp Loc Ninh to rescue the beleaguered advisors at the Loc Ninh sub-sector compound after daybreak on October 29, 1967. *(George Pawlaczyk/USA)* **Top right:** A view from the sandbagged parapets along the southern side of Camp Loc Ninh shows how the field of battle looked to the defenders. The .30-cal. machine gun fired from the top of the embankment can be seen in foreground. *(21st MHD Pictorial Sec.)* **Center left:** Capt. Florencio Berumen, commander of Detachment A-331, directed the successful defense of Camp Loc Ninh with his mixed Vietnamese, Chinese, Montagnard, and Nung garrison during the battle. *(21st MHD Pictorial Sec.)* **Center right:** The Viet Cong attacked from the woods behind the runway and charged into this wire barrier, shown before the battle. More than 1,000 Viet Cong were killed in this sector by a combination of camp automatic-weapons fire and helicopter gunships. *(Author's Collection)* **Bottom:** Defensive bunkers at Camp Loc Ninh repelled all attempts by enemy sappers to reach the main camp wall. *(Author's Collection)*

Top: The opening of Camp Bunard was initiated on April 2, 1967, by a parachute assault conducted by Mike Force elements from the Nha Trang base and led by Special Forces Detachment A-503. Known as Operation Harvest Moon, the drop was the first mass Special Forces-led CIDG combat parachute jump of the Vietnam conflict. The mission of the Harvest Moon operation was securing and building Camp Bunard along the Song Be River in Phuoc Long Province. *(Scott J. Whitting)* **Bottom:** Special Forces parachutist leaders used radio transmissions to link up scattered forces on the drop zone shortly after the Harvest Moon jump. *(5th SFG PIO)*

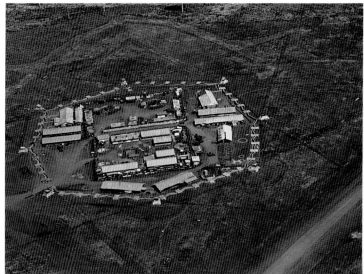

Top left: Once the Operation Harvest Moon parachutists landed, they secured a landing zone, so that a larger force could be landed by helicopter close to the projected campsite. Although ten jumpers were injured in the dense foliage, the operation proceeded smoothly, and the drop zone was secured immediately by Capt. Wilson's Detachment A-503 Mike Force warriors. *(5th SFG PIO)* **Top right:** Camp Bunard was built in order to strengthen the line of Special Forces camps stretching along Highway 14 from Chon Thanh to Ban Me Thuot, and it denied Viet Cong access to local VC rice fields and War Zone D to the south. *(Author's Collection)* **Center right:** Helicopters arrived only minutes after the parachute jump, and enough troops were in position to resist Viet Cong probes on the following day. Throughout the construction of Camp Bunard, Detachment A-344 depended on supplies and provisions delivered by helicopter. *(Scott J. Whitting)* **Bottom:** Mobile strike-force paratroopers hook up static lines from their T-10 parachute-pack assemblies prior to exiting the door of a C-130 aircraft during the Harvest Moon jump. They wear reserve parachutes in front. *(5th SFG PIO)*

Top: The entrance to Camp Bu Dop, a Special Forces border-surveillance camp in III Corps Tactical Zone near Cambodia, garrisoned by Detachment A-341. This camp served as a forward Army artillery bastion and launching site for operations against remote enemy base areas throughout the Vietnam conflict. Bu Dop was also a vital intelligence-gathering station for Project Gamma, the top-secret reconnaissance program that monitored developments in neighboring Cambodia. *(Steinken)* **Bottom:** Camp Bu Dop was the focus of heavy combat throughout 1967. Reengineered to avoid reliance on outdated moats and corner blockhouses, the fortified camp featured an elaborate array of zigzag trench lines, reinforced automatic-weapon bunkers, and artillery positions. *(Author's Collection)*

FIGHTING CAMPS ON THE OFFENSE

Top left: Special Forces took every precaution to insure camp self-sufficiency. This well drilled inside Camp Bu Dop provided fresh water for the garrison, even if enemy action prevented access to the nearby streams. *(Stephen Hembree)* **Top right:** The best camp protection involved offensive operations to keep the enemy out of range. Led by Special Forces sergeants of Detachment A-343, CIDG irregulars from Camp Duc Phong patrol the jungle near Highway 14 at the junction of II and III Corps Tactical Zones. Camp Duc Phong intercepted two enemy lifelines: a major infiltration route from Cambodia to War Zone D and another corridor from II CTZ to Bien Long Province. *(James Donahue)* **Center left:** Special Forces veterinary experts examine a water buffalo at Camp Bu Dop. A plentiful supply of healthy livestock was vital to the self-sufficiency of remote Special Forces forts along the undeveloped Vietnamese frontier. *(Stephen Hembree)* **Bottom:** Special Forces increased the firepower of their camp strike forces in order to engage the well-armed NVA regulars increasingly being encountered. Here, Staff Sgt. Jack Henderson of Detachment A-333 trains an indigenous mortar man at Camp Chi Linh, an important interior camp on War Zone D's northern edge. *(Jack Henderson)*

Top: The broad expanse of the Mekong Delta flatland was the scene of continual combat between Special Forces of the IV Corps Tactical Zone and Viet Cong guerrillas. *(James DeRego/USA)* **Bottom:** Viet Cong forces in the Mekong Delta, who specialized in attacking isolated ''Ruff-puff'' outposts under Special Forces jurisdiction, conducted a battalion raid against Tan Chau on March 6, 1967. Control Detachment B-42 sergeants display captured Viet Cong weapons used in the attack, which included ten-kilo turtle mines, eight-kilo cylindrical mines, and bangalore torpedoes. *(Author's Collection)*

MEKONG DELTA CAMPS ON THE OFFENSE

Top left: Camp Ba Xoai was located strategically along the western side of a small hill dominated by neighboring mountains in the contested Seven Mountains region of the Mekong Delta, the homeland of its sizeable Khmer Kampuchea Krom (KKK) garrison. *(Author's Collection)* **Top right:** During the early spring of 1967, signs of VC activity around Camp Ba Xoai increased, and the Special Forces stepped up patrols throughout the surrounding marshland. *(Author's Collection)* **Bottom left:** The Viet Cong conducted an all-out attack against Camp Ba Xoai on May 19, 1967. The camp's well-placed machine gun positions and hilltop 81mm mortars stopped all enemy attempts to cross the flat rice paddies toward the main perimeter. *(Author's Collection)* **Bottom right:** Camp Ba Xoai's critical corner machine gun, a sandbag platform held by Master Sgt. Alligood and Staff Sgt. Eckard of Detachment A-429 during the May 1967 battle, was rebuilt as a reinforced bunker in the fall. *(Author's Collection)*

Top: Camp My Dien II, located in Dinh Tuong Province, was projected as the southern anchor of the box around the Plain of Reeds during 1967. It was completed in January 1968. Detachment A-416 conducted search operations and night ambushes in an effort to reduce Viet Cong control of the region. *(Ensign/USA)* **Center:** The operational area around Camp My Dien II was typical of the Mekong Delta. Open areas required crossing but exposed CIDG troops to enemy observation, and heavily vegetated canals intersected the region. My Dien II was located adjacent to a Viet Cong stronghold known as ''The Pocket,'' shown here, where as many as four VC regiments were based. *(Author's Collection)* **Bottom left:** Throughout 1967 the IV CTZ (Can Tho) Mike Force expanded its reaction capacity to safeguard camps like My Dien II. Detachment C-4 commander Lt. Col. Robert Hassinger pins jump wings on Lt. Chau Thun, leader of the Cambodian 42d Mike Force Company. *(Author's Collection)* **Bottom right:** ''The Four Corps Mafia,'' top bosses of the Special Forces IV Corps region, line up on Pearl Harbor Day, December 7, 1967. They are (left to right) IV CTZ Mike Force commander Maj. George Marecek, LLDB executive officer Maj. Quan, LLDB commander Lt. Col. Chuan, Detachment C-4 commander Lt. Col. Robert Hassinger, and IV CTZ Mike Force executive officer Lt. Scales. *(George Marecek)*

Top left: Sgt. Ike Dolezel, radio operator at Camp Kinh Quan II, proudly displays an enemy Czechoslovakian machine gun captured during a waterborne operation south of Ap Bac. *(George Marecek)* **Top right:** The Special Forces team at Camp Kinh Quan II, which was underwater for five months during the 1966 flood. *(George Marecek)* **Bottom:** Camp Kinh Quan II was a border-surveillance camp located near Cambodia in Kinh Tuong Province. Detachment A-412 had the dual mission of conducting offensive operations to stifle enemy cross-border activity in its area—often employing CIDG-trained boat crews to accomplish this task—and assisting the district chief in military security, intelligence gathering, and radio-communications improvement. *(Author's Collection)*

Top: Detachment A-413 at Camp My Da conducted interdiction operations against Viet Cong supply routes and engaged in pacification projects for the My An district. The camp was opened on March 20, 1967, and it was attacked on seven occasions by Viet Cong battalion-sized units before the end of the year. This CIDG .50-cal. machine gun crew maintains a vigilant lookout during July 1967. *(Thomas Larsen/USA)* **Bottom:** Camp My Da, also known as My An, was situated 17 miles north of Vinh Long in the vast Plain of Reeds swamp, located in the Kien Phong Province at the junction of the So Nam and Tong Doc Loc canals. The camp's primary mission was blocking main enemy-infiltration routes from Cambodia into the Viet Cong ''Pocket'' base area within the Mekong Delta. *(Author's Collection)*

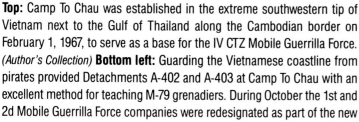

Top: Camp To Chau was established in the extreme southwestern tip of Vietnam next to the Gulf of Thailand along the Cambodian border on February 1, 1967, to serve as a base for the IV CTZ Mobile Guerrilla Force. *(Author's Collection)* **Bottom left:** Guarding the Vietnamese coastline from pirates provided Detachments A-402 and A-403 at Camp To Chau with an excellent method for teaching M-79 grenadiers. During October the 1st and 2d Mobile Guerrilla Force companies were redesignated as part of the new

IV Corps Mobile Strike Force Command. Advanced training commenced during December, when airborne courses were introduced at To Chau. *(Author's Collection)* **Bottom right:** Detachment A-431 was initially responsible for instructing native recruits in the techniques of guerrilla warfare and recruited its CIDG members from ten camps throughout the Mekong Delta. When training commenced on February 20, 1967, the 1st ''G'' (Guerrilla) Company began physical conditioning. *(Author's Collection)*

Top: The Special Forces village health program at Camp Vinh Gia was a vital part of the successful area-development program in this Cambodian-border vicinity. These LLDB medics dispense medicine during April 1967. *(Author's Collection)* **Center:** Camp Vinh Gia, the only CIDG border-surveillance camp in the Mekong Delta that was operated solely by the Vietnamese LLDB after its final transfer on June 27, 1967, was located just south of Cambodia in the extreme western portion of Chau Doc Province. *(Author's Collection)* **Bottom left:** LLDB commander Gen. Quang reviews the Vinh Gia honor guard with LLDB camp commander Capt. Tram Ngoc Nam. *(Author's Collection)* **Bottom right:** Detachment A-422, commanded by Capt. Alvin B. Morris, prepares to leave Camp Vinh Gia after the first turnover of a Special Forces camp to complete LLDB authority in the IV Corps Tactical Zone. *(Author's Collection)*

Top left: This communist flag and poster of Ho Chi Minh were captured by Special Forces-led CIDG forces from Camp Vinh Gia during a March 1967 sweep near the Vinh Te canal that paralleled the Cambodian border and marked the northern boundary of the camp's tactical responsibility. *(Author's Collection)* **Top right:** Camp Vinh Gia's CIDG forces, which excelled in extended overnight missions, gained a reputation among the enemy for aggressive defense. On May 19, 1967, one CIDG night-ambush platoon overhead a Viet Cong scout tell his comrade, ''We had better spread out here because we are entering the area where the ambushes start.'' Immediately, the CIDG patrol opened fire and disrupted a Viet Cong company moving in two columns. The CIDG victors display the captured enemy material. *(DOD)* **Bottom:** Camp Vinh Gia was positioned astride a major enemy-infiltration route leading from Cambodia into the Seven Mountains region. These CIDG forces sweeping around Nui Giai pause as Sgt. Gilchrist coordinates with other advancing units over his radio. *(Author's Collection)*

Top left: Camp My Phuoc Tay construction began in February 1967 but was hampered by Viet Cong bombardments and mines. Here, Staff Sgt. Cary C. Ward, Detachment A-411 weapons supervisor, sweeps the Cai Lay road with an AN/PRS-3 metallic mine detector before a convoy heading into camp. *(Author's Collection)* **Top right:** Camp My Phuoc Tay was located in Dinh Tuong Province near the Viet Cong "Pocket" stronghold. *(Author's Collection)* **Center left:** A dozer positions the versatile CONEX steel freight container as a camp bunker at My Phuoc Tay. The sturdy structure's inside volume of 290 cubic feet and overall height of 6 feet 10 inches made it an ideal fighting position, once weapons apertures were cut. *(Author's Collection)* **Center right:** The CONEX bunker at Camp My Phuoc Tay is cushioned by a sandbagged shellburst-absorption wall. Its full-access double doors are swung open in back—the normal "front" of the logistical receptacle. *(Author's Collection)* **Bottom:** Sp4 Hubert R. Anderson and CIDG troops cross a rice paddy while searching for Viet Cong troops who launched a two-hour mortar and rocket barrage against My Phuoc Tay on November 5, 1967. *(James Hatton/USA)*

Top: During 1967 North Vietnamese and Viet Cong contingents received additional modern Sino-Soviet weapons, which vastly outmatched the arms carried by CIDG camp forces. Among the more effective enemy weapons were the RPG-2 and RPG-7 hand-held anti-tank launchers, used against bunkers and vehicles. Here, Special Forces Maj. Jones inspects captured rocket-propelled grenade rounds. *(5th SFG PIO via R. W. Utegaard)* **Bottom:** Sgt. First Class Charles E. Hosking Jr. (center), a leader of the 3d Mobile Strike Force, earned the Medal of Honor for his heroic sacrifice during a reaction mission in Don Luan district on March 21, 1967, when he wrestled to the ground a Viet Cong prisoner, who suddenly brandished a live grenade, and saved his men by absorbing the blast. *(Hosking Children's Collection)*

Top left: Blackjack 32 was conducted in eastern Phuoc Tuy Province from March 15 to April 3, 1967, by Mobile Guerrilla Task Force 966 of the III CTZ (Bien Hoa) Mike Force, led by Capt. Thomas G. Johnson. Here, one of the Cambodian mobile guerrillas crosses a small stream on the rugged slopes east of Nui May Tao and Nui Be. *(James Donahue)* **Top right:** Master Sgt. Billy Waugh of the III CTZ Mike Force prepares to depart on an airmobile mission into enemy-held territory. *(Jerry Kringel)* **Bottom:** Blackjack 32 participants included 12 Special Forces members (nine shown here after the mission), six interpreters, and 126 Cambodian mobile guerrillas. During this operation, Viet Cong trackers maneuvered larger forces against the mobile guerrilla force, resulting in a fire fight at the extraction zone. Special Forces disengaged quickly and called in air strikes that devastated the Viet Cong attackers. *(James Donahue)*

Top left: Blackjack 31 was conducted in War Zone D from January 8 to February 7, 1967, by Mobile Guerrilla Task Force 957 of the III CTZ (Bien Hoa) Mike Forces. A Montagnard trooper recovers a container packed full of food and ammunition. *(James Donahue)* **Top right:** Members of Blackjack 31 standing (left to right) are Sgt. First Class Richard Kindoll, Sgt. First Class George Ovsak, Sgt. First Class Aloysius Doyle, Staff Sgt. Dennis Montgomery, Sgt. First Class Patrick Wagner, Staff Sgt. Dale England, Staff Sgt. Richard Jarvis, and Sgt. James Donahue; kneeling (left to right) are Master Sgt. James Howard, Capt. Steven Yedinak, Capt. James Gritz, and Lt. Joseph Cawley. *(James Donahue)* **Bottom left:** Posing for a picture after a month in War Zone D are Blackjack 31 members Sgt. First Class George Ovsak (left), killed days later at Trang Sup, and Sgt. James C. Donahue (right), who wrote the gripping true account of his experience with the mobile guerrilla forces, *No Greater Love. (James Donahue)* **Bottom right:** Special Forces break radio silence deep in enemy territory by hoisting radio antennas in the trees. *(5th SFG PIO)*

Top left: Blackjack 34 was conducted in northeastern Binh Long and northwestern Phuoc Long Provinces during July 16-21, 1967, by Mobile Guerrilla Force 966 of the III CTZ (Bien Hoa) Mike Force, led by Lt. James J. Condon, shown here. The operation discovered a Viet Cong regiment and killed 126 of the enemy while suffering light casualties in exchange. *(James Donahue)* **Top right:** A Cambodian mobile guerrilla force member waits for the enemy during Blackjack 34. On July 18 newly laid enemy commo wire was found that led to the destruction of two Viet Cong platoons by ambush. *(James Donahue)* **Bottom:** The indigenous Blackjack reconnaissance team wore Viet Cong soldiers attire and surprised Viet Cong wiremen checking their land communication lines. *(James Donahue)*

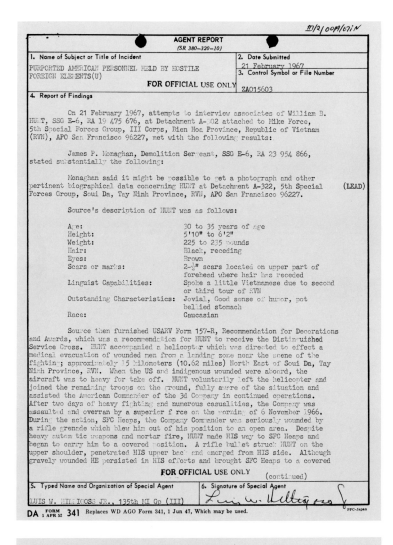

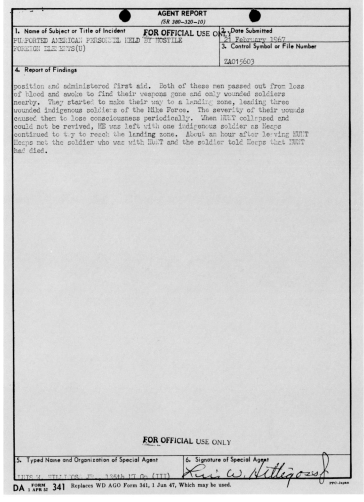

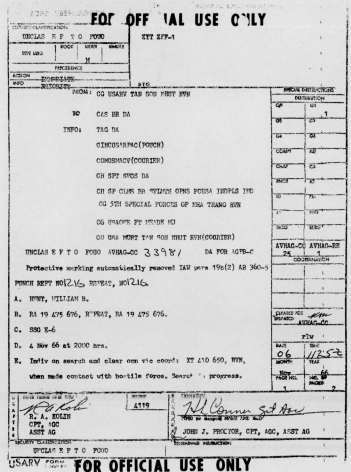

The heroic deeds of Staff Sgt. William B. Hunt, a replacement platoon leader airlifted to the III CTZ (Bien Hoa) Mike Force during the midst of battle, typified the fate of Special Forces troops who never returned. The circumstances surrounding his disappearance are related in the military intelligence report, illustrated above, including the recommendation for his Distinguished Service Cross, which was never awarded. The initial U.S. Army Vietnam Missing in Action notice to the Department of Army Casualty Branch is reproduced at bottom left. (Author's Collection)

Top left: One of the most successful Special Forces Blackjack operations conducted during the Vietnam conflict was the retrieval of a highly secret instrument, known as the "black box," from a Lockheed U-2 reconnaissance aircraft downed during December 1966 in triple-canopy jungle along the Cambodian border. In this picture (left to right) Detachment A-303 medical Staff Sgt. Dennis Montgomery, section leader Lt. Joseph Cawley, and Sgt. First Class Patrick Wagner point to their location—deleted by wartime censors—on a map while sitting on the wreckage of the plane. *(James Donahue)* **Top right:** Capt. Steven Yedinak stands next to the recovered "black box," the key to the high-altitude, long-range surveillance capability of the downed U-2 aircraft. Although the instrument was rigged for self destruction, there was strong evidence that the auto-destruct mechanism had failed. Blackjack forces led by Capt. James G. Gritz, acting on MACV commander Gen. Westmoreland's orders in response to Pentagon directives, found the intact instrument during January 1967. *(James Donahue)*

Top left: Many Special Forces control detachments continued their important role as sector advisors at the province level during 1967. An important aspect of this duty was disaster relief. When An Phu village in Chau Doc Province was destroyed by fire on July 8, 1967, Detachment B-42 rushed in fire fighters and civic-action personnel. Special Forces ensured that temporary shelter tents were available that same day. *(Author's Collection)*
Top right: The An Phu waterfront was still smoldering when Special Forces arrived with fire equipment. *(Author's Collection)* **Center left:** Maintaining local defenses against Viet Cong attack was a vital sector responsibility. Here, Control Detachment B-42 members survey a Tri Ton ''Ruff-puff'' outpost during February 1967. *(Author's Collection)* **Center right:** Special Forces trained many new security units for province protection. During March 1967 the 816th Regional Force Company renewed its pledge to support the South Vietnamese regime, under the sacred pall of joss candle sticks. *(Author's Collection)*
Bottom: Special Forces skills instruction continues, even in province advisory detachments. Here, Sgt. First Class Chase teaches advanced first aid to B-42 members at Chau Doc in February 1967. *(Author's Collection)*

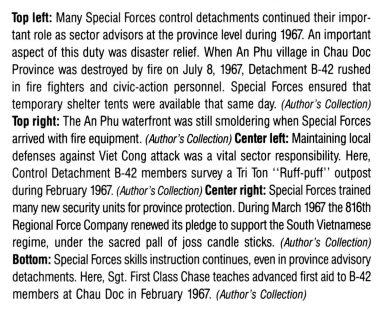

Top: Special Forces humanitarian civic action not only generated favorable conditions, but it prepared the way for psychological operations that promoted a sense of village loyalty to the government and deterred the Viet Cong insurgency. Lt. Jay Rickman shares a long Vietnamese-style handshake with a village elder after discussing civil-assistance measures at Camp Bunard on October 6, 1967. *(Robert Lafoon/USA)* **Center:** Col. Jonathan F. Ladd (second from left), commander of the 5th Special Forces Group from June 1967 to June 1968, discusses special warfare deployments with LLDB commander Maj. Gen. Doan Van Quang, beside him, at Dong Ba Thin. *(John Borgman)* **Bottom:** Special Forces Control Detachment B-42 had the dual mission of being both a combat headquarters and a sector advisory team for Chau Doc Province. Scattered outposts were part of Special Forces provincial responsibility, and these successful defenders are decorated by Detachment B-42 commander Maj. Earl Thieme during March 1967. *(Author's Collection)*

Countering the Viet Cong Tet-68 offensive, a 5th Special Forces Group patrol from Camp Tra Cu disregards high water and monsoon weather as it relentlessly chases the retreating insurgents deep into the Plain of Reeds near the Cambodian border. *(Author's Collection)*

SPECIAL FORCES COUNTEROFFENSIVE, 1968

The Viet Cong struck towns and cities throughout South Vietnam at the end of January in a sudden onslaught known as the Tet-68 campaign, and their attack sparked a bitter year-long series of offensives and counteroffensives. The Tet-68 military confrontation initiated intense urban battles, mandated sustained clearing operations, and heightened struggles for possession of the strategic borderlands. Protracted levels of heavy combat caused widespread camp and village destruction, sapped irregular combat strength, and drained personnel resources of the elite but relatively small Special Forces establishment. As a result the enemy's 1968 Tet offensive and the ensuing allied counteroffensive represented a decisive year of Special Forces service in Vietnam.

Two sentinel border-surveillance camps were destroyed early in the year at Lang Vei and Kham Duc, and the loss of both forts tore a massive gap out of Special Forces' frontier monitoring capability. The battle of Lang Vei began in early January 1968, when several North Vietnamese Army divisions crossed into northwestern South Vietnam from Laos. Camp Lang Vei, located in a sparsely populated woodland area occupied by a few Bru Montagnard villages, had been relatively quiet for several months. On February 7, 1968, the enemy mounted an overwhelming armored-infantry assault.

Local security outposts outside Lang Vei heard tank engines 15 minutes after midnight. The North Vietnamese tank-escorted infantry successfully charged the short distance to the outer perimeter, although recoilless rifle fire destroyed two tanks, and defensive automatic weapons killed many supporting sappers and infantrymen. Other enemy tank forces rapidly penetrated to the inner perimeter where they destroyed the ammunition storage and petroleum points and leveled most of the key bunkers. Special Forces troops, armed with hand-held Light Antitank Weapons (LAWs), valiantly pursued the vehicles and knocked them out using LAWs fired at point-blank range or grenades tossed down pried-open hatches. Unfortunately, many of the shoulder-fired LAWs either misfired or failed

to detonate after striking their targets. Enemy flamethrower parties, demolitions teams, and infantrymen followed in the wake of the tanks and isolated the remaining defenders.

The Lang Vei command bunker was besieged by sappers, but demolition charges failed to kill the Special Forces troops trapped inside. Several allied counterattacks to reach this bunker were led by Special Forces Sergeant First Class Eugene Ashley Jr., before he was killed at the head of his troops. Continual air strikes enabled MACV-SOG troops from nearby Marine Khe Sanh combat base to rescue the camp survivors, but Lang Vei was vacated and never reestablished.

Camp Kham Duc was an important cross-border raiding station located along the Laotian border about 150 miles south of Lang Vei. Early in 1968 aerial surveillance determined that the North Vietnamese were connecting their main Laotian infiltration route to Vietnam's Route 14 southwest of Kham Duc. During March Special Forces opened a patrol base at Ngoc Tavak, reinforced by Marine artillery, to monitor these developments and provide early warning of enemy advances toward Kham Duc. On May 10 Ngoc Tavak was attacked by the North Vietnamese and partially overrun, but Air Force gunship fire over the site allowed the defenders to restore the position after daylight. The North Vietnamese sealed off the patrol base with heavy fire and prevented aerial reinforcement, forcing the Special Forces and Marines to abandon the compound and retreat into the jungle, where the survivors were extracted by helicopters.

The main enemy attack on Kham Duc began on the early morning of May 10 with heavy mortar barrages. Kham Duc was one of several Special Forces camps in the Americal Division sector of responsibility, and it was reinforced by an infantry battalion that afternoon. The North Vietnamese Army 2d Division surrounded the camp and successfully stormed allied mountain outposts encircling Kham Duc early on the morning of May 12. Shortly before 10 a.m. enemy ground attacks were launched from the northeast, northwest, and southwest. These infantry charges were repulsed by coordinated tactical air strikes, artillery, and ground fire. The Americal Division, however, decided to evacuate Kham Duc rather than continue the battle.

The aerial evacuation of Kham Duc was conducted in spite of intense anti-aircraft machine-gun fire directed against the Air Force transports. At noon a major North Vietnamese ground attack was staged from the low gullies east of the camp, but air strikes in that area slowed the enemy advance. At 2 p.m. enemy troops breached the main compound's outer wire. Cluster bomb units and napalm temporarily stalled the enemy attack, and the evacuation continued, although it became disorderly after several cargo transports were shot down. The evacuation of Kham Duc was concluded in the late afternoon of May 12, as enemy riflemen overran the airfield.

The final incident at Kham Duc occurred at 4:45 p.m., when Air Force Lieutenant Colonel Joe M. Jackson flew his C-123 (call-sign Bookie 771) into the shattered airfield to rescue the combat control team. Despite a hail of enemy gunfire, Jackson landed his aircraft and manuevered down the cratered and fragment-littered airstrip. The combat control team members leaped from their ditch and raced to the aircraft while Jackson turned the plane to take off from the same end of the runway that he had landed on. He taxied around a 122mm rocket, which had struck in front of the nose wheel but failed to detonate, and used jet-assisted takeoff to climb sharply away from the exploding airfield. A photograph of this final episode is reproduced on page 231.

The battles of Lang Vei and Kham Duc were the most serious Special Forces reverses, but they were fought outside the mainstream of the Tet-68 campaign. The Viet Cong Tet-68 offensive initially achieved a degree of success because of the tactical surprise and confusion that resulted from launching hundreds of attacks countrywide, some of considerable magnitude.

Major allied counterattacks—many of them assisted by Special Forces native contingents—erased these enemy gains and defeated the insurgents, forcing them to retreat with devastating losses. Although Tet-68 produced adverse political ramifications that weakened American home-front willpower,

the allies and Special Forces emerged highly victorious on the tactical battlefield.

The Tet-68 campaign impacted against Special Forces most directly in Vietnam's central II and southern IV Corps Tactical Zones. From January 30 through February 4, the western Central Highlands provincial capital of Kontum was subjected to enemy attacks, which engaged each allied compound in its own defensive struggle. The perimeter of Kontum-based Control Detachment B-24 was isolated, but its defenders repelled several charges that originated from nearby building complexes, which had turned into enemy strongpoints early in the battle.

Other localities in Vietnam's central sector also saw extended Special Forces action. Mobile Strike Force reaction units conducted a hard-fought operation to clear the outskirts around the pro-VC port city of Phan Thiet. In the highland interior Control Detachment B-20 became involved in a week of significant house-to-house fighting while mopping up Pleiku City. Perhaps the most difficult Tet-68 combat for Special Forces transpired in the coastal battle of Qui Nhon, fought January 30 through February 5, 1968. The combat was often more typical of World War II street fighting than Vietnam warfare. The successful clearing of the Qui Nhon railroad yard—held by die-hard Viet Cong entrenched in the engine shed's lubrication pits beneath the locomotives—became a classic instance of Special Forces professionalism in combining conventional fire support and infantry maneuver to clear a well-defended urban objective.

The Viet Cong also hit a wide number of targets throughout the Mekong Delta during the Lunar New Year, and numerous Special Forces camps in IV Corps Tactical Zone were engaged in heavy action. From January 29 through February 5, Company D sustained major damage from enemy artillery and sapper attacks directed against the Can Tho airbase. Although the Viet Cong made a well-rehearsed, all-out attempt to win a decisive military victory, they sustained heavy losses and ultimately failed to secure their objectives because the populace—many of whom benefited from years of patient Special Forces work—failed to rally in large numbers to the communist cause. Most Viet Cong battalions never received sufficient assistance from district companies, a factor later attributed to Special Forces civic-action and patrolling intervention in many local rural areas.

Throughout the Vietnam conflict, Special Forces operations in the Mekong Delta were tailored for swamp warfare across the marshes and flood areas that dominated the greater part of South Vietnam's vast, waterlogged flatland. The Viet Cong insurgents maintained major support bases and strongholds within these Delta swamp forests and canal-crossed wetlands. Such enemy sanctuaries were relatively safe from allied intrusion before the advent of the unique "Green Beret Navy." The Special Forces employed a wide range of sampans and other watercraft to reach and engage the enemy, including light and sleek fiberglass airboats powered by 180-horsepower aircraft engines.

The swift and maneuverable airboats were employed for a multitude of tasks including river reconnaissance, canal surveillance, boat formation screening, and rapid displacement of blocking forces. The airboats could enter shallow or vegetation-choked waterways where propeller-driven patrol boats became bogged down. Airboats attained their greatest utility, however, during the rainy seasons, because they were able to skim over flooded rice fields, jump paddy dikes, and cut across marsh grasses. Armed with light machine guns and grenade launchers, the aggressive airboat crews could outrun and outmaneuver most enemy vessels, and they trounced enemy sampan forces in numerous naval clashes. Perhaps of equal importance, Special Forces waterborne interdiction of Viet Cong border crossings and Delta hideouts provided another combat demonstration of special warfare versatility.

The condition of Special Forces during 1968 reflected years of continual combat and high cumulative losses that inevitably eroded the overall quality of Special Forces personnel. Many replacements were inexperienced and untried, and they lacked fundamental qualifications like parachutist ratings. Fortunately, the high physical standards and intelligence prerequisites for Special Forces selection were not slackened. Newer members did not have the benefit of prolonged peacetime training ar-rangements typical of pre-Vietnam Special Forces, but combat orientation courses and "on-the-job" training in forward operational detachments enabled them to learn their jobs quickly.

The pace of the war in 1968 intensified again when the long-anticipated communist Third Offensive began on August 18 in Tay Ninh Province and then spread to other regions of the country. The most significant battle of this offensive occurred in the Central Highlands at Camp Duc Lap. From August 23 to 29 three North Vietnamese Army regiments (66th, 95C, 320th) attempted to destroy the civilian irregular defense camp as well as a nearby South Vietnamese district headquarters. Camp Duc Lap was partially overrun, but the camp defenders eventually regained all fallen positions with the help of counterattacking elements from both 2d and 5th Mobile Strike Force Commands. The North Vietnamese were forced to retreat.

Seven other Special Forces camps were also targeted by major enemy ground assaults during this period. They ranged from Ha Thanh and Thuong Duc in northern South Vietnam, past Dak Seang in the Western Highlands, to Katum, Loc Ninh, Ben Soi, and Thien Ngon in the III Corps Tactical Zone west of Saigon. In each case the enemy was repulsed but retreated to regroup in Cambodian or Laotian base areas.

Throughout the year Special Forces continued to apply pressure through small-unit actions and saturation patrolling of enemy base areas and border-crossing points located near Civilian Irregular Defense Group camps. Sustained efforts were made to increase the intelligence gathering capabilities of the native forces and to react aggressively against identified enemy targets. The North Vietnamese and Viet Cong forces often responded violently, but they were deterred from inflicting severe damage on more isolated camps by a combination of artillery firepower, prompt Air Force support, and Mobile Strike Force reinforcement. The Special Forces continued its diverse Civilian Irregular Defense Group mission with a high rate of overall success despite increased North Vietnamese infiltration, the introduction of more powerful enemy weapons, and fewer camps to patrol a wider battlefield.

Top: Camp Lang Vei, not far from the Laotian border, was overrun by an armored infantry assault, spearheaded by NVA tanks, on the morning of February 7, 1968. In this view of the gutted campsite, looking south just after the battle, Route 9 can be seen exiting toward Khe Sanh on the left. The main attack came down the road in the upper right, and enemy tanks destroyed by Sgt. First Class James W. Holt's 106mm recoilless rifle are circled in this area. The command bunker is in the center next to another circled tank wreck. *(Author's Collection)* **Bottom:** The command bunker at Camp Lang Vei, where Capt. Frank C. Willoughby and several team members of Detachment A-101 made their last stand—continuing to broadcast for air support and Marine reinforcements that never arrived—while the camp was completely overwhelmed. A heroic reinforcing mission by MACV-SOG Maj. George Quamo and a handful of Special Forces volunteers from nearby Khe Sanh saved the remaining Americans. *(Author's Collection)*

Top: The hulk of a North Vietnamese PT-76 tank, center, rests beside the smashed Special Forces command bunker at Camp Lang Vei. The final protective barrier of gravel-filled barrels to the left beside the bunker was blasted apart by direct tank fire, and the large crater resulted from enemy demolition charges shoved down the bunker's vent shaft. *(Author's Collection)* **Bottom left:** Survivors of Detachment A-101 receive decorations for their valor in defending Lang Vei: (left to right) Capt. Frank Willoughby, LLDB Lt. Quy, Staff Sgt. Emanuel Phillips, Staff Sgt. Peter Tiroch, Sgt. Nikolao Fragos, Sgt. Richard Allen, Sp4 Franklin Dooms, and Sp4 Joel Johnson. *(Author's Collection)* **Bottom right:** Team intelligence Sgt. First Class Eugene Ashley Jr. led five valiant counterattacks that almost reached his trapped comrades inside the command bunker before he was killed. His widow, Barbara P. Ashley, received his posthumous Medal of Honor from Vice President Spiro Agnew almost two years later, on December 2, 1969. *(Louis Reinhardt/USA)*

Top: The siege of the Marine combat base at Khe Sanh by elements of four North Vietnamese Army divisions from January 21 to April 7, 1968, became one of the pivotal battles of the Vietnam conflict. In this picture taken during the height of the siege, Special Forces veterans of the Lang Vei battle—wearing green berets—race to a C-123 Provider. The aircraft kept its engines running to minimize ground time while under sporadic mortar fire. *(USAF)*

Bottom: Khe Sanh had been upgraded during 1967 on the orders of MACV commander Gen. Westmoreland, who saw the camp as a major launching point for his projected multi-divisional invasion into Laos. These plans caused a massive buildup that overwhelmed the original Special Forces camp, shown here. However, Special Forces continued to maintain a presence within the Marine compound because MACV-SOG continued to maintain a forward operating base (FOB #3) at Khe Sanh. *(USAF)*

Top: The communist countrywide offensive known as Tet-68 affected Special Forces camps in coastal I CTZ to a lesser extent than other regions, but it still caused considerable damage. Camp Ba To was located at the confluence of the Song Tra No (background) and Suoi Dec Lien (foreground) in southern Quang Ngai Province. On February 1, 1968, Detachment A-106 defeated perhaps the most bizarre Tet-68 enemy attack, conducted by 700 Viet Cong armed with tribal spears and knives. *(Author's Collection)* **Bottom:** Blasted structures and upturned earth at Khe Sanh combat base, seen during March 1968, testified to the impact of prolonged enemy heavy bombardment that often exceeded 1,000 rounds a day. Although never generally credited, Special Forces also endured the Khe Sanh siege. A SOG contingent was present as part of the larger Marine garrison throughout the campaign and played an active role in defending the base against enemy infantry probes. *(Alton Gaston)*

Top: The communist Tet-68 offensive struck Special Forces units throughout South Vietnam, but elements in II CTZ sustained the brunt of the fighting. Control Detachment B-24 was cut off at Kontum and defended its compound against enemy artillery barrages and ground assaults from January 30 to February 4, 1968. The North Vietnamese staged their attacks against the Special Forces perimeter from this Buddhist temple located only a few hundred yards from the B-24 compound. *(Author's Collection)*
Center: The Special Forces northeastern trench line at Kontum, with the enemy-occupied Prisoner Interrogation Center in the background, was used as a North Vietnamese fire-direction center during the battle. *(Author's Collection)* **Bottom:** The Special Forces perimeter at Kontum was surrounded by North Vietnamese regulars during Tet-68, and supplies had to be parachuted to the isolated defenders. *(Author's Collection)*

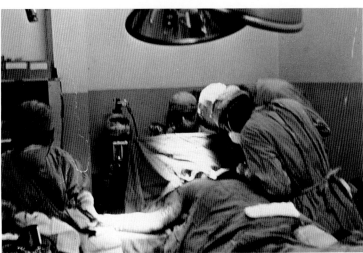

Top: Phan Thiet, the capital of Binh Thuan Province, was an important Viet Cong objective during the Tet-68 offensive, because the Viet Minh movement traced some of its earliest connections to this coastal town. The 26th Mobile Strike Force Company fought to recapture Phan Thiet in conjunction with other allied units in heavy combat from February 3-20, 1968. *(Author's Collection)* **Center left:** Deliberately ignoring the proximity of North Vietnamese forces storming Pleiku city, Special Forces Dr. William M. Cheatum performs skin grafting on a seriously wounded Montagnard CIDG soldier, who was burned by an enemy phosphorous-grenade explosion at the onset of Tet-68. The surgery was performed at the Pleiku CIDG hospital. *(Lynn Dievendorf)* **Center right:** The Pleiku security-zone compound was defended by Special Forces during Tet-68. *(Gerald Foy)* **Bottom left:** Control Detachment C-2 headquarters at Pleiku, shown here, ordered the 23d and 24th Mobile Strike Force Companies into heavy urban combat to recapture the main city district during January 30 to February 4, 1968. *(Author's Collection)*

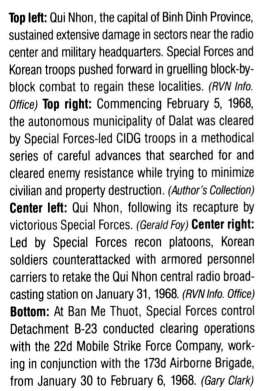

Top left: Qui Nhon, the capital of Binh Dinh Province, sustained extensive damage in sectors near the radio center and military headquarters. Special Forces and Korean troops pushed forward in gruelling block-by-block combat to regain these localities. *(RVN Info. Office)* **Top right:** Commencing February 5, 1968, the autonomous municipality of Dalat was cleared by Special Forces-led CIDG troops in a methodical series of careful advances that searched for and cleared enemy resistance while trying to minimize civilian and property destruction. *(Author's Collection)* **Center left:** Qui Nhon, following its recapture by victorious Special Forces. *(Gerald Foy)* **Center right:** Led by Special Forces recon platoons, Korean soldiers counterattacked with armored personnel carriers to retake the Qui Nhon central radio broadcasting station on January 31, 1968. *(RVN Info. Office)* **Bottom:** At Ban Me Thuot, Special Forces control Detachment B-23 conducted clearing operations with the 22d Mobile Strike Force Company, working in conjunction with the 173d Airborne Brigade, from January 30 to February 6, 1968. *(Gary Clark)*

Top left: One of the hardest-fought Special Forces actions of the Vietnam war involved the counterattack at the Qui Nhon railway security compound marshalling yard on January 31, 1968. *(Author's Collection)* **Top right:** The D-10 Sapper Battalion defended the yard's locomotive works against Special Forces in conventional combat. This diesel engine, located over lubrication pits inside the maintenance shed during the battle, was used as an enemy base of fire that broke up a counterattack by two CIDG companies, causing severe casualties. *(Author's Collection)* **Bottom left:** Detachment A-227 Master Sgt. Victor G. Franco blasted the engine shed with direct recoilless rifle fire, enabling CIDG troops to charge through the smoke, overrunning the Wickham trolley and clearing out the grease pits in close combat. *(Author's Collection)* **Bottom right:** Wickham trollies in the Qui Nhon railway yard just after the battle. Control Detachment B-22 recaptured the complex with a composite reinforced CIDG battalion mustered from Camps Cung Son, Phu Tuc, Ha Tay, and Vu-Van-Tho. *(Author's Collection)*

Top: Following the surprise attack of January 31, 1968, a Special Forces-led patrol passes through a village outside Saigon to cordon off enemy reinforcements from reaching the capital. *(Army News Features)* **Center:** After the Tet-68 campaign, high-priority supplies to replace battle losses were unloaded directly from Sea-Land cargo containers into Special Forces warehouses at Bien Hoa. The Sea-Land vans were sealed before leaving the United States and unlocked only at their destination, alleviating much of the cargo theft that often occurred during transit, especially at the Saigon docks. *(Author's Collection)* **Bottom left:** Dense jungles not far from Saigon, exemplified by this bamboo thicket near Chau Thanh in Bien Hoa Province, offered excellent concealment to Viet Cong infiltrators. *(USIS)* **Bottom right:** The communist Tet-68 offensive threatened to disrupt the construction of Camps Thien Ngon and Katum, under the jurisdiction of Control Detachment B-32 at Tay Ninh, shown here. However, the main enemy thrusts were aimed at populated Vietnamese centers and only marginal raids were made to damage engineer equipment at the new campsites. *(Author's Collection)*

Top left: The enemy Tet-68 offensive in the Mekong Delta struck Camp Moc Hoa, which suffered heavy bombardment as Viet Cong troops attempted to seize Moc Hoa City on February 2, 1968. *(Author's Collection)* **Top right:** Special operations reconnaissance leader Staff Sgt. Drew D. Dix earned the Medal of Honor for several acts during Tet-68, including the rescue of captives at Chau Phu. *(Carl Schneider/USA)* **Center left:** On January 29, 1968, the VC attacked Special Forces Camp Can Tho and caused heavy damage, including this charred CH-47 Chinook helicopter. *(Author's Collection)* **Center right:** Detachment A-431 Sgt. Gordon D. Yntema defended a trench near Thong Binh until his ammunition was exhausted. He then used his rifle as a club until he was killed in close combat on January 18, 1968. Vice President Agnew presented his posthumous Medal of Honor to his wife Mrs. Peggy Yntema Fischrupp. *(Louis Reinhardt/USA)* **Bottom:** The Can Tho headquarters of Special Forces in the IV Corps Tactical Zone during Tet-1968. *(Author's Collection)*

Top left: Airboats from Camp Thuong Thoi in the open marshes of the Plain of Reeds near Cambodia during September 1967. The highly maneuverable boats were powered by 180-horsepower Lycoming aircraft engines. *(Author's Collection)* **Top right:** The flexibility of airboat operations is demonstrated as CH-47 Chinooks airlift two sections of IV CTZ Mike Force airboats from Don Phuc to the Seven Mountains region during November 1966. *(George Marecek)* **Center:** An airboat formation of Special Forces Company D travels along the Mekong River near the Cambodian border in late 1966. The Hurricane Company Aircats were capable of going 38 miles per hour when carrying 300 pounds. *(5th SFG PIO)* **Bottom:** Special Forces monitoring of the waterways included using Vietnamese officials aboard airboats, such as this national policeman checking the identity papers of a fishing couple in the Delta during September 1970. *(Ensign/USA)*

Top: Airboats could leap over rice-paddy dikes, skim across swamp grass, and glide through aquatic vegetation that would foul boat propellers. *(MACV PIO)* **Center left:** Special Forces worked closely with the Navy in the Delta. These mobile strike-force personnel embark on Mark II River Patrol Boats. *(USN)* **Center right:** Sgt. First Class David S. Boyd (second from right) waits while mechanics clean the air filter on his airboat north of Tuyen Nhon, early on the morning of November 14, 1966. He was killed while providing airboat flank security for assault boats and sampans from Camp Moc Hoa one hour and ten minutes after this photograph was taken. *(George Marecek)* **Bottom left:** Camp Tra Cu airboats are guided into dock by CIDG boat handlers after an operation west of Trang Bang during 1969. *(Author's Collection)* **Bottom right:** Boat crews from Camp My Phuoc Tay perform river reconnaissance using engineer-assault craft. *(James Hutton/USA)*

Top left: A guard tower overlooks the Rach Cao Lanh, the main canal in front of Camp Boyd, home of the airboat training center at Cao Lanh. *(USA)* **Top right:** Camp Cao Lanh was located near the capital of Kien Phong Province and served as headquarters for Detachment B-43 and the Special Forces mobile airboat force. After February 1967 most airboat reaction missions were staged from this complex. *(Author's Collection)* **Center:** Detachment B-41 was located at Camp Moc Hoa, an important Special Forces regional advisory post since November 1963 and a major airboat complex after October 1966. The camp was located near the canal-segmented capital of Kien Tuong Province, just south of the enemy-held Elephant's Foot protrusion of Cambodia. *(Ensign/USA)* **Bottom:** In this view of Moc Hoa during the flood of 1966, vehicles have been abandoned in favor of sampans. *(Author's Collection)*

Top left: Mekong Delta flooding partially submerged Camp Thuong Thoi in Kien Phong Province during September 1967. *(Author's Collection)*
Top right: Camp Thuong Thoi was located less than four miles from the Cambodian boundary and was an important border-surveillance and airboat site. Capt. Jeffrey Fletcher, Detachment A-432 commander (back to camera), receives a captured Viet Cong flag from the Special Forces-advised 843d Regional Forces Company leader after a successful mission in the Hong Ngu district. *(Author's Collection)* **Bottom:** Camp Thuong Thoi was located on the northern shore of the wide Mekong River, along the first great bend of the large tributary inside South Vietnam not far from its crossing point with Cambodia. Note the landing jetty extending from the camp wall in the extreme lower portion of the picture. *(Author's Collection)*

Top: An airboat, its twin rudders painted with the shield of the Special Forces Mobile Strike Force Command, carried a standard crew consisting of a driver, grenadier, and machine gunner. The Hurricane Company Aircats were modified versions of the Florida Everglades swamp buggies. *(Ensign/USA)*
Center: Wounded CIDG troops are evacuated by boat from a battle site in the Plain of Reeds to medical facilities at Moc Hoa. *(George Marecek)* **Bottom left:** The Special Forces modified several water craft for fire-support purposes. This boat from Vinh Gia is fitted with a 57mm recoilless rifle and light machine gun during 1966. *(Bogart)* **Bottom right:** A pursuit attack boat loaded with ammunition and sandbags at Camp Vinh Gia in October 1967. *(Author's Collection)*

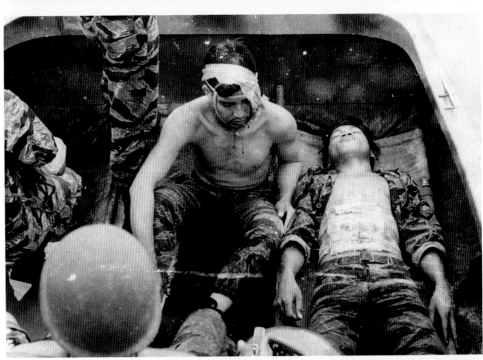

Top: Camp Dong Tre was located in the central portion of II Corps Tactical Zone in the middle of the hilly Ha Boung River valley, just inland from the coast. Detachment A-222 conducted saturation patrolling throughout this valuable rice-producing region and also guarded the district capital of Le Hai. This camp strike-force soldier leaps from a helicopter during a search-and-destroy mission northwest of Tuy Hoa. *(Richard Parker/USA)* **Bottom:** The Vietnamese LLDB headquarters inside Camp Dong Tre. These fixed installations dated from Dong Tre's origin as a major training center of President Diem's strategic hamlet program, before the post was transferred to Special Forces during June 1963. *(Berry/USA)*

Top: Camp Dong Tre had responsibility for securing a wide area of coastal Phu Yen Province. Here, Detachment A-222 prepares to issue equipment prior to a routine company-sized night operation. *(Berry/USA)* **Center left:** The fire direction arrow at Camp Dong Tre, which was completely enclosed with a system of communication and firing trenches and fortified checkpoints. *(Berry/USA)* **Bottom left:** Camp Dong Tre maintained a forward company to the north outside Qui Nhon following the battles of Tet-68. These CIDG troops are being transported to this rotational duty station. *(Berry/USA)*

Top: Camp Tieu Atar was located nearly 100 miles due west of Dong Tre, near the Vietnamese-Cambodian border along the jungle boundary of Darlac and Pleiku Provinces. Detachment A-231 escorts a patrol deep into the tropical rain forest during an interdiction mission. *(Gerald Foy)* **Bottom:** The highland interior camp at Tieu Atar was built by the 299th Engineer Battalion and completed on December 20, 1967. Tieu Atar was the last Special Forces Fighting Camp constructed during the year, and it began active operations in early 1968. The camp guarded enemy approach routes through the forested Cao Nguyen Dac Lac, the Darlac Plateau heartland between Ban Me Thuot and Pleiku, for the duration of 5th Special Forces Group service in Vietnam. *(Author's Collection)*

Top: Originally established as a South Vietnamese regimental frontier post and used by Special Forces beginning in September 1963, Camp Kham Duc was a vital Special Forces cross-border site along the Laotian border in western Quang Tin Province. *(USAF)* **Bottom:** The approaches to Kham Duc were guarded by the remote outpost of Ngok Tavak. On May 10, 1968, the 2d NVA Division overran this post and drove its joint Australian-American-led 11th Mobile Strike Force Company and supporting Marine howitzer crews into the jungle, clearing the way for a major advance against Kham Duc itself. *(Author's Collection)*

Top: On May 12, 1968, North Vietnamese soldiers captured the high ground around Camp Kham Duc, and their artillery bombardment and periodic ground assaults made the compound untenable. The camp was evacuated under fire with several aircraft shot down at close range. *(Author's Collection)* **Bottom left:** The final picture of the battle at Kham Duc, taken as NVA troops overran the runway against the last ditch resistance offered by Special Forces and Air Force combat-control teams. *(USAF)* **Bottom right:** Vietnamese camp followers are helped off one of the last transports to leave Kham Duc. *(USAF)*

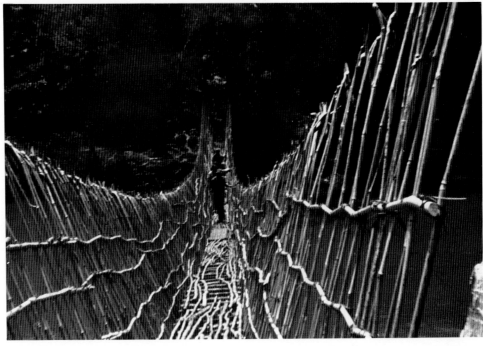

Top: Camp Ben Het was established by Detachment A-244 in western Kontum Province during February 1968, but intensive enemy mortar and rocket barrages delayed completion of the complex until the following year. This view shows the 299th Engineer Battalion working on Camp Ben Het and West Hill during late 1968. *(Author's Collection)* **Bottom:** Camp Ben Het was located within the rugged tri-border region of South Vietnam, Laos, and Cambodia. This Special Forces patrol crosses a suspension bridge over a swift mountain stream in the triple-canopy jungle during a hazardous border-surveillance operation. *(William Cruse)*

Top left: Detachment B-33 relieved Camps Loc Ninh, Minh Thanh, Chi Linh, and Tong Le Chon north of Saigon of many administrative burdens. It was responsible for team or personnel changes within camps; the funding and scheduling of projects; overall employment of strike forces, guards, interpreters, and laborers; and camp relocations within its jurisdictional area. Capt. Thomas Myerchin relaxes at the B-33 Hon Quan complex. *(Thomas Myerchin)* **Top right:** The B-Detachment was an intermediary command

organization that implemented the decisions of higher company headquarters and coordinated Special Forces tasks with Vietnamese province authorities and other government agencies. The CIA Phoenix compound was located beside Camp Widder inside Hon Quan. *(Thomas Myerchin)* **Bottom:** Control Detachment D-33 headquarters was located at Hon Quan in upper Binh Long Province.*(Author's Collection)*

Top: Camp Tra Cu experienced a major Viet Cong assault on April 21, 1968. The Viet Cong delivered sustained barrages across the Binh Gay canal, followed by a ground assault that reached the camp parapets. The Viet Cong were repulsed by heroic Special Forces and LLDB leadership, and the CIDG performed well despite several acts of individual sabotage by VC sympathizers within the compound. *(Bryant/USA)*
Center: The Detachment A-352 medical personnel at Camp Tra Cu performed herculean service during the battle of April 1968. *(Brian Peterson)* **Bottom:** During August 1968 5th Special Forces Group commander Col. Harold R. Aaron (front left), flanked by Vietnamese LLDB commander Maj. Gen. Doan Van Quang, held a major conference with his mobile strike-force commanders. One of the main topics was the acceleration of response time for getting military reinforcements into camps under attack. *(John Borgman)*

Top: The Special Forces goal of converting its CIDG program to Vietnamese control suffered some setbacks during 1968. The most conspicuous failure during the year was Camp Ben Soi (A-321), turned over to South Vietnamese LLDB authorities in July. Unfortunately, Vietnamese leaders in the compound were content to languish behind their wire barriers, and the camp's offensive reliability quickly diminished. *(Author's Collection)* **Bottom:** The conversion of Camp Ben Soi from Special Forces to full Vietnamese control failed because of the LLDB commander's unwillingness to engage in aggressive combat operations against the enemy. So many problems were experienced that the 5th Special Forces Group was forced to resume control of the camp. *(Author's Collection)*

Top left: During 1968 the personnel situation within 5th Special Forces Group became critical. There were serious shortages of experienced senior officers with special-warfare experience in Vietnam, such as this field officer arriving at Cam Ranh Bay during January 1968. *(Author's Collection)* **Top right:** Recruiting shortfalls and a declining Army retention rate lessened the ability of Special Forces to maintain pre-war standards. Volunteers who accepted Special Forces assignment upon entering Vietnam often had to be taught basic parachuting. *(5th SFG PIO)* **Center left:** The Special Forces also lacked enough qualified noncommissioned officers with medical, signal, engineering, and other field skills. As a temporary remedy, Special Forces authorized grade substitutions up to three levels. Troopers with the rank of Specialist Fourth Class, such as this replacement wearing the Green Beret at the Cam Ranh Bay depot, filled positions normally reserved for staff sergeants or higher. **Bottom:** The strength of Special Forces was constantly eroded by high battlefield casualties, such as this patrol leader receiving emergency treatment after being hit by a sniper during December 1968. *(Vance Harnes/USA)*

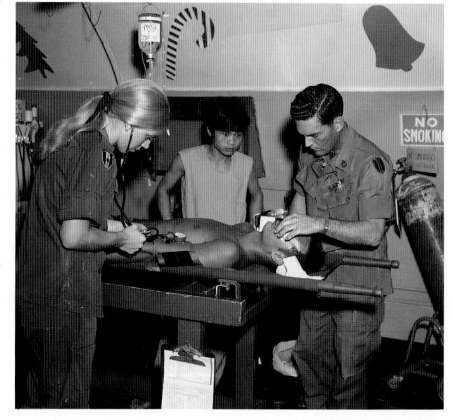

Top: In an effort to keep its field A-Detachments up to strength, Special Forces resorted to direct recruitment of selected soldiers arriving in Vietnam at the Long Binh and Cam Ranh Bay replacement centers. Special Forces did not relax its rigid mental and physical standards, but it did accept non-paratroopers with little knowledge of required specialties such as communications or engineering. These troops were sent through a parachute crash-course at Dong Ba Thin for basic jump qualification, and then learned special-warfare skills ''on the job'' after being assigned to a camp. *(5th SFG PIO)* **Bottom left:** A Special Forces trainee exits the mock tower as he learns the basics of parachuting at Dong Ba Thin, Vietnam. *(5th SFG PIO)* **Bottom right:** The Special Forces also conducted advanced training courses in Vietnam, to ensure that necessary proficiency was retained in such fields as pathfinder operations, shown here. *(Army News Features)*

REQUIRED STRENGTH
1st QTR CY 68

	OFF	WO	EM	AGG
5TH SFG (ABN)	486	24	2078	2588
MI AUGMENTATION	11	19	80	110
SIGNAL AUGMENTATION	4	–	12	16
31st ENGR DET	6	–	31	37
B-52 (DELTA)	11	–	82	93
RECONDO	5	–	41	46
C&C DET	102	–	465	567
PROJECT DANIEL BOONE	24	–	132	156
B-53	7	–	24	31
TOTAL:	656	43	2945	3644

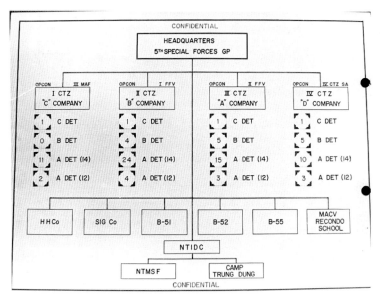

Top left and center left: The requirements for enough personnel to fill the myriad assortment of Special Forces camp A-Detachments, control B-Detachments, and corps-level C-Detachments, as well as various high-priority projects and organizations, imposed a tremendous strain on Special Forces to fill its ranks without sacrificing quality. These 5th Special Forces Group briefing charts for the 1st Quarter, January-March, of the Calendar Year 1968—the most critical point of Special Forces service in Vietnam from a manpower perspective—reveal required personnel levels. *(Author's Collection)* **Top right:** Battle-hardened, highly qualified special warfare sergeants were the backbone of the 5th Special Forces Group, but cumulative combat losses and the need for supervisors and instructors decreased their presence at the operational detachment level with each passing year of the seemingly interminable Vietnam war. *(Kenneth Powell/USA)* **Bottom right:** Special Forces in Vietnam made use of its excellent Korean special-warfare connections to provide advanced Tae Kwon Do instruction in the martial arts. This examination is being held for indigenous team members at Long Thanh in III Corps Tactical Zone during September 1968. *(Author's Collection)*

Top: New Camp Thuong Duc was established by Detachment A-109 in Quang Nam Province during August 1966 and endured almost constant action from Viet Cong forces entrenched within its operational zone. From May 5-20, 1968, the compound was subjected to intense daily rocket and mortar barrages. On September 28 the Special Forces defenders repulsed a major North Vietnamese Army ground assault. Enemy infantry probes and periodic bombardments continued until October 6, when Marine Operation Maui Peak finally succeeded in breaking the siege. *(Author's Collection)* **Bottom:** The land route to Thuong Duc, Highway 4, required heavy patrolling and engineer support, because most of its bridges were usually washed out, and it was almost impossible to cross the river in the rainy season. Here, Staff Sgt. L. Brooks "Stik" Rader patrols the dense jungle. *(James Donahue)*

Top: Camp Ha Thanh in Quang Ngai Province was subjected to a fierce assault and partially overrun on September 10-11, 1966, but it was rebuilt by Detachment A-104. Following the loss of Kham Duc in May 1968, a new I CTZ training facility for cross-border movements was established at Ha Thanh and commenced operations in the middle of July. From August 23-30, 1968, Camp Ha Thanh was subjected to barrages and enemy ground attacks against its outposts, which resulted in the closing of the training facility. Here CIDG camp soldiers carry crates of ammunition from a C-7 Caribou. **Bottom:** The land route, Highway 5B, was closed most of the time by enemy action and adverse weather. Like other camps in the northern region of South Vietnam, extensive aerial support was essential to keep the camp supplied. This C-7 Caribou of the 459th Tactical Airlift Squadron brings in emergency supplies to Ha Thanh from Da Nang. *(USAF)*

Top: Detachment A-102 was reestablished at Camp Tien Phuoc after the battle of A Shau. The land route, Highway 533 shown here, was often mined, and the 104th South Vietnamese Engineer Battalion constructed an airfield that opened in April 1966. Nearly all camp supplies were air delivered directly from Da Nang or Chu Lai. *(Author's Collection)* **Bottom:** Camp Tien Phuoc came under heavy attack on February 23, 1969, when one of its outposts was overrun. Although a prompt counterattack recaptured the position, the siege of the camp was not lifted until March 24. Here, an enemy prisoner awaits interrogation after the battle at the A-102 detention facility at Camp Tien Phuoc. *(David Epstein/USA)*

Top left: Highway 537 leading to Camp Nong Son was lined with several active VC ambush sites and interrupted by a river ferry crossing at the Song Thu Bon. *(Author's Collection)* **Top right:** Camp Nong Son was built by the Navy 3d Mobile Construction Battalion and garrisoned by Detachment A-105 with a full Vietnamese CIDG camp force. The camp had no airfield and depended on helicopter deliveries brought in through its small helipad. The 5th Marines at An Hoa served as the over-watch unit for this Special Forces post. *(Author's Collection)* **Bottom:** The coal mine at Nong Son in Quang Nam Province, with its grading building shown here, supplied the An Hoa industrial complex in northern South Vietnam. The 5th Special Forces Group was ordered to protect this vital facility after Tet-68, and it established Camp Nong Son with team personnel from Kham Duc on June 24, 1968. *(USIS)*

Top left: Camp Dak Seang in northern Kontum Province was assaulted by the 101D NVA Regiment on August 18, 1968. Rainstorms and low clouds hampered Air Force AC-47 Dragonship support, but these aircraft later proved instrumental in saving Camp Duc Lap. *(USAF)* **Top right:** 14th Special Operations Wing Col. Conrad S. Allman discusses the difficulties of air support over Camp Dak Seang with Lt. Col. Samuel E. Blessing. *(USAF)* **Center:** Enemy sappers breached the perimeter, but Detachment A-245 counterattacks prevented enemy penetration of the camp. Medical aidman Sgt. Gary B. Beikirch set the highest example of bravery: At (1) he retrieved wounded Lt. Christensen despite his own wounds and dragged him to (2) the emergency medical bunker, and at (3) he was critically wounded in the back while carrying fallen Montagnard defenders from (4) the area where the enemy breakthrough was defeated. *(Author's Collection)* **Bottom:** Sgt. Beikirch is awarded the Medal of Honor by President Richard M. Nixon. *(Wayne O'Neill/USA)*

Top left: The battle for border-surveillance Camp Duc Lap, nine miles from Cambodia and southwest of Ban Me Thuot, was fought August 23-31, 1968. The NVA 95C Regiment captured a large portion of the camp, but Detachment A-239 held out with its Rhade and Mnong tribal defenders until the reinforcing 2d Mobile Strike Force Command arrived and drove the enemy out. Here, CIDG victors take helmets and bangalore torpedoes from the battlefield. *(13 MHD)* **Top right:** One of the heroes at Duc Lap was Sgt. Michael B. Dooley, killed by a sniper, whose last cartoon depicts a prisoner claiming that the draft forced him to fight. *(13 MHD)* **Center:** View of Camp Duc Lap from the enemy-occupied northern hill, looking toward the southern hill held by Special Forces throughout the battle. Bunkers in the upper left center were retaken by Sp5 Donald Childs on August 25. *(13 MHD)* **Bottom:** The lower enemy trench at Duc Lap where Capt. Joseph Trimble, Staff Sgt. Manuel Gonzales Jr., Staff Sgt. Arnulfo Estrada, and Sgt. Walter Hetzler led Mike Force soldiers in a valiant charge that cleared it in close combat. *(13 MHD)*

Top left: Wives of Montagnard irregulars killed at Duc Lap mourn the loss of their husbands. *(13 MHD)* **Top Right:** After the battle of Duc Lap, a CIDG troop poses behind one of the weapons used against the counterattacking Mike Force troops on the northern hill. *(Author's Collection)* **Center left:** A patrol pushes outside the Duc Lap perimeter after the battle. *(13 MHD)* **Center right:** Camp Duc Lap as viewed from the enemy side of the southern wire, looking toward the Special Forces-controlled main hill with machine gun bunker on left. Logs in the wire provided some cover for the advancing NVA infantry, and their helmets and gear still mark the path of advance after Special Forces removed the dead. *(13 MHD)* **Bottom:** One of numerous NVA graves found after the battle of Duc Lap, marked by the boots of the fallen soldier. *(13 MHD)*

Top: The battle of Duc Lap provided another case of Special Forces excellence in standard infantry warfare. On August 25, 1968, several Mike Force companies composed of Rhade, Raglai, and Jarai Montagnards clambered out of their trenches to retake the enemy-occupied northern hill as Lt. Norman Baldwin shouted, ''Over the top! Let's Go!'' They made this front charge uphill despite the raking fire of enemy heavy machine guns (one such machine gun can be seen on the previous page). Lt. Baldwin, Sp5 Forestal Stevens, and Staff Sgt. Leslie Brucker Jr. were among those killed. The conventional nature of the warfare at Duc Lap was also demonstrated by this native gun crew firing a 105mm howitzer within the camp. *(Steven Hembree)* **Bottom:** Camp Duc Lap was shelled incessantly throughout the battle. A dud North Vietnamese mortar round struck the parking ramp of the Duc Lap airfield during one of the countless bombardments. *(13 MHD)*

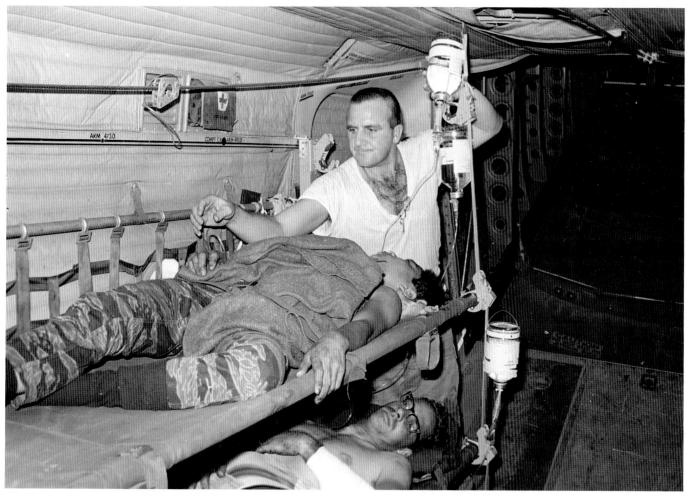

Top left: The pilot of this wrecked Air Force F-100 shot down over Duc Lap on August 23 was rescued by daring camp defenders who drove two 3/4-ton trucks outside the camp perimeter wire and through a startled enemy company dug in on both sides of the road. On their return to camp after rescuing the pilot, the trucks were covered by a wall of destructive fire from Air Force gunships that discouraged enemy reaction. *(13 MHD)* **Top right:** Detachment A-239 commander Lt. William J. Harp with 21st

Tactical Air Support Squadron FAC pilot Capt. Wayne F. Arnold, who flew an observation aircraft over Duc Lap for 50 hours and called in more than 60 air strikes during the battle. *(13 MHD)* **Bottom:** Tech. Sgt. Wilbur V. Hosman attends seriously wounded American and Montagnard defenders taken from Camp Duc Lap aboard a 903d Aeromedical Evacuation Squadron flight to Nha Trang. *(USAF)*

Top: The enemy attempted to destroy several Special Forces camps north of Saigon in late 1968. The border-surveillance camp of Camp Katum in upper Tay Ninh Province was rocketed and mortared throughout August and September and close-assaulted twice by the 5th VC Sapper Battalion. The determined enemy ground attacks were defeated only after heavy combat. Streaking in at treetop level, an Air Force F-100 Supersabre carries out an airstrike against Viet Cong forces surrounding Camp Katum. *(DOD)* **Center:** On September 25, 1968, Detachment A-322 survived its most difficult battle by defeating an enemy breakthrough with howitzer canister charges fired point-blank at Viet Cong swarming over the parapets. Here, Special Forces commander Capt. Francis W. Kane reflects on defensive requirements. *(DOD)* **Bottom:** Camp Loc Ninh was also targeted by bombardments and ground assaults conducted August 9-22, 1968, but Detachment A-331 defeated the enemy maneuvers with backup from the 1st Infantry Division and 11th Armored Cavalry. *(Author's Collection)*

Top: Camp Tuyen Nhon was an important border-surveillance camp located just below the enemy-controlled Parrot's Beak region of Cambodia that jutted into South Vietnam's Plain of Reeds. The camp's Detachment A-415 airboat companies were engaged in continual combat patrolling along the frontier canals and waterways. *(Author's Collection)* **Bottom:** The vast Plain of Reeds, as seen from Camp Tuyen Nhon. The vessel in the foreground is a Navy armored monitor converted from a LCM-6 landing craft and detached from the Mobile Riverine Force to provide added protection to the Special Forces compound's amphibious expeditions. The forward turret of the monitor, the starred structure in lower left, was armed with 40mm weapons. *(Author's Collection)*

SPECIAL FORCES REACTION AND RECONNAISSANCE

Reconnaissance-specialized units, formed to locate and track elusive Viet Cong and North Vietnamese forces within the tropical wilderness of Southeast Asia, were an important facet of Special Forces operations. Detachment B-52 Project Delta pioneered long-range reconnaissance concepts inside South Vietnam and acquired a high degree of jungle operating expertise. During May 1964 Project Delta established an internal unit-training program to streamline its patrolling techniques. Throughout the next two years, this program was expanded as more conventional Army formations deployed to Vietnam.

During mid-1966 MACV commander General Westmoreland decided to formalize this instruction as part of his increased emphasis on Army reconnaissance operations. He directed Special Forces to establish a permanent three-week school, based on the Project Delta training concept, to instruct allied reconnaissance personnel. The Special Forces-run MACV Recondo School opened officially on September 15, 1966. General Westmoreland personally chose the Recondo title as a derivative of three well-known terms associated with soldiering: reconnaissance, commando, and doughboy.

The MACV Recondo School emphasized physical conditioning, military-map reading, medical training, radio skills, intelligence gathering, patrol organization, weapons familiarization, and helicopter operations. The first phase of training consisted of academic subjects and confidence tests conducted at the Nha Trang training area. During the second phase, practical exercises using helicopter support were employed in conjunction with a four-day field training exercise on Hon Tre island, located five miles off the coast of Nha Trang. During the third and final phase, the students were deployed as six-man teams on extended reconnaissance patrols in hostile areas west of Nha Trang or on Hon Tre island. The total program lasted 20 days and was taught by Special Forces instructors supplemented by a Thai, Korean, and Australian liaison staff.

During 1964 Special Forces boosted its own reconnaissance of the Nha Trang area with a specially recruited Nung security platoon, which was expanded to three full companies in the following year. The Nung security force was designated as a "Mike Force," or Mobile Strike Force, for quick reaction to emergency situations. During early 1966 this original force was decimated in the battle for Camp A Shau. Detachment A-503 was raised to reconstitute the Mobile Strike Force with Nung and Montagnard volunteers and received a two-fold mission: to act as a Group reaction force to support besieged Special Forces camps, and to serve as a special reserve for any threatened sector within South Vietnam.

This response force was designated as the 5th Mobile Strike Force Command and gained heightened combat experience throughout 1967 at Tan Rai, Phu Nhon, and Buon Blech. During Tet-68 the command excelled in defending Nha Trang, and in March the command began reorganization under Detachment B-55 and expanded to four battalions by July. Demonstrating its parachute capability in 1967 jumps at Nui Giai and Bunard, the command conducted its third combat parachute assault over Nui Coto during November 1968.

One of the greatest achievements of the 5th Mobile Strike Force Command transpired in the enemy-fortified Seven Mountains region of the Mekong Delta. During March 1969 the command successfully stormed the Viet Cong mountain bastion of Nui Coto, despite heavy casualties and days of uphill fighting, which culminated in the capture of "impregnable" Tuk Chup Knoll. The mountain-warfare proficiency of the group's Mobile Strike Force was demonstrated again during the first half of 1970. The 1st Battalion wrested Nui Khet from enemy control in the Mekong Delta during March and April, while the 2d Battalion retook the Central Highlands fortress of Nui Ek in another intense battle lasting from April through June.

In addition to the Nha Trang Mobile Strike Force Command, each Special Forces C-1 operational control detachment also controlled a multi-purpose reserve for its own Corps Tactical Zone. Detachment B-16 formed the 1st Mobile Strike Force Command with two battalions for operations in northern South Vietnam. The five-battalion 2d Mobile Strike Force Command

A Special Forces flamethrower team of the 5th Mobile Strike Force Command advances past sniper fire up the boulder-strewn slope of Nui Coto in March 1969. The successful storming of this Viet Cong bastion by Special Forces verified its high degree of mountain warfare expertise, a military skill historically associated with special-operations units. *(James Ross)*

served under Detachment B-20 in the Central Highlands. The approaches to the Vietnamese capital and western-border districts were guarded by three battalions of the 3d Mobile Strike Force Command of Detachment B-36. The 4th Mobile Strike Force Command, also containing three battalions but partially equipped with airboats, covered the Mekong Delta.

Projects Delta, Sigma, and Omega also used ethnic minority troops of demonstrated courage and political reliability—similar to the Mobile Strike Forces—but employed them in the long-range reconnaissance role.

Project Delta, originally an outgrowth of covert Project Leaping Lena, grew from a single A-Detachment of 12 personnel in 1964 to an Army-level special warfare component under Detachment B-52 by 1966, containing nearly 100 assigned Special Forces troops and more than 1,200 indigenous warriors. Project Delta continued to perform a wide range of missions that encompassed detection of enemy units, operational intelligence, bomb-damage assessment, artillery and air-strike coordination, and special-purpose raiding.

Project Sigma was organized at Ho Ngoc Tao from August to October 1966 as an unconventional warfare unit under Project B-56 to provide corps-level special reconnaissance for II Field Force in the war zones of III Corps Tactical Zone west of Saigon. The project contained eight reconnaissance teams, three commando companies, and one camp defense company of ethnic Cambodian and Chinese troops under Special Forces direction. Project Omega, formed at the same time by Detachment B-50 to provide specialized reconnaissance for I Field Force in the Central Highlands of II Corps Tactical Zone, used Montagnard, Cham, and Chinese troops. These twin Greek-letter projects each contained more than 100 Special Forces and nearly 900 indigenous personnel.

During November 1967 Projects Omega and Sigma were reassigned to MACV-SOG, creating a gap in the II and III Corps Tactical Zone reconnaissance screens where each previously operated. The former Project Omega recon area was covered by Detachment B-20. In the latter zone Detachment B-36 Rapid Fire was established to provide a substitute reaction and exploitation force, and employed two Mobile Guerilla Force companies as well as mixed Special Forces-indigenous recon teams. Special Forces wartime projects like Delta, Omega, Sigma, and Rapid Fire rendered vital divisional, corps, and army-level field reconnaissance that uncovered enemy movements and intentions of great military value to several campaigns.

Specialized control headquarters were established by 5th Special Forces Group to perform specific assignments. Detachment B-51 was responsible for the South Vietnamese Special Forces training center at Dong Ba Thin from 1964 through 1971. The detachment had the primary mission of advising and assisting the school and its Lục-Lượng Dặc-Biệt contingent. Courses at Dong Ba Thin included basic parachuting and jumpmaster skills, communications techniques, urban warfare, Tae Kwon Do martial arts, and Mobile Strike Force airborne and reconnaissance tactics.

Detachment B-57 Project Gamma was a Special Forces-controlled military intelligence project working directly for the U.S. government. Project Gamma was created in June 1967 to provide strategic reconnaissance assessments on North Vietnamese Army penetration of Cambodia and make use of neutral Cambodian territory for bases and resupply networks to fuel the war in South Vietnam. The project depended on intelligence collection agents and teams based at forward campsites such as Duc Co, Bu Dop, Loc Ninh, Thien Ngon, Duc Hue, Moc Hoa, and Chau Doc along the Vietnamese-Cambodian border.

The Military Assistance Command, Vietnam, Studies and Observation Group (MACV-SOG) was the only theater-level special reconnaissance project fielded during the Second Indochina War. The ''studies and observation'' title was part of a cover deception designed to mislead people into believing that the joint staff was analyzing lessons of the Vietnam conflict. In actual fact MACV-SOG was a highly classified, high-command task force with authority over a multitude of unconventional warfare operations throughout Southeast Asia.

Activated in April 1964—simultaneously with the creation of

the South Vietnamese Special Exploitation Service—MACV-SOG continued the special activities formerly directed by the Central Intelligence Agency and carried out by Special Forces and indigenous personnel. The organization reinforced Special Forces assets assigned to these projects and became responsible for a wide range of clandestine sabotage, psychological operations, and special-warfare objectives in North and South Vietnam, Laos, Cambodia, and southern China.

MACV-SOG tasks included regular cross-border sorties to disrupt Viet Cong, Khmer Rouge, Pathet Lao, and North Vietnamese forces operating in their own territory. The locations of imprisoned and missing Americans were also monitored. Where possible, "Bright Light" raiding teams assisted downed airmen or struck prison camps as part of the escape and evasion mission for all captured allied military personnel. MACV-SOG also trained and dispatched agents and teams into North Vietnam to run resistance movements. These measures were assisted by sophisticated psychological operations, ranging from false enemy broadcasting stations to powerful propaganda transmitters. MACV-SOG also maintained the capability to undertake additional special missions as required, such as kidnapping, assassination, and insertion of defective munitions to contaminate enemy supply systems.

Special Forces troops were assigned primarily either to the Nha Trang-based air-studies group or the ground-studies group and worked under the direction of control launch sites established at Hue-Phu Bai, Khe Sanh, Da Nang, Kontum, and Ban Me Thuot. In addition to some concurrent basing with control sites, additional forward mission launch sites existed at Quang Tri, Kham Duc, Dak Pek, Ben Het, Dak To, Duc Co, and Quang Loi in South Vietnam as well as Ubon and Nakhon Phanom in Thailand. The MACV-SOG training and airborne operations center was located at Long Thanh.

The internal structure of MACV-SOG stabilized after November 1, 1967, when three command and control units were established for missions outside South Vietnam. The three field commands were composed of spike recon teams, hatchet forces, and search-location-and-annihilation mission (SLAM) companies that could be flexibly switched between them depending on mission requirements. There were a total of about 90 recon teams, and these formed the backbone of the Special Forces cross-border raiding enterprise. Each team included three Special Forces members and nine indigenous troops chosen for their jungle warfare knowledge. The recon teams were named after states, territories, Asian reptiles, tools, and other assorted designations. The stronger hatchet forces were platoon-sized organizations containing five Special Forces and 30 natives that could perform larger missions or reinforce individual recon teams. The SLAM companies were designed to exploit situations requiring concentrated commando tactics or emergency response.

The largest of the three field commands was Command and Control North (CCN), created by consolidating Special Forces resources at forward operations bases FOB-1 at Phu Bai, FOB-3 at Khe Sanh, and FOB-4 at Da Nang. This unit conducted special warfare missions into Laos, the Demilitarized Zone, and North Vietnam. Command and Control Central (CCC) was responsible for the highly dangerous operational area around the tri-border junction of Laos, Cambodia, and Vietnam and was formed by expanding the forward operations base FOB-2 at Kontum. Finally, Command and Control South (CCS) was raised by expanding Project Daniel Boone to give unconventional warfare coverage over the eastern half of Cambodia.

Although many aspects of MACV-SOG remain classified, enough has been released on their operational success to verify a major strategic impact against enemy forces while only involving a fraction of the total Special Forces effort in Vietnam. The Special Forces contribution to MACV-SOG's lengthy campaign of cross-border raiding and other extraterritorial missions revolutionized modern concepts of high-level ground reconnaissance and earned Special Forces a legacy of proven strategic performance. The success of all Special Forces reaction and reconnaissance elements provided an unblemished record of mission accomplishment and was of decisive importance in furthering development of the U.S. special-warfare community.

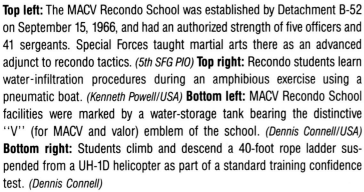

Top left: The MACV Recondo School was established by Detachment B-52 on September 15, 1966, and had an authorized strength of five officers and 41 sergeants. Special Forces taught martial arts there as an advanced adjunct to recondo tactics. *(5th SFG PIO)* **Top right:** Recondo students learn water-infiltration procedures during an amphibious exercise using a pneumatic boat. *(Kenneth Powell/USA)* **Bottom left:** MACV Recondo School facilities were marked by a water-storage tank bearing the distinctive ''V'' (for MACV and valor) emblem of the school. *(Dennis Connell/USA)* **Bottom right:** Students climb and descend a 40-foot rope ladder suspended from a UH-1D helicopter as part of a standard training confidence test. *(Dennis Connell)*

Top left: Students rappel from a UH-1D helicopter. *(Dennis Connell)* **Top right:** The MACV Recondo School trained selected U.S. and allied personnel to conduct long-range reconnaissance operations in Vietnam. As part of the training, recondo students, seen passing through the main gate, were required to complete a seven-mile endurance run while wearing a 30-pound backpack and carrying a weapon. *(Kenneth Powell/USA)* **Bottom left:** Instructors demonstrate an immediate action drill on Hon Tre Island. *(Dennis Connell/USA)* **Bottom right:** Students learn to use the Stabo harness, designed for fast extraction from terrain not suited for helicopter landings. *(Dennis Connell)*

Top left: A recondo student practices descending from a helicopter. *(Gordon Gahan)* **Top right:** Mobile Strike Force Command troops practice hand-to-hand take-down techniques. *(James Morrison)* **Center left:** Students climb up ropes to the tower during training in rappelling methods. *(Kenneth Powell/USA)* **Center right:** Hon Tre Island, a large and isolated area covered by tropical wilderness, was located within helicopter-ferrying distance of Nha Trang. *(Donald Miller/USA)* **Bottom right:** From the time the MACV Recondo School opened until its closure in December 1970, 5,625 personnel attended training, but only 3,357 graduated, despite tough entrance requirements. *(Robert Tuttle)*

Top: During the third and final phase of the MACV Recondo School, students were deployed as six-man teams on three- to four-day reconnaissance patrols in hostile areas west of Nha Trang or on Hon Tre Island. *(David Friedrich)* **Bottom:** Recondo Operations Master Sgt. Louis Le Page explains the use of blasting caps to students on Hon Tre Island. The recondo instructors taught map reading, medical aid, communications, intelligence gathering, patrolling, weapons, and air operations as part of its program to impart combat-reconnaissance skills. Only those students who achieved the required academic points and who demonstrated overall proficiency in the first two phases of the course were permitted to participate in the final combat phase. *(Dennis Connell)*

Top: The Nha Trang-based 5th Mobile Strike Force Command was controlled by Detachment B-55, and it served as the 5th Special Forces Group's countrywide reserve reaction force. Originally created in August 1965 by expanding the original Nung security company recruited during 1964, it consisted of Cholon Chinese, Vietnamese, and Rhade, Raglai, and Koho Montagnards organized into three reinforced battalions under Detachments A-502, A-503, and A-551. The command was primarily intended for camp-relief missions, but it conducted battalion-sized reinforcing missions to secure difficult areas and sometimes maneuvered as a full brigade. During November 1968 these mobile strike-force paratroopers made a combat jump over Nui Coto to reinforce Mekong Delta operations. *(Jerry Kringel)* **Bottom:** 5th Special Forces Group commander Col. Aaron presents Duc Lap battle streamers to 5th Mobile Strike Force Command guidons in recognition of Detachment B-55 service during the August 1968 battle. *(John Borgman)*

Top: Nui Coto was the Viet Cong-held southernmost mountain of the Seven Mountains region of Chau Doc Province. Allied attempts to secure its steep, cave-studded, boulder-strewn slopes were unsuccessful until March 16, 1969, when battalions from the 4th and 5th Mobile Strike Force Commands stormed the enemy bastion. *(Doug Baribeau)* **Bottom:** Special Forces leaders on the battlefield of Nui Coto after securing the Viet Cong stronghold. The Special Forces direct assault against this formidable enemy citadel represented the supreme Vietnam example of special-warfare attributes associated with mountain warfare, first manifested by the Special Forces predecessor organization, the First Special Service Force of World War II. *(21 MHD)*

Top left: Wounded soldiers are brought down the slope during the Special Forces attack on Nui Coto, which commenced March 16, 1969. *(21 MHD)* **Center left:** On March 17 Special Forces psychological operations and broadcast appeals convinced nine Viet Cong to rally to the allied cause as ''Hoi Chanhs.'' Capt. Henry Sturm, commanding the 2d Battalion, 5th Mobile Strike Force Command, interrogates a Hoi Chanh prisoner who later led them to the main enemy cave complex on Nui Coto. *(21 MHD)* **Bottom left:** During the attack, strike-force soldiers encountered heavy resistance from enemy gunners hidden among the thousands of granite boulders littering the fractured mountainside. *(21 MHD)*

Phosphorous shells rain down on enemy strongpoints on Nui Coto. The local population believed that the Viet Cong stationed on Nui Coto were immune from death, so they called it ''Superstition Mountain.'' Tuk Chup knoll, the highest elevation of the mountain, was known as ''Million-Dollar Knoll'' after the amount of costly ordnance used against it. *(21 MHD)*

Top left: Staff Sgt. Benedict M. Davan, seen behind Staff Sgt. Scrobbs just before the battle, was killed by a sniper while retrieving wounded troops on Tuk Chup knoll. The Detachment B-55 compound at Nha Trang was renamed in his honor. *(Author's Collection)* **Top right:** Nui Coto burns under napalm strikes delivered by F-100s on March 16, as the 4th and 5th Mobile Strike Force Commands commence their attack on the mountain fortress. During the first assault up the mountain, the enemy suddenly opened fire on the lead company with B-40 rockets, grenades, and automatic weapons—causing a 20-percent casualty rate among the attackers in the first two minutes of battle. *(James Ross/USA)* **Bottom left:** On March 16 and 17 mobile strike-force soldiers consolidated their newly won positions on the west side of Tuk Chup knoll and prepared for the main flank assault against the remaining enemy defenses. *(21 MHD)* **Bottom right:** This soldier goes into battle on March 18, as part of a general sweep by the mobile strike-force battalions around the Nui Coto mountainside. *(James Ross)*

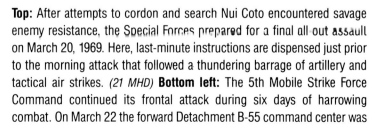

Top: After attempts to cordon and search Nui Coto encountered savage enemy resistance, the Special Forces prepared for a final all-out assault on March 20, 1969. Here, last-minute instructions are dispensed just prior to the morning attack that followed a thundering barrage of artillery and tactical air strikes. *(21 MHD)* **Bottom left:** The 5th Mobile Strike Force Command continued its frontal attack during six days of harrowing combat. On March 22 the forward Detachment B-55 command center was alerted that a large cave system, guarded by boobytraps, had been discovered. Throughout the next day, Special Forces anxiously monitored reports from a volunteer exploration team that was traveling through the underground passages to determine enemy dispositions. *(21 MHD)* **Bottom right:** Special Forces-led reinforcements trek into combat. On March 26 the Mobile Strike Force Command seized the final point of enemy resistance and concluded the battle of Nui Coto. *(21 MHD)*

Top left: During the three-day battle of Nui Khet that commenced April 3, 1970, Sgt. Brian L. Buker led numerous heroic charges against the crucial hilltop-bunker complex before being mortally wounded by a combination of rocket and mortar return fire on April 5. *(5th SFG PIO)* **Top right:** Part of the enemy bunker system on the summit of Nui Khet, showing Sgt. Buker's path of advance and the enemy bunker he was attempting to eliminate when killed. *(5th SFG PIO)* **Bottom:** The Viet Cong-dominated mountain fortress of Nui Khet in the Seven Mountains region was captured by the 1st Battalion, 5th Mobile Strike Force Command. *(5th SFG PIO)*

Top: While the 1st Battalion, 5th Mobile Strike Force Command, fought at Nui Khet in the Mekong Delta, the 2d Battalion, shown here, fought in the highlands battle of Nui Ek from April 28 to June 15, 1970. Nui Ek was a craggy mountain post overrun by enemy troops on March 29. The hill's recapture involved a steep climb by Special Forces-led troops over rock formations that channeled movement into enemy firing zones, crowned by the costly reduction of 12 concrete bunkers on the peak. *(5th SFG PIO)* **Bottom:** Two Rhade warriors of the 5th Mobile Strike Force Command near Dak Seang. The difficulty of Nui Khet's terrain and the battle's severity caused racial tensions to flare between the Vietnamese and Montagnards contingents, but these disturbances were quelled by Special Forces leaders. *(5th SFG PIO)*

Top left: A 3d Mobile Strike Force Command sergeant signals an evacuation helicopter into a clearing near the Cambodian border during 1969. *(William Gates)* **Top right:** Capt. Robert C. Beckman (left), Detachment B-36 commander of the 2d Battalion, 3d Mobile Strike Force Command, calls for reinforcements after coordinating with Operations Sgt. Ernest Fant (right). Just days later, Capt. Beckman was killed. *(Lee Mize)* **Bottom:** During a March 1969 skirmish southeast of Ban Me Thuot, 2d Mobile Strike Force Command Lt. Dave E. Moley (left) and Detachment B-20 Capt. Martin L. Green Jr. (top) hoist wounded aboard a UH-1 helicopter. *(Darryl Arizo/USA)*

Top: Special Forces leaders of the 1st Battalion, 3d Mobile Strike Force Command, after their return from 1969 Operation Centurion, an extended reconnaissance-in-force mission through the Apache area of operations in War Zone D. *(William Gates)* **Bottom left:** 5th Mobile Strike Force Command medical Sgt. George Funk moves down a mountain trail behind a seventeen-year-old Montagnard irregular named Dani, who weighed 95 pounds but still carried the radio on all missions. *(Christopher Funk)* **Bottom middle:** Special Forces Lt. George Turney (right) calls in a communication check as Sp5 Jeff E. Anadon provides patrol information near Bu Prang. *(Frank Sullivan III/USA)* **Bottom right:** Master Sgt. Soublet designed the Detachment B-55 monument at Nha Trang. It was erected in the winter of 1969 and "dedicated in honor of the men killed in action with Detachment B-55, 5th Mobile Strike Force Command." The Company's pennant is flanked by company guidons of the 1st Battalion on the left and 2d Battalion on the right. *(5th SFG PIO)*

Top: The greatest advantage of the mobile strike-force concept for Special Forces group and company commanders was its ability to conduct far-ranging operations in areas beyond traditional tribal homelands. Indigenous mobile strike-force members were volunteers who received better training, higher pay, and equipment superior to those in normal camp defense forces. The flexibility and high proficiency of strike-force operations were highlighted by parachute jumps on Bunard, Nui Giai, and Nui Coto and the encounters at A Shau, Tong Le Chon, Duc Lap, and Katum. These troopers of the 3d Mobile Strike Force Command board a C-123 aircraft of the 309th Special Operations Squadron at Phan Rang during 1969 Operation Centurion. *(DOD)* **Bottom:** Native troops of the 3d Mobile Strike Force Command are being flown to a forward camp for operations in War Zone D. *(USAF)*

MOBILE STRIKE FORCE COMMANDS

Top: Detachment B-52 provided command and control for Project Delta, a covert special-reconnaissance operation in Vietnam under Special Forces jurisdiction. Project Delta infiltrated into hostile territory or difficult regions normally inaccessible to regular troops, with the purpose of locating enemy units, gathering intelligence, detecting infiltration routes and base areas, making bomb-damage assessments, directing air and artillery strikes, guiding reaction forces, and conducting other special missions such as harassing and deception raids. Project Delta normally contained about 90 Special Forces members. *(Jason T. Woodworth)* **Bottom:** Special Forces Project Delta was the only Army-level special-reconnaissance unit deployed during the Vietnam conflict, and it operated in response to directives from MACV. The hazards of Project Delta service, reflected by the Purple Hearts being awarded to Detachment B-52 members here, were outweighed by Project Delta's success in detecting many major NVA/VC elements, thus saving a far greater number of American lives in conventional formations. *(5th SFG PIO)*

Top: Project Delta patrol member Staff Sgt. Russell P. Bott (far right) was part of a reconnaissance team sent more than a mile into Laos west of the Demilitarized Zone in late November 1966. On December 2, after several skirmishes, the patrol was surrounded by superior enemy forces. Sgt. Bott was listed as Missing in Action after Vietnamese patrol survivors reported that he was last seen attending a wounded comrade, Sgt. First Class Willie Stark, whom he refused to abandon. *(Eleanor Bott Gregory)* **Center:** Warrant Officer John W. Korsbeck, with the aid of a Vietnamese interpreter, provided Project Delta aerial radio relay from a U-1 Otter aircraft. *(John Korsbeck)* **Bottom:** Project Delta reconnaissance teams uncovered this enemy jungle way station full of Chinese-marked recoilless rifle ammunition during Operation Samurai expeditions into the A Shau Valley from March to May 1968. *(DOD)*

Top: During October and November 1969, Project Delta conducted Operation Trojan Horse, which used helicopters from the 101st Airborne Division to insert reconnaissance teams along the northwestern fringes of Vietnam. This Detachment B-52 member rappels from a helicopter into the mist-shrouded, triple-canopy jungle below. He carries a spool of communications wire that will be used as a land line for an outpost picketing an ambush site. Teams often stretched their observation capability by having personnel relay the signal for ambush through a series of clicks on field hand-phones. *(Author's Collection)* **Bottom:** Project Delta Roadrunner Thach Huong posed for this picture in July 1968; he was killed in action three months later. Detachment B-52 Roadrunner teams consisted of indigenous scouts attired in enemy clothing and equipment. They were well paid and received extra privileges but often did not survive. *(Author's Collection)*

INDIVIDUAL EARNINGS RECORD
HỒ SƠ LỢI TỨC CÁ NHÂN

NAME OF EMPLOYEE: DINH VENH	CAMP and TEAM DESIGNATION: DETACHMENT B-52		Type of Action: Per.	Grade: Recon Member

Month Tháng	Base Pay Lương chính	Family Allow Phụ cấp gia-đình	High Cost of Living Phụ đất-đỏ	Language Allow Phụ cấp Sinh ngữ	Total Amt. Due Tổng cộng	Subsistence Deductions Trừ tiền ăn ở	Net Amt. Due Số tiền còn được lãnh	Remarks Bị chú
Jul.	5,100$				5,100$		5,100$	14085
Aug	5,100$	400$			5,500$		5,500$	
Sep	5,100$	400$			5,500$		5,500$	
Oct	5,100$	400$			5,500$		5,500$	
Nov	5,300$	400$			5,700$		5,700$	
Dec	5,300$	400$			5,700$		5,700$	
Jan	5,700$	400$			6,100$		6,100$	
Feb	5,700$	400$			6,100$		6,100$	
Mar	5,700$	400$			6,100$		6,100$	
Apr	5,700$	400$			6,100$		6,100$	
May	5,900$	400$			6,300$		6,300$	
Jun	5,900$	400$			6,300$		6,300$	

ASFFI-06

Top, center, and bottom right: The individual pay cards of Project Delta Roadrunners Recon Member Dinh Venh, Cpl. First Class Van Dinh Vinh, and Master Sgt. Dao Em are representative of the hundreds of Chinese Nung and other native special-warfare experts employed by Detachment B-52 during the war. The success of mounting special operations always hinged heavily on their remarkable bravery. Special Forces paid these indigenous fighters with secret funds and kept careful photographic records of recipients in an effort to reduce fraud. *(Author's Collection)* **Bottom left:** Project Delta Roadrunners with Staff Sgt. Paul V. Tracy stand in regular formation to guard their forward operating base after a 1966 mission. These troops were among the elite of the special-warfare personnel who undertook the most hazardous missions by posing as NVA/VC troops behind communist lines to reconnoiter the trails, streams, and roads between Viet Cong-controlled villages. *(Jason T. Woodworth)*

INDIVIDUAL EARNINGS RECORD
HỒ SƠ LỢI TỨC CÁ NHÂN

NAME OF EMPLOYEE: VAN DINH VINH	CAMP and TEAM DESIGNATION: DETACHMENT B-52		Type of Action: Road Runner	Grade: CPLI

Month Tháng	Base Pay Lương chính	Family Allow Phụ cấp gia-đình	High Cost of Living Phụ đất-đỏ	Language Allow Phụ cấp Sinh ngữ	Total Amt. Due Tổng cộng	Subsistence Deductions Trừ tiền ăn ở	Net Amt. Due Số tiền còn được lãnh	Remarks Bị chú
Sep	5,700$				5,700$		5,700$	
Oct	5,700$				5,700$		5,700$	
Nov	5,700$				5,700$		5,700$	
Dec	5,900$	400$			6,300$		6,300$	
Jan	2,350$	1,200$	1,350$	1,000$	5,900$		5,900$	

ASFFI-06

INDIVIDUAL EARNINGS RECORD
HỒ SƠ LỢI TỨC CÁ NHÂN

NAME OF EMPLOYEE: DAO EM	CAMP and TEAM DESIGNATION: DETACHMENT B-52		Type of Action: Road Runner Per	Grade: MSG

Month Tháng	Base Pay Lương chính	Family Allow Phụ cấp gia-đình	High Cost of Living Phụ đất-đỏ	Language Allow Phụ cấp Sinh ngữ	Total Amt. Due Tổng cộng	Subsistence Deductions Trừ tiền ăn ở	Net Amt. Due Số tiền còn được lãnh	Remarks Bị chú
Jul	6,300$				6,300$		6,300$	
Aug	6,300$				6,300$		6,300$	
Sep	6,300$				6,300$		6,300$	
Oct	6,300$				6,300$		6,300$	
Nov	6,300$				6,300$		6,300$	
Dec	6,300$				6,300$		6,300$	
Jan	1,900$		675$	500$	3,075$		3,075$	

ASFFI-06

Top: Special Forces Project Omega was a Corps-level special-reconnaissance unit controlled by Detachment B-50 and operated in response to directives from I Field Force, Vietnam. In addition to Western Highland activities, Project Omega also worked with the Navy to patrol specified zones along the central Vietnamese coast. Sometimes target areas were reconnoitered by traveling aboard innocuous cargo vessels, such as the landing craft and LSTs (Landing Ship, Tank) shown here. *(Charles Darnell)* **Center left and two bottom photos:** These three views show (top to bottom) the Project Omega parachute training area at Ban Me Thuot, a hastily prepared recoilless rifle position at a temporary Omega field location, and Omega elevated tent quarters located beside the fighting position. *(Charles Darnell)* **Center right:** Project Omega contained Roadrunner and reconnaissance teams, as well as three commando companies. Indigenous personnel were selected from Sedang, Jeh, and Rhade Montagnards, as well as Chinese Nungs. This Chinese shrine was maintained fervently by the Nungs on Project Omega. *(Charles Darnell)*

Top left: Detachment B-51 advised and assisted the Vietnamese *Lực-Lượng Đặc-Biệt* Training Center and parachute course at Dong Ba Thin, located five miles north of the major military port base at Cam Ranh Bay. Special Forces Sgt. Ernest A. Jensen watches 4th Mobile Strike Force Command airborne trainees as they jump through the Mock Aircraft Door during the last phase of ground training, preparatory to actual parachuting, in April 1969. *(Joseph Primeau)* **Top right:** A graduation ceremony for Vietnamese students who have completed parachutist training. *(John Borgman)* **Center:** This Special Forces instructor demonstrates a parachute landing fall from the Swing Landing Trainer to native airborne trainees. *(Joseph Primeau)* **Bottom:** Special Forces Sgt. Thomas A. Nelson, right, watches as a Vietnamese instructor helps a parachute candidate assume the proper position in the Mock Aircraft Door during the ground phase of airborne school. *(Joseph Primeau/USA)*

Top: Airborne training was part of advanced infantry training that Detachment B-51 sought to provide for all *Lúc-Lúong Dặc-Biệt* and specialized units under Special Forces command in Vietnam. Here, 3d Mobile Strike Force Command paratroopers, graduates of the Dong Ba Thin course, exit their C-123 aircraft during a routine proficiency jump over Saigon. *(USAF)* **Bottom:** Detachment B-51 Sgt. First Class Gilmer White checks the parachute harness of a soldier who is about to make his first jump during a basic airborne training course conducted for American personnel at Dong Ba Thin. *(Floyd Harrington)*

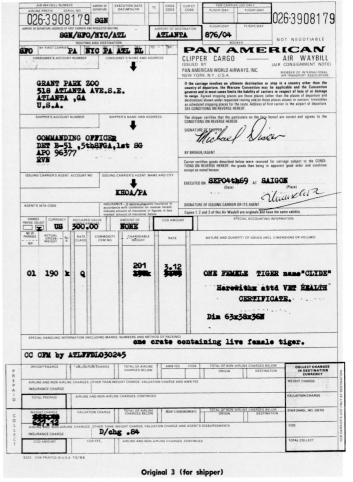

Top: Lt. Col. John Borgman's Detachment B-51 with tiger cub "Clyde" before she was shipped to the Grant Park Zoo in Atlanta, Georgia. *(John Borgman)*
Bottom left: Detachment B-51 fielded its own elite combat recon platoon that served as an Airborne Commando Demonstration unit for the LLDB and Special Forces in Vietnam. This parachutist-qualified, karate-trained unit was composed of experts in specialized unconventional-warfare tactics. *(John Borgman)*
Bottom right: Cargo manifest for tiger cub Clyde, "the first refugee from Vietnam to arrive in the United States—courtesy of Detachment B-51." *(Author's Collection)*

LÚC-LÚONG DĂC-BIỆT TRAINING CENTER

PHỤNG HOÀNG
yết thị

Tên họ. NGUYỄN-THUA
35 tuổi.

Nơi sinh: Xã Thượng-Hóa, Quận Nam-Hóa
Tỉnh Thừa-Thiên.

Chức vụ Việt-Cộng. Cán bộ Nông-Hội xã, hoạt động
tại xã Thượng-Hóa.

Anh Thua,

Anh không thể lẫn tránh mãi vì mọi người đều có thể nhận diện được anh. Sớm muộn gì anh cũng bị sa lưới pháp-luật. Hãy tỉnh-ngộ và quay về với Chính Nghĩa Quốc Gia. Chỉ có hồi chánh mới giúp anh thoát được tù tội, chết chóc.

Đồng bào nào biết được tin tức của Nguyễn-Thua hãy mật báo cho Cảnh Sát Quốc-Gia hoặc Uỷ-Ban Phụng Hoàng. Người cho tin được tưởng thưởng và tên tuổi sẽ được giữ Kín.

Uỷ Ban Phụng Hoàng Tỉnh Thừa Thiên.

P7-400W-70.

Top: Project Phoenix (Phung Hoang) was designed to destroy the Viet Cong infrastructure as part of the Accelerated Pacification Program of President Nguyen Van Thieu after the Tet-68 offensive. The Special Forces became involved in Phoenix Provincial Reconnaissance Unit operations by transferring personnel from the CIA-MACV Intelligence Coordination and Exploitation (ICEX) program. This Project Phoenix wanted poster targets Nguyen Thua, a suspected VC cadre member of the black-listed Thuong Hoa Village Farmers' Association, by warning: ''Mr. Thua, You can no longer hide since you have been identified. Sooner or later you will be trapped by law. Wake up to reality and rally to national just cause. Only the Hoi-Chanh way can keep you from imprisonment and death. Anyone who knows any information about this Viet Cong, report it to the National Police or Phung Hoang Committee. The informant will be well rewarded and his name will be kept confidential.'' *(Author's Collection)* **Bottom left:** Provincial Reconnaissance Unit soldiers paint warnings and pro-Saigon regime slogans after eliminating a VC cadre member in Hung Phat. *(Author's Collection)* **Bottom right:** A Provincial Reconnaissance Unit propaganda technician posts a general warning to Hung Phat village. These posters were deliberately posted to instill fear and suspicion, and they often divided village loyalties prior to actual Project Phoenix sweeps. *(Author's Collection)*

Top left: This Project Phoenix operations officer (center, wearing black uniform) of the MACV Civil Operations and Rural Development Support Territorial Security Directorate was one of many personnel loaned from Special Forces to the program because of their language and native expertise. He is shown at Vam Lam in Ninh Thuan Province. *(Author's Collection)*
Top right: An aircraft takes government agents to Nha Trang for coordination with Special Forces intelligence officers during a classified Project Phoenix mission. *(Author's Collection)* **Center left:** Project Phoenix officials at Phan Rang chart out a Provincial Reconnaissance Unit raid against a suspected Viet Cong residence in Minh Thuan Province. *(Author's Collection)*
Center right: A Project Phoenix wanted poster is nailed to a central tree by a Special Forces-led Provincial Reconnaissance Unit member. It offers a sizable cash reward for an identified communist party cell official—dead or alive. *(Author's Collection)* **Bottom:** A Project Phoenix case officer makes a last-minute check on his target map inside the Phung Hoang compound at Saigon. Orders for selective mission strikes were often sent to Special Forces, based on data gathered and analyzed here. *(Author's Collection)*

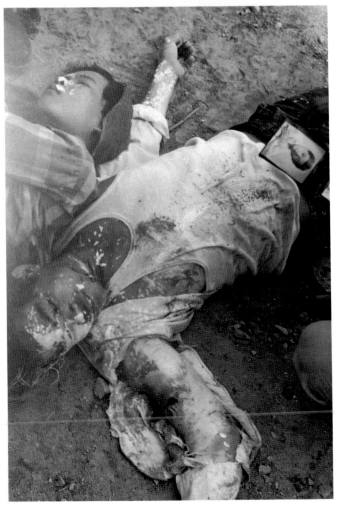

Top: Two members of a Project Phoenix Provincial Reconnaissance Unit patrol, wearing the black peasant attire of Revolutionary Development cadre, check a woman's belongings in Qui Thuan hamlet in northern Binh Dinh Province. A Special Forces Phoenix agent wearing a plain tropical uniform devoid of markings, headgear, or individual equipment, stands guard with his M16 rifle. *(Author's Collection)*
Bottom: Project Phoenix targeted this suspected Viet Cong cadre member, who was shot dead in the marketplace and unceremoniously photographed at the scene for ''evidence of elimination.'' A Phoenix target dossier including suspect photographs was used for convenience in identifying the body. The victim's bodyguard, also killed in the incident, lies beside his comrade. Project Phoenix was a very effective campaign, and after the war top communist officials testified to their fear of the program, because it wiped out many of their local bases in South Vietnam. *(Author's Collection)*

Top: Special Forces Project Sigma was a Corps-level special-reconnaissance unit controlled by Detachment B-56 and operated in response to directives from II Field Force, Vietnam. Project Sigma contained eight reconnaissance teams, three commando companies, and a camp defense company located at Ho Ngoc Tao, shown here, utilizing ethnic Cambodians and Chinese personnel. At the beginning of November 1967, Detachment B-56 assets were transferred to Project Daniel Boone and devoted to higher-level cross-border missions. *(Author's Collection)* **Bottom left:** Hand-to-hand combat instruction at Ho Ngoc Tao. *(James Donahue)* **Bottom right:** Carbine firing practice at Ho Ngoc Tao. *(James Donahue)*

Top left: Col. Harold R. Aaron decorates members of Project Rapid Fire, created under Provisional Detachment B-36, during its conversion to the 3d Mobile Strike Force Command at Long Hai in June 1968. Project Rapid Fire temporarily replaced Projects Omega and Sigma while the latter organizations were merged into MACV-SOG. Col. Aaron served as commander of the 5th Special Forces Group from June 1968 to May 1969. *(Author's Collection)* **Top right:** Project Gamma used some of the Army's most efficient military-intelligence personnel to collect information on enemy activities from border-surveillance camps near Cambodia. Capt. Allen B. Clark Jr., who later became Assistant Secretary for Veterans Liaison within the U.S. Department of Veterans Affairs, is seen here at an operational field outpost. *(Allen Clark Jr.)* **Center left:** Detachment B-57 Project Gamma was established by the 5th Special Forces Group as an ultra-secret intelligence operation that monitored North Vietnamese bases and infiltration into Cambodia, as well as Cambodian support to both the NVA and VC. *(Allen Clark)* **Center right:** Project Rapid Fire Sergeants First Class Bob Cole, Frank Hillman, and Ernest ''Duke'' Snider of Provisional Detachment B-36 during 1967. *(James Donahue)* **Bottom right:** Col. Robert B. Rheault, a dynamic and highly respected Special Forces officer, took command of the 5th Special Forces Group on May 29, 1969. *(USA)*

Top: As early as 1961 the Central Intelligence Agency retained one reinforced Special Forces A-Detachment at Thu Duc outside Saigon, which was dedicated to preparing cross-border expeditions in Laos and North Vietnam. This photograph shows the CIA's paramilitary branch training center at Thu Duc. *(Author's Collection)* **Bottom:** Detachment A-413 was sent to Thu Duc from Okinawa on temporary duty in April 1963 and opened a advanced training camp at Long Thanh. Detachment elements were also based at the Agency's deep-penetration site in Long Khanh Province. This photograph of A-413 includes team Master Sgt. Hardy Allen (extreme left) and team Capt. Clint Hayes (fifth from left). The Military Assistance Command, Vietnam, Studies & Observation Group (MACV-SOG) was established in January 1964 to continue the highly classified, unconventional-warfare activities of the CIA-sponsored Pacific Ocean project. MACV-SOG, composed in large part of Special Forces personnel, was the only theater-level strategic reconnaissance project deployed during the Vietnam conflict. *(George Houston/ Adam Dintenfass Collection)*

Top left: One of MACV-SOG's greatest unresolved legacies concerned the disappearance of special project operations officer Maj. Larry Thorne, whose helicopter was never found following transmissions over a patrol inserted inside Laos on October 18, 1965. One of the final photographs taken of Maj. Thorne at the Kham Duc launch site shows (left to right) Larry Thorne, with Model 1903 Springfield rifle; Maj. Emmons, launch site commander with M-2 carbine; Master Sgt. George Petry with Swedish ''K'' 9mm M-45 submachine gun; Vietnamese pilot Capt. Dinh; and a Vietnamese known as ''Cowboy,'' who was killed less than a year later. *(Charlie Norton)* **Top right:** MACV-SOG Capt. Michael Eiland and Master

Sgt. Dick Pegram. *(Michael Eiland)* **Bottom left:** Despite serious wounds, MACV-SOG reconnaissance patrol leader Staff Sgt. Franklin D. Miller repelled several attacks on his patrol in Laos on January 5, 1970, and he was later awarded the Medal of Honor in recognition of his valor. *(John Plaster)* **Bottom right:** Special Forces SOG team commander Master Sgt. Dick Warren makes final coordination with other U.S. team leaders, all armed with Swedish ''K'' 9mm M-45 submachine guns, as they prepare to launch into Laos during the fall of 1965. Capt. Dinh (waving to camera), commander of the Vietnamese 219th Squadron, will fly the raiding team across the border. *(Charlie Norton)*

Top left: Special Forces personnel were posted secretly to MACV-SOG under cover orders assigning them to the Special Operations Augmentation of the 5th Special Forces Group. Rich Hoffman of MACV-SOG Command and Control Center, one of the first Special Forces commandos to sport an earring, is seen here at the Dak Pek launch site. *(Jeff Harris)*

Top right: The success of MACV-SOG intelligence-gathering raids was exemplified by the capture of this North Vietnamese cook by Staff Sgt. Robert J. Graham and David Paul north of Svay Rieng, Cambodia, during 1970. The cook provided valuable information regarding NVA logistical arrangements. *(Robert Graham)* **Bottom:** MACV-SOG ground operations were conducted primarily by mobile-launch "Spike" Reconnaissance Teams, consisting of three Special Forces personnel and nine indigenous troops, backed up by SLAM (Search-Location-Annihilation Monitor or Mission) reaction companies. Recon Team Michigan patrols inside Laotian territory during 1968. *(Kenneth Bowra)*

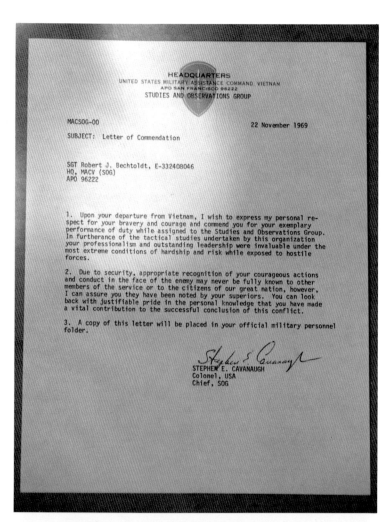

HEADQUARTERS
UNITED STATES MILITARY ASSISTANCE COMMAND, VIETNAM
APO SAN FRANCISCO 96222
STUDIES AND OBSERVATIONS GROUP

MACSOG-OO   22 November 1969

SUBJECT: Letter of Commendation

SGT Robert J. Bechtoldt, E-332408046
HQ, MACV (SOG)
APO 96222

1. Upon your departure from Vietnam, I wish to express my personal respect for your bravery and courage and commend you for your exemplary
performance of duty while assigned to the Studies and Observations Group.
In furtherance of the tactical studies undertaken by this organization
your professionalism and outstanding leadership were invaluable under the
most extreme conditions of hardship and risk while exposed to hostile
forces.

2. Due to security, appropriate recognition of your courageous actions
and conduct in the face of the enemy may never be fully known to other
members of the service or to the citizens of our great nation, however,
I can assure you they have been noted by your superiors. You can look
back with justifiable pride in the personal knowledge that you have made
a vital contribution to the successful conclusion of this conflict.

3. A copy of this letter will be placed in your official military personnel
folder.

                                    STEPHEN E. CAVANAUGH
                                    Colonel, USA
                                    Chief, SOG

Top left: Col. Stephen E. Cavanaugh took over command of MACV-SOG on August 3, 1968. He realized that the gallant deeds of his mobile-launch team members might go unrecognized because of security restrictions surrounding the secrecy of cross-border operations, so he issued personal letters of commendation to his troops. *(Robert Bechtoldt)* **Top right:** MACV-SOG Sgt. Robert J. Bechtoldt in his Vietnam barracks, flanked by the major leaders of both warring countries. *(Robert Bechtoldt)* **Bottom left:** Sgt. Bechtoldt of Recon Team Auger advances across a stream in the dense jungle of the ''Golf-80'' target area within the Cambodian ''Fishhook'' region. *(Robert Bechtoldt)* **Bottom right:** Staff Sgt. Robert J. Graham (right), armed with a modified grenade launcher, and his interpreter Na-Ku wear North Vietnamese pith helmets prior to conducting a MACV-SOG Command and Control South mission into Cambodia. The North Vietnamese helmets caused the enemy to hesitate during chance encounters with patrols long enough to allow split-second reaction and a burst of opening fire that often saved the entire team. *(Robert Graham)*

Top: MACV-SOG, which routinely staged operations outside South Vietnam to disrupt North Vietnamese, Viet Cong, Pathet Lao, and Khmer Rouge units inside their own territory, used a force that averaged 2,000 Americans, mostly Special Forces, and more than 8,000 hand-picked indigenous troops. The Ground Studies Group (SOG 35) included Army military intelligence, psychological operations, and approximately 70 mobile-launch Recon Teams, such as RT Louisiana gathered at the Quang Tri launch site in northern South Vietnam. Seen here are (top row, left to right) Sp4 Ken Van Arsdel, Sgt. David A. Maurer, and Sgt. David Badger. *(Jeffry Junkins)* **Bottom:** MACV-SOG Recon Team Hawaii, with Staff Sgt. John Plaster at center, trains in helicopter boarding procedures using a downed Huey converted into a practice platform at the Command and Control Center base at Kontum during 1970. Note the rappelling tower in the background. *(John Plaster)*

SPECIAL OPERATIONS

Top left: One of the Vietnamese CH-34 helicopters used by MACV-SOG lands in Vientam with battle damage sustained during a cross-border insertion. Vietnamese Capt. Tuong (center) flew numerous missions taking FOB-1 teams into the DMZ and neighboring countries. Known as an outstanding pilot who possessed unbounding courage, he had several helicopters shot out from under him and grins over shell hits taken while extracting Spike Team Idaho under fire. *(J. Stryker Meyer)* **Top right:** MACV-SOG Recon Team Pick demonstrates the individualized range of extraordinary weapons carried on some specialized raiding patrols. Seen (left to right) are team leader Staff Sgt. Robert J. Graham with longbow and quiver of arrows, Sgt. Mike Crimmings, Lt. Ash with M-79 grenade launcher, and Staff Sgt. Frank Oppel, who normally carried a trench knife and a silenced grease gun. *(Robert Graham)* **Bottom:** Staff Sergeants John Plaster (far left) and Glenn Vemura (far right), members of Sgt. Franklin Miller's Command and Control Center recon team, are shown under fire in Laos. *(John Plaster)*

Top left: Indigenous troops of Recon Team Nevada. *(Adam Dintenfass Collection)* **Top middle:** Recon Team Idaho being extracted by ladder hookup to a UH-1H during November 1971. *(Kenneth Bowra)* **Top right:** Sgt. Ken Quackenbush, the MACV-SOG launch site medic at Duc Co with Command and Control South, after a Bright Light team extraction of two Americans killed during a border crossing patrol. One Montagnard of the Bright Light team was killed during the extraction mission. Heavy automatic weapons ammunition expenditures in sudden firefights with superior numbers of enemy troops forced SOG members to utilize special ammunition rigs, such as this BAR belt that could hold 24 magazines. *(Ken Quackenbush)* **Bottom left:** MACV-SOG Sgt. Ed Wolcoff wore World War II-era combat leggings that stopped leeches from entering clothing above the boot but also caused fellow Americans to mistake team members at the Dak Pak launch site for Special Air Service personnel of Australian or New Zealand origin. *(Ray Harris)* **Bottom right:** The MACV-SOG Leghorn radio-relay point on a Laotian mountain summit within the dangerous tri-border region was steadfastly maintained throughout the war, despite continual North Vietnamese regimental attempts to overrun the vital communications site. *(Clyde Sincere Jr.)*

SPECIAL OPERATIONS

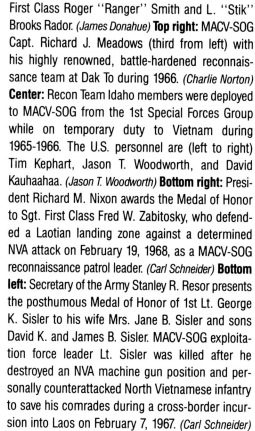

Top left: Recon Team Hawaii members Sergeants First Class Roger "Ranger" Smith and L. "Stik" Brooks Rador. *(James Donahue)* **Top right:** MACV-SOG Capt. Richard J. Meadows (third from left) with his highly renowned, battle-hardened reconnaissance team at Dak To during 1966. *(Charlie Norton)* **Center:** Recon Team Idaho members were deployed to MACV-SOG from the 1st Special Forces Group while on temporary duty to Vietnam during 1965-1966. The U.S. personnel are (left to right) Tim Kephart, Jason T. Woodworth, and David Kauhaahaa. *(Jason T. Woodworth)* **Bottom right:** President Richard M. Nixon awards the Medal of Honor to Sgt. First Class Fred W. Zabitosky, who defended a Laotian landing zone against a determined NVA attack on February 19, 1968, as a MACV-SOG reconnaissance patrol leader. *(Carl Schneider)* **Bottom left:** Secretary of the Army Stanley R. Resor presents the posthumous Medal of Honor of 1st Lt. George K. Sisler to his wife Mrs. Jane B. Sisler and sons David K. and James B. Sisler. MACV-SOG exploitation force leader Lt. Sisler was killed after he destroyed an NVA machine gun position and personally counterattacked North Vietnamese infantry to save his comrades during a cross-border incursion into Laos on February 7, 1967. *(Carl Schneider)*

Top: The alleged Special Forces disposal of a double-agent, Thai Khac Chuyen—whose turncoat activities during Project Gamma threatened several hundred lives—received widespread attention when MACV commander Gen. Creighton W. Abrams Jr. insisted on arresting and charging 5th Special Forces Group personnel with ''premeditated execution of a Vietnamese national.'' Unable to produce any evidence, Army Secretary Stanley Resor ordered all charges dropped. Celebrating this decision at Long Binh are (left to right) II Field Force Vietnam chief defense counsel Capt. John Stevens Berry; Chief-of-counter-intelligence Capt. Leland J. Brumley; Intelligence Chief Maj. Thomas C. Middleton; and B-57 team leader Capt. Robert F. Marasco. *(Wide World)* **Center:** This high-level July 1969 Saigon conference included (left to right) Joint Chiefs of Staff chairman Earle G. Wheeler, MACV commander Gen. Abrams, and Pacific Command Adm. John S. McCain, all conventional line officers who opposed the CIDG concept and sought to remove the 5th Special Forces Group from Vietnam, because they failed to comprehend the guerrilla nature of the war. *(Dwight Carter/DOD)* **Bottom left:** The general American public perception of the Green Beret murder case. *(Herblock/Washington Post)* **Bottom right:** Col. Alexander Lemberes was selected by Gen. Abrams to lead Special Forces, but he was replaced just a month after assuming command. *(USA)*

"I'll Fight My Way Out Of This! Where Am I? Who Turned Out The Lights?"

THE GREEN BERET CASE

PENTAGON

©1969 HERBLOCK

COPYRIGHT © 1969 BY HERBLOCK IN *THE WASHINGTON POST.*

THE DOUBLE AGENT MURDER CASE

COMPANY IDENTIFICATION Combat Recon Platoon 1

PAYROLL FOR PERSONAL SERVICE Số lương nhân công. CIDG Payroll	DO VOU Nr # Biên lai DO số 901	AGENT VOU Nr # Biên lai phát ngân số	PAGE Trang OF Trong số trang

DETACHMENT Nr. AND LOCATION Số phân-đội và địa điểm A-108 Minh Long Camp	PERIOD OF PAYROLL (FROM – TO) Kỳ lương từ 1 Jun đến 30 Jun PAYROLL Nr.

Pursuant to authority vested in me, I certify that within payroll in _____
pages is correct and proper for Payment and approve payment for 1 3 4 ,4 3 0 vn
Chiếu theo quyền hạn dành cho tôi, tôi chứng thực rằng trong bản lương gồm có
trang là đúng, số tiền trả là chính đáng và chấp thuận số tiền trả là _____

PAID BY :
Tiền trả bởi :

SIGNATURE (SIGN ORIGINAL ONLY)chỉ ký bản-chánh thôi
Ký tên
JAMES V. KENNEDY, 1st/Lt Inf

FINANCE OFFICER
CIDG FINANCE OFFICE
5th SFGA
APO 96240

DATE Ngày tháng 30 June 68	OFFICIAL TITLE Chức vụ Agent Funds Officer	(FOR USE OF FIN OFF)

I have Paid the ___54___
personnel listed on the attached payroll.
Tôi đã trả lương những nhân viên liệt kê trong bảng lương
kèm theo đây

I certify that I have witnessed the payment
and signatures (or fingerprints) of all personnel
listed on attached payroll
Tôi thực rằng tôi đã chứng kiến việc trả lương
và chữ ký ký nhận (hay điểm chỉ) của tất cả nhân viên trong
bảng lương đính kèm theo đây

SIGNATURE (SIGN ORIGINAL ONLY)chỉ ký bản chánh Chữ ký	SIGNATURE Chữ ký
JAMES V. KENNEDY,1st/1t Inf	Trung-úy NGC-Trung-Hồ

DATE Ngày, tháng 30Jun68	OFFICIAL TITLE Chức vụ Agent Funds Officer	DATE Ngày tháng 30Jun68	OFFICIAL TITLE Chức vụ LLDB Paying Officer

PAYROLL SUMMARY (Bảng chiết tính lương)

1. Base Pay (Lương chính)	69,100 vn
2. Family Allowance (Phụ cấp gia đình)	48,300 '
3. High Cost of Living	31,000 '
4. Miscellaneous (Identify) Linh tinh (liệt kê) Incentive pay	15,750 '
GROSS PAYMENTS (Tổng số tiền trả)	164,430 vn
DEDUCTIONS (Trừ)	
1. Subsistence (Ăn ở)	
2. Miscellaneous (Identify) Linh tinh (liệt kê)	
NET PAYMENTS (Số tiền thực lãnh)	164,430 vn

COSTING	TITLE RECAPITULATION (Tóm tắt các khoản)	AMOUNT (Số tiền)
901	STRIKE FORCE SALARIES Lương dân sự chiến đấu	164,430 vn
902	SUBSISTENCE COSTS Tiền ăn ở	
903	ADM SALARIES, AND LABOR COSTS Tiền quản trị và nhân công	
	OTHER (SPECIFY)	

REMARKS : Nr. OF STRIKE FORCE PERSONNEL 54
Chú ý   Số nhân viên Dân Sự chiến đấu
OTHER
Các khoản khác

: 1

ASFFI - 6
REVISED 10 JUL 1966

AGENT OFFICERS COPY

RECEIPT FOR CASH — SUB - VOUCHER
Biên lai nhận tiền — Biên lai phụ
(TO BE USED WHEN INVOICE IS NOT AVAILABLE)
(Chỉ dùng khi không có hóa đơn)

Vou. Nr # 398
Biên lai số
Date 20 JUN
Ngày tháng

RECEIVED IN CASH FROM Lt DANIEL F. VAN GUND
Nhận tiền mặt do
21,250 $ VN FOR THE FOLLOWING :
về khoản sau đây :

JAMES E. ROSE
Capt   FC
CIDG   Fin Off
SFGA
APO 96240

QUANTITY Số lượng	ARTICLES OR SERVICES Phẩm vật hoặc công việc	Unit price Giá đơn vị	AMOUNT Số tiền
46	CHICKENS (LIVE)	GENERAL	15,850 #VN
8	DUCKS (LIVE)	GENERAL	2,400
1	PIG (LIVE)		3,000
	The above items bough from farmer, no unit price costum of VN Farmer.		
	TOTAL (cộng)		21,250 #VN

VENDOR LE VAN LOC
Người bán   (Printed Name) (Tên Bằng Chữ In)   (Signature) (Ký Tên)
ADDRESS MINH TAM, MINH LONG
Địa chỉ

COST CODE DATA
Dữ kiện về vật giá
902

I HEREBY CERTIFY THAT A RECEIPT WAS NOT OBTAINABLE AND FUNDS IN THE AMOUNT OF 21,250 #VN
WERE EXPENDED FOR THE PURPOSE STATED ABOVE
398
SIGNATURE OF WITNESSING OFFICER   SIGNATURE OF PAYING OFFICER

Top left: The Special Forces employed a flexible and militarily unorthodox funding system to support its activities in Vietnam. Local purchases were authorized at all levels, using cash from current operating funds, and formal accountability was covered by a system of internal cost codes. Illustrated here is the summary page of the personnel payroll for Camp Minh Long, charged to Cash Code 901: Strike Force Pay and Allowances. *(Author's Collection)* **Top right:** Camp strike force individual identification card. *(Author's Collection)* **Center right:** Cash receipt for foodstuffs used by Camp Minh Long. *(Author's Collection)* **Bottom:** Capt. Lief Kjonnerod (right) counts out money as Camp Ben Het CIDG troops sign the personnel payroll during pay call administered by Detachment A-244. Those who could not sign their names on the form placed their thumbprint in the required space. *(Gilley/USA)*

Top: The Special Forces purchased food items but often encouraged the LLDB to dispense these products to the local communities in an effort to generate goodwill toward the central government. *(Thomas Myerchin)* **Bottom left:** Disbursements by field detachments were categorized by use of accounting or cost-code numbers. A 900-series of accounts was provided for identifying the various types of expenditures. Subsistence expenditures were charged to Cost Code 902, like this periodic invoice for general subsistence supplies at Camp Gia Vuc. *(Author's Collection)* **Bottom right:** A death gratuity settlement paid to the wife of a CIDG master sergeant killed when Camp Lang Vei was overrun by North Vietnamese Army tanks on February 6-7, 1968. Special Forces death gratuities for native dependents were charged exclusively to Cost Code 911. *(Author's Collection)*

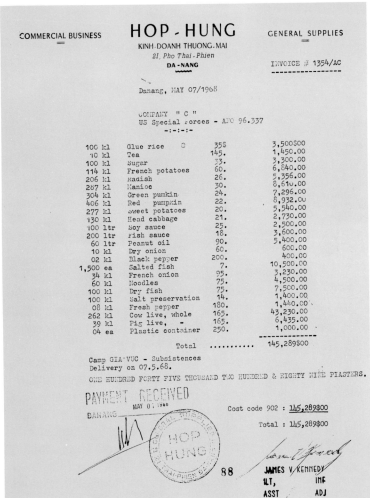

COMMERCIAL BUSINESS

HOP - HUNG

GENERAL SUPPLIES

KINH-DOANH THUONG-MAI
21, Pho Thai-Phien
DA-NANG

INVOICE # 1354/AC

Danang, MAY 07/1968

COMPANY " C "
US Special Forces - APO 96.337

100 kl	Glue rice	35$	3,500$00
10 kl	Tea	145.	1,450.00
100 kl	Sugar	33.	3,300.00
114 kl	French potatoes	60.	6,840.00
206 kl	Radish	26.	5,356.00
287 kl	Manioc	30.	8,610.00
304 kl	Green pumkin	24.	7,296.00
406 kl	Red pumpkin	22.	8,932.00
277 kl	Sweet potatoes	20.	5,540.00
130 kl	Head cabbage	21.	2,730.00
100 ltr	Soy sauce	25.	2,500.00
200 ltr	Fish sauce	18.	3,600.00
60 ltr	Peanut oil	90.	5,400.00
10 kl	Dry onion	60.	600.00
02 kl	Black pepper	200.	400.00
1,500 ea	Salted fish	7.	10,500.00
34 kl	French onion	95.	3,230.00
60 kl	Noodles	75.	4,500.00
100 kl	Dry fish	75.	7,500.00
100 kl	Salt preservation	14.	1,400.00
08 kl	Fresh pepper	180.	1,440.00
262 kl	Cow live, whole	165.	43,230.00
39 kl	Pig live, -	165.	6,435.00
04 ea	Plastic container	250.	1,000.00

	Total	....	145,289$00

Camp GIA-VUC - Subsistences
Delivery on 07.5.68.
ONE HUNDRED FORTY FIVE THOUSAND TWO HUNDRED & EIGHTY NINE PIASTERS.

PAYMENT RECEIVED
DANANG MAY 07 1968

Cost code 902 : 145,289$00

Total : 145,289$00

88

JAMES V. KENNEDY
1LT, INF
ASST ADJ

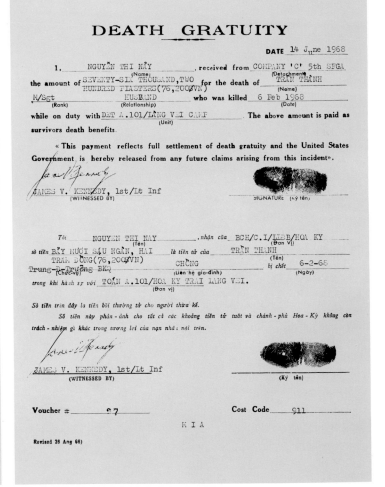

DEATH GRATUITY

DATE 14 June 1968

1. NGUYEN THI NAY , received from COMPANY 'C' 5th SFGA
(Name)   (Detachment)
the amount of SEVENTY-SIX THOUSAND, TWO for the death of TRAN THANH
HUNDRED PIASTERS (76,200/VN)   (Name)
M/Sgt   HUSBAND   who was killed 6 Feb 1968
(Rank)   (Relationship)   (Date)
while on duty with DET A.101/LANG VEI CAMP . The above amount is paid as
(Unit)
survivors death benefits.

« This payment reflects full settlement of death gratuity and the United States Government, is hereby released from any future claims arising from this incident».

JAMES V. KENNEDY, 1st/Lt Inf
(WITNESSED BY)

SIGNATURE (ký tên)

Tôi NGUYEN THI NAY , nhận của BCH/C.I/LLBB/HOA KY
(Tên)   (Đơn vị)
số tiền BẢY MƯƠI SÁU NGÀN, HAI là tiền tử của TRAN THANH
TRAM ĐỒNG (76,200/VN)   CHỒNG   bị chết 6-2-68
Trung-Sĩ Trưởng BK,   (Liên hệ gia-đình)   (Ngày)
(Chức-vụ)
trong khi hành sự với TOÁN A.101/HOA KY TRAI LANG VEI.
(Đơn vị)

Số tiền trên đây là tiền bồi thường tử cho người thừa kế.

Số tiền này phản-ảnh cho tất cả các khoảng tiền tử tuất và chánh-phủ Hoa-Kỳ không còn trách - nhiệm gì khác trong tương lai của nạn nhân nói trên.

JAMES V. KENNEDY, 1st/Lt Inf
(WITNESSED BY)

(Ký tên)

Voucher #_____ 27

Cost Code_____ 911

M I A

Revised 26 Aug 66)

Top left: Cash rewards for captured weapons were covered by Cost Code 915: Equipment Capture Bonuses. The offering of financial incentives cancelled CIDG reluctance to attack enemy positions. Special Forces cost codes were cleverly distributed to cover everything from 906 Camp Construction to 916 Heroic Action and Camp Celebrations. *(Author's Collection)* **Center right:** Special Forces weapons-reward stationery was issued nine per sheet on light green paper. More than 500,000 sheets were printed in this series on October 16, 1968, by Special Forces psychological operations personnel at Saigon. *(Author's Collection)* **Bottom:** A CIDG native looks forward to a hefty reward as he brings a captured communist RPD squad automatic weapon, in this case a Chinese 7.62mm Type 56 light machine gun, from the field. *(USA)*

Top: Air Force tactical air support, like this F-100 of the 31st Tactical Fighter Wing over the Central Highlands, continued to be a vital source of firepower for Special Forces operations. *(USAF)*
Bottom: The precision targeting ability of the A-1E Skyraider provided Special Forces with essential aerial support throughout the war. This Skyraider of the 633d Special Operations Wing releases a 500-pound bomb near a Special Forces element fighting in the Western Highlands during November 1968. *(USAF)*

AERIAL SUPPORT

Top left: South Vietnamese H-34 helicopter pilot Capt. Phan Van Tuan and co-pilot Tran Van Phen of the Vietnamese 74th Wing prepare to fly across the Cambodian border on an emergency mission to extract a MACV-SOG team during January 1969. *(James Polner)* **Top right:** Vietnamese H-34 helicopters return to base after placing a MACV-SOG hatchet platoon across the Vietnamese border in December 1968. They pass over a downed Huey helicopter being salvaged by crane-assisted retrieval personnel near the forward launch site. *(USAF)* **Center left and bottom left:** A North Vietnamese Army convoy, attempting to resupply enemy troops after the Tet-68 campaign, was spotted in Laos by a MACV-SOG patrol that promptly called for Air Force support. The resulting bombing sortie is shown here, demonstrating the close working relationship forged by Special Forces and Air Force during the war. *(USAF)* **Center right:** During 1969 the O-2 Super Skymaster forward air control aircraft (left) replaced the O-1 Bird Dog (right) at the task of providing support for many Special Forces long-range patrols. In this rare photograph both aircraft types fire rockets in support of a Special Forces patrol engaged on a jungle hillside in the tri-border region. *(Donald Dirksing)*

Top left: A South Vietnamese O-1 Bird Dog, shot down over Laos while supporting a MACV-SOG mission, is lifted from its crash site by a Vietnamese 41st Wing H-34 helicopter during March 1968. The small pilot chute on the tail of the Bird Dog helped to prevent oscillation. *(USAF)* **Top right:** Air Force Capt. Lee R. Cook, the navigator of an AC-47 Spooky at Bien Hoa Air Base, checks the three MXU-470 7.62mm miniguns preparatory to a night mission. Air Force gunships provided critical ordnance and illumination assistance to isolated Special Forces camps throughout the Vietnam conflict. *(USAF)* **Bottom left:** An AC-119K Stinger of the 18th Special Operations Squadron at Phan Rang Air Base, armed with four 7.62mm miniguns and two 20mm cannons, provided armed reconnaissance and interdiction firepower in response to Special Forces target requests. *(USAF)* **Bottom right:** An Air Force AC-47 Spooky of the 14th Air Commando Squadron fires rapid volleys at the rate of 6,000 rounds per minute in support of a beleaguered border Special Forces camp within II Corps Tactical Zone. *(USAF)*

Top left: The mortar served as the primary Special Forces "artillery" in Vietnam. This 81mm M1 mortar crew includes Sgt. First Class Philip Kramer (left) and Sgt. Thomas E. Miles (kneeling) with Air Force security police troops on Hon Tre Island in 1969. *(USAF)*
Top right: An 81mm M29 mortar on an M23A1 mount at Camp Buon Mi Ga in January 1965, typical of early-war emplacements. *(Jack Abraham)* **Center:** A 4.2-inch M30 mortar blasts enemy positions close to Camp Bu Prang during July 1968. *(Hector Robertin/USA)* **Bottom left and bottom right:** Many camps featured unusual weapons systems devised by team members. Camp Plateau Gi demolitions supervisor Staff Sgt. Jackson built this rocket launcher nicknamed "Little Sure Shot," which utilized 2.75-inch aviation rockets and was mounted on the perimeter wall, complete with wiring system. *(Author's Collection)*

Left, top to bottom: (1) A 57mm M18 recoilless rifle being shoulder-fired by CIDG troops attacking Viet Cong bunkers. *(Author's Collection)* (2) 7.62mm M60 machine guns rarely reached Special Forces, but some were employed in camp bunkers. Note the weapons lubricant nearby. *(Author's Collection)* (3) Quad Browning .30-cal. machine guns occupied key defensive positions in some early camps and made use of the Army T165 multiple machine gun mount. *(Author's Collection)* **Right, top to bottom:** (1) A Browning Automatic Rifle at Camp Ban Don. *(USA)* (2) A Browning .30-cal. M1919 machine gun at Camp Ban Don, used extensively for Special Forces position defense. *(USA)* (3) CAR-15 submachine guns often became ''personalized'' within MACV-SOG. Note the Montagnard luck bracelet doubling as a strap-holder, green anti-dirt tape over the ejector port, improvised foregrip on the forward hand guard, Chu Van ''swastika'' of Vietnamese Buddhist faith, and the 30-round magazine, hit by enemy fire in Laos. *(Robert Graham)* (4) The M2 .50-cal. machine gun was a Special Forces favorite due to its reliability and operational simplicity, seen here at Camp Bu Dop. *(Frank Sullivan III/USA)*

Left, top to bottom: (1) The M16 standard Special Forces rifle in use at Vietnam. *(Dennis Connell/USA)* (2) An AN/PAS-8 aiming light on the M16 rifle, combined with head-mounted SU50 night vision goggles, used by MACV-SOG and 46th Special Forces Company nocturnal operations during 1971 and 1972. *(Author's Collection)* (3) The XM177E2 5.56mm submachine gun, or CAR-15, had a shortened barrel, telescoping stock, stronger flash-hider, and revised hand guard. Field-tested by 5th Special Forces Group from November 1966 to August 1967, it was issued to long-range reconnaissance patrols. *(USA)* (4) An M16A1 rifle with noise suppressor. *(USA)* **Right, top to bottom:** (1) An M16A1 special-missions rifle with silencing, recoil, and flash suppressor devices. *(Bob Bechtoldt)* (2) The Light Antitank Weapon (LAW), a 66mm M72 high-explosive weapon, failed to function properly against tanks during the battle for Camp Lang Vei, but it still proved useful in eliminating enemy bunkers. *(Army News Features)*

Left, top to bottom: (1) This lightweight .30-cal. carbine, favored by CIDG troops, is fired by Staff Sgt. Harold Dreblow at Camp Buon Mi Ga in February 1965. *(Jack Abraham)* (2) The Night Vision Sight Subassembly PVS-2A "Starlight Scope" amplified low-light levels during the night and was either hand-held or mounted on small weapons. *(Eric R. Schmiedlin/USA)* **Right, top to bottom:** (1) During 1964 the 5.56mm M16 rifle was authorized as the standard rifle in Special Forces organizations. Here, Capt. Edwin Rybat leads a CIDG force in the Iron Triangle on November 12, 1964. *(Al Chang/USA)* (2) The M79 40mm grenade launcher was a reliable, compact weapon covering the area between the reach of a hand grenade and the range of a mortar. *(Dennis Connell/USA)* (3) The Soviet-designed Kalashnikov AK-47 assault rifle was widely used by North Vietnamese and Viet Cong infantry and was sometimes employed by Special Forces, such as this MACV-SOG recon member during a sterile weapons mission. *(Army News Features)*

300

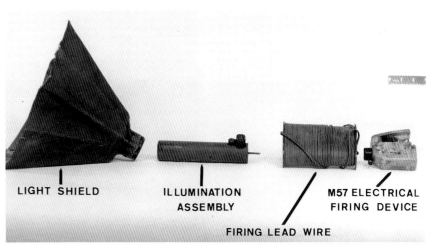

LIGHT SHIELD   **ILLUMINATION ASSEMBLY**   **M57 ELECTRICAL FIRING DEVICE**

FIRING LEAD WIRE

Left, top to bottom: (1) The Ek Commando-type, double-edged fighting knife; (2) a rare variant of the World War II British Fairbairn-Sykes fighting knife without blackened blade; (3) a SOG Bowie etched with the Special Forces insignia and 5th SFG logo; (4) the V42 Stiletto "Force Knife" depicted on the Special Forces crest; (5) mint-condition SOG Bowies with bright hilt mounts; and (6) a SOG Bowie shown as originally issued with rust-protective wax paper over the blade. *(All knives, Robert Buerlein/American Historical Foundation)* **Right, top to bottom:** (1) The disposable Pyrotechnic Ambush Light illuminated the kill zone with two M127A1 white star candles arranged to burn sequentially. *(Robert Buerlein/American Historical Foundation)* (2) Electroplate Cell-Timing Devices, used for arming and disarming mines emplaced around Special Forces protected villages, were ten-day devices with alternating 8-hour "on" and 16-hour "off" cycles. *(USA)*

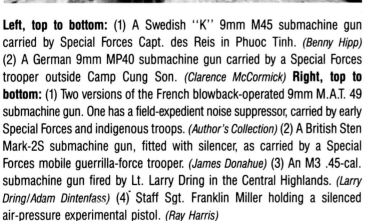

Left, top to bottom: (1) A Swedish "K" 9mm M45 submachine gun carried by Special Forces Capt. des Reis in Phuoc Tinh. *(Benny Hipp)* (2) A German 9mm MP40 submachine gun carried by a Special Forces trooper outside Camp Cung Son. *(Clarence McCormick)* **Right, top to bottom:** (1) Two versions of the French blowback-operated 9mm M.A.T. 49 submachine gun. One has a field-expedient noise suppressor, carried by early Special Forces and indigenous troops. *(Author's Collection)* (2) A British Sten Mark-2S submachine gun, fitted with silencer, as carried by a Special Forces mobile guerrilla-force trooper. *(James Donahue)* (3) An M3 .45-cal. submachine gun fired by Lt. Larry Dring in the Central Highlands. *(Larry Dring/Adam Dintenfass)* (4) Staff Sgt. Franklin Miller holding a silenced air-pressure experimental pistol. *(Ray Harris)*

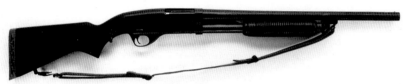

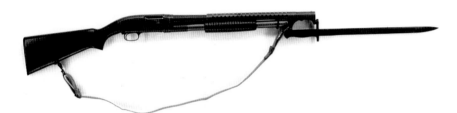

Left, top to bottom: (1) An XM21 sniper rifle with bipod and noise suppressor, often used by Special Forces marksmen along a camp's outer wall to eliminate enemy snipers. *(USA)* (2) The Stevens Model 77E riot-type shotgun, the most common military shotgun in Southeast Asia, was issued in large quantities to CIDG forces. Its short buttstock and the factory-fitted recoil pad reflect its intended use by indigenous personnel. *(Eric Archer)* (3) A World War II-vintage Winchester Model 12 riot-type shotgun rebuilt at Rock Island Arsenal to the ''trench gun'' configuration and fitted with an M1917-style Enfield bayonet for Special Forces use in Vietnam. *(Eric Archer)* (4) An XM21 sniper rifle with range-finder scope used by a Special Forces sharpshooter practicing in camp for a night patrol. *(Author's Collection)* **Top right:** Special Forces sidearms included a diverse mix of specialized military and commercial pistols. The AN-M8 pyrotechnic pistol was a signalling device that fired flares, especially for aircraft when Special Forces teams could not gain radio contact. *(Lynn Ligon)*

Top: The PRC-25 and PRC-77 series of FM radios were widely used by Special Forces. Externally they were very similar, but the PRC-77 was greatly improved by its completely solid-state design and more reliable performance with less power. *(James Donahue)* **Bottom left:** PRC-74 radio set with Special Forces-developed nickel-cadmium battery case (left) and an original factory-manufactured dry-battery pack (right) that required 70 BA-30 batteries. In the event that some batteries went bad, all 70 had to be changed, because there was no time to test individual batteries under combat conditions. *(DOD)* **Bottom middle:** The Canadian-produced PRC-66 portable transceiver provided an AM communications mode between aircraft and Special Forces ground elements during the mid-war period, 1967 to 1968. The rechargeable battery package used nickel-cadmium cells, and the alternate "throw-away" battery package used alkaline cells. *(DOD)* **Bottom right:** A lightweight PRC-70 man-portable and vehicular combination transceiver tested during 1967. It provided a single common set for a combat patrol using both internal FM control and long-range AM or single-sideband for base-camp communication. *(DOD)*

Top: The Air Force multichannel survival radio was often carried by Special Forces long-range patrols to contact reconnaissance aircraft, provide spot reports, and relay emergency-extraction instructions. *(USAF)* **Center:** The PRC-74 single-sideband radio was used by Special Forces patrols operating beyond the range of portable radios issued to regular troops. In October 1966 the nickel-cadmium battery case was introduced by Special Forces to increase the radio's utility. *(Richard Nieland/USA)* **Bottom left:** Introduced in 1968, the Beacon System used by Special Forces long-range patrols determined a patrol's position for precise fire support. The Patrol Station Assembly, shown here, used a low radar frequency to penetrate through heavy foliage and communicate with two other base stations to determine ranging. *(DOD)* **Bottom right:** Communications chiefs of the 5th Special Forces Group with signal officer Maj. Bowles at Nha Trang in February 1970. These high-ranking sergeants were responsible for the vital field-communications link between far-flung elements of the Special Forces empire in Vietnam. *(5th SFG PIO)*

SPECIAL FORCES COMMUNICATIONS

Top left: Special Forces used the McGuire extraction rig to lift patrol members from difficult terrain or situations that prevented helicopter landing. The rig's limitations are evident in this training photograph. Personnel had to be seated in the harness and use both hands during extraction, a situation that prohibited easy retrieval of wounded troops or soldiers who needed to use their weapons for return fire. *(Author's Collection)* **Top right:** The improved Stabo extraction harness allowed both hands to remain free, as demonstrated by Sergeants First Class Walter Hawley, Agostine Chiarielio, and Clifford Roberts at Nha Trang during 1968. *(5th SFG PIO)* **Bottom left:** The Stabo rig, modeled by a Special Forces Recondo School instructor, shows the carabineer attachment to the lift rope, normally extended from a helicopter hovering overhead. *(Author's Collection)* **Bottom right:** A Project Delta recon sergeant wears the Stabo extraction harness and stands behind a display of lowering lines and helicopter ladders used for extractions in 1969. *(Author's Collection)*

EQUIPMENT OF SPECIAL FORCES

Top: The Special Forces employed indigenous women in a wide variety of duty positions during the Vietnam war. Although female personnel were restricted primarily to the nursing and medical fields, all were potential combatants in forward Special Forces camps and received the same weapons drill as other civilian base workers. *(Author's Collection)* **Bottom:** This female combat interpreter-translator of Project Delta was a graduate of the Combat Interpreters Course in October 1969. Project Delta employed a number of female personnel in forward locations, many of whom were parachute qualified. *(Author's Collection)*

"CIDG girl" — **Band!**

INDIVIDUAL EARNINGS RECORD
HỒ SƠ LỢI TỨC CÁ NHÂN

NAME OF EMPLOYEE / Tên nhân viên: Đàn. Thang
NUMBER : SS
CAMP and TEAM DESIGNATION / Trại và số Phân-đội: A.502
DOB:

Month / Tháng	Base Pay / Lương chính	Far / Phụ		Language Allow Phụ cấp Sinh ngữ	Total Amt. Due / Tổng cộng	Subsistence Deductions / Trừ tiền ăn ở	Net Amt. Due / Số tiền còn được lãnh	Remarks / Bị chú
Aug	2200	1600	1850		5150		5750	A.ltc
09	2200	1600	1350		5150		5150	
10	2200	1600	1350		5150		5750	
11	2200	1600	1350		5150		5150	b.
12	2200	1600	1350		5150		5150	
Jan	2350	1600	1350		5300		5300	
Feb	Bonus						20000	
03	2350	1600	1350		5300		5300	

ASFF1-66

Singer in camp

INDIVIDUAL EARNINGS RECORD
HỒ SƠ LỢI TỨC CÁ NHÂN

NAME OF EMPLOYEE / Tên nhân viên: Hồ thị Dân-Ngọc
NUMBER : SS
CAMP and TEAM DESIGNATION / Trại và số Phân-đội: Trung Dung Det-A-502

Month / Tháng	Base Pay / Lương chính	Phụ cấp gia-đình	Phụ đất đô	Language Allow Phụ cấp Sinh ngữ	Total Amt. Due / Tổng cộng	Subsistence Deductions / Trừ tiền ăn ở	Net Amt. Due / Số tiền còn được lãnh	Remarks / Bị chú
July	1800	250	800		2850	300	2550	
08	1800	250	800		2850	300	2550	
09	1600	500	750		2850	300	2550	
10	1600	500	750		2850	300	2550	
11	1600	500	750		2850	300	2550	
12	1600	500	750		2850	300	2550	
13	1800	700	800		3300	300	3000	
Jan	2200	700	800		3700	300	3100	
Feb	1950	700	800		3400		3400	

ASFF1-66

Top left: This Vietnamese girl was killed during Tet-68 by Viet Cong cadre entering Kontum with "lists" of those who had befriended American Special Forces. *(Roger Pierson)* **Top right:** Identified by the Viet Cong as "female agents and mistresses of Special Forces," these young girls were executed by enemy raiders at Suoi Chan on April 16, 1967, before Detachment B-31 could recapture the Long Khanh Province hamlet. The National Liberation Front imposed automatic death sentences for collaboration between Vietnamese women and American Special Forces. *(Author's Collection)* **Center left:** LLDB commander Gen. Quan and Col. Ladd talk to one of the CIDG female parachute graduates at the Detachment B-51 Airborne Course in Dong Ba Thin during October 1967. *(John Borgman)* **Center right:** 2d Mobile Strike Force Command Staff Sgt. Stephen L. Putthoff and Capt. Bill Albracht relax after a field operation in the Central Highlands with women realistically identified by Sgt. Putthoff as, "Local VC?" *(Stephen Putthoff)* **Bottom right photos:** The individual earning records of female personnel hired as political-warfare agents by Special Forces Detachment A-502, 5th Mobile Strike Force Command. They were paid directly by American funds. Note their cover designations as "CIDG Girl of the Band" or "Singer in Camp" *(Author's Collection)*

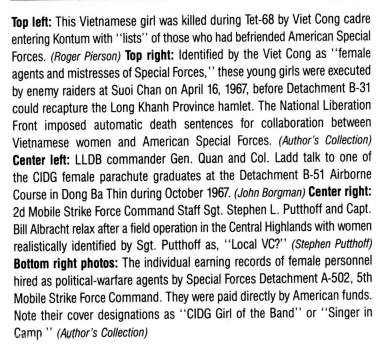

Top: The 5th Special Forces Group headquarters at Nha Trang was also responsible for installation protection, and it maintained an array of outposts to give advance warning of enemy proximity to the main base. These were set up from west to east at Nui Thi, Suoi Dau, Trung Dung, Kinh Trung, Thuy Tu, Dong Bo, Binh Tan, Tuong Phat, and Nui Chut. The heightened conventional defense arrangements of the late-war period are typified by this V-100 security vehicle parked outside the group command building. *(Author's Collection)* **Center:** The communications complex at the Nha Trang Defense Installation command bunker, a massive fort structure that discouraged direct enemy attack on the coastal port city. *(Author's Collection)* **Bottom left:** Detachment A-502, responsible for a string of defensive sites around the Nha Trang base, continually conducted sweep operations to occupy key terrain and block enemy infiltration. *(Chris Shelly)* **Bottom right:** Sector-sweeping operations by Detachment A-502 resulted in some sharp clashes during the war. Here, Special Forces Sgt. First Class Chris Shelly directs a counterattack during a reaction mission west of Nha Trang. *(Chris Shelly)*

One of the greatest Special Forces accomplishments in Vietnam was the contribution of the widespread medical program that treated millions of village inhabitants and saved thousands of battlefield lives. Special Forces medical assistance was the most influential and productive of the various civic-action efforts and by far the biggest success with the people. Here, Special Forces medics help load indigenous casualties into an ambulance at Ha Tien during 1963. *(Author's Collection)*

Top: The heart of the Special Forces medical organization consisted of two medical non-commissioned officers in each A-Detachment. The burden of humanitarian treatment in Vietnam fell on their shoulders, as they were often the only medically skilled personnel in a given area of operations. Here, a wounded CIDG trooper is attended on the battlefield while awaiting helicopter evacuation. *(5th SFG PIO)* **Center:** Two highly qualified Special Forces medical personnel—Sergeants First Class George Hofftrien, anesthetist, and Stan Shank, surgical assistant—help a Nung recon trooper who had been seriously burned by white phosphorous explosions during a MACV-SOG mission. They are assisted by a Vietnamese nurse. *(Mike Dwyer)* **Bottom:** The main II Corps Tactical Zone CIDG Hospital at Pleiku treated most Montagnard battle casualties in Vietnam. It was administered and staffed by Special Forces medical personnel. *(Lynn Dievendorf)*

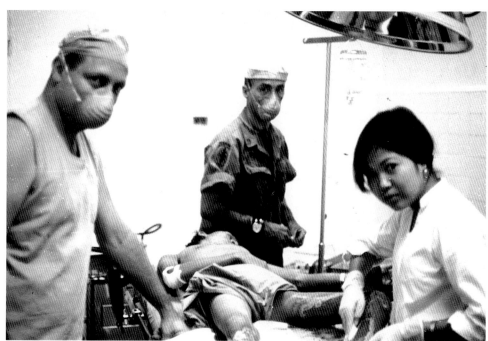

Top left: Special Forces Sgt. First Class Millard Chavers and Staff Sgt. Edward Lawson, members of the Walter Reed Army Institute of Research Field Epidemiological Research Team (FEST), study entomological aspects relating to tropical diseases at Ba Xoai. *(Louis Dorogi)* **Top right:** Medical Capt. Ray Parson, a FEST entomologist, dips for mosquito larvae near Song Be during July 1967. *(Louis Dorogi)* **Center left:** Detachment A-239 Lt. James Narregan assists a young Montagnard boy near Duc Lap in July 1968. *(Eugene Randon/USA)* **Center right:** Medical Capt. Craig H. Llewellyn, who later became the chairman of the Department of Military Medicine at the Uniformed Services University of the Health Sciences, discusses the urgent medical situation in a disease-ridden native cluster of villages with Capt. Coleman at Mai Linh during January 1966. *(Gerald Foy)* **Bottom:** CIDG troops guard a Special Forces veterinarian and his Air Force senior master-sergeant assistant as they perform a post-mortem on a water buffalo in VC-controlled territory outside of Dalat. *(44th Med Bde Info Office)*

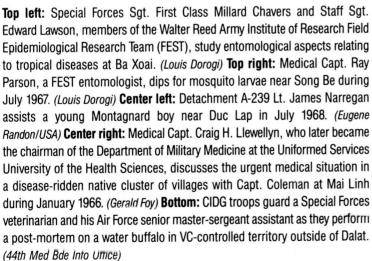

SPECIAL FORCES MEDICAL

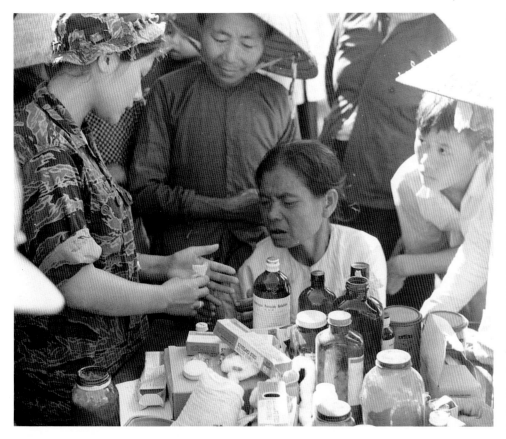

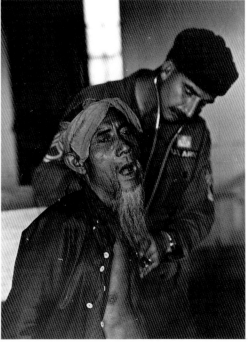

Top left: Special Forces medics and their Vietnamese assistants treated wounds, fractures, sores, and infections, and gave immunizations and pills for many diseases and illnesses. These CIDG nurses dispense a variety of medicines to native villagers near Mai Loc in October 1969. *(Gualt/USA)* **Top right:** Sgt. First Class Kenneth D. Stinkly, a member of the Special Forces team at Camp Van Canh training center, examines a malaria-stricken Montagnard villager in January 1963. *(Henry Backes/USA)* **Center:** A Special Forces medic conducts a triage as casualties are brought in by 101st Airborne Division helicopters to a temporary field aid station in northern South Vietnam during 1969. *(Author's Collection)* **Bottom:** Special Forces medics apply life-sustaining emergency measures as intravenous fluid replacement from a saline bottle is applied to a critically wounded trooper. *(Scott Whitting)*

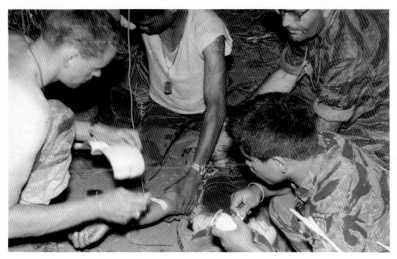

South Vietnamese infantrymen of the 42d Regiment, advancing to relieve the isolated Special Forces garrison at Ben Het, watch bombs dropped by B-52s explode over enemy lines south of the beleaguered camp on June 19, 1969. The North Vietnamese abandoned their attack on Camp Ben Het two weeks later and withdrew inside Cambodia. *(DOD)*

SPECIAL FORCES DEPART VIETNAM, 1969-1970

During 1969 and 1970 the 5th Special Forces Group fought its final campaign in Vietnam. The Southeast Asian conflict was dominated by the politically mandated ''One War'' policy that sought to expand South Vietnamese participation in the war effort while expediting U.S. military withdrawals. Special Forces was ordered to maintain fewer and fewer campsites throughout the country, and it scaled back its Civilian Irregular Defense Group program accordingly. Realizing that American withdrawal was imminent, Special Forces troops concentrated on upgrading the capability of Montagnard tribal and ethnic groups to defend their home territories alone. The final years were highlighted by several battles along the border, where the North Vietnamese Army took advantage of a lessened American presence to press major attacks against isolated frontier posts.

During this long and difficult extraction campaign, the 5th Special Forces Group was commanded by Colonel Michael D. ''Iron Mike'' Healy. He was a long-term Special Forces officer who rose through the ranks during World War II combat, led ranger units in the Korean war, and served nearly three years as a paratrooper battalion commander in Vietnam. Widely regarded as one of the Army's finest battlefield commanders, Colonel Healy took over the group at the end of August 1969 and remained in charge until its Vietnam departure.

The danger of overwhelming enemy attack against the string of isolated Special Forces border camps along the Cambodian and Laotian borders increased greatly with the reduction of American force levels. The North Vietnamese Army began an ambitious construction program to improve their Ho Chi Minh trail supply lines, and it sent fresh regiments to reinforce the tri-border front of the Central Highlands. Commencing in late February 1969, following a three-month lull of enemy activity in this area, Camp Ben Het was bombarded by 85mm field guns and other artillery weapons stationed just inside Cambodia.

On March 3 five infantry-escorted PT-76 light amphibious tanks from the NVA 202d Armored Regiment, supported by artillery fire and tear-gas shelling, launched an attack against Ben Het. The garrison was reinforced by Army medium tank crews and Special Forces-led native rocket crews, who duelled the approaching enemy armor successfully and prevented a close assault. The North Vietnamese retreated after losing two tanks in a firestorm of exploding rockets, anti-tank mines, and Army tank cannon fire. Although this main assault on the compound was defeated, infantry skirmishes continued to erupt around the Ben Het vicinity, and the camp was shelled incessantly for the next four months.

Taking advantage of dismal monsoon weather over the western mountains during May and June, the North Vietnamese Army next applied regimental pressure against Camps Ben Het and Dak To. The camps were completely cut off from allied reinforcement, and the defensive garrisons depended on aerial support and parachuted resupplies for ammunition and sustenance. The Military Assistance Command, Vietnam (MACV), was aware of the desperate plight of both camps, but it decided to make the South Vietnamese counterattacks a political showcase for ''Vietnamization.'' As a result, the Ben Het and Dak To defenders were forced to hold out alone while South Vietnamese regiments marched to relieve them. Special Forces fighting courage, native tenacity, and air power finally succeeded in discouraging further enemy attacks during late June, although the South Vietnamese Army was given credit for lifting both sieges that July.

The next major battle in the Central Highlands erupted in October 1969, when two North Vietnamese regiments moved against Camps Bu Prang and Duc Lap. Both camps were again left to defend themselves while MACV commander General Abrams relied on South Vietnamese command promises to defeat the enemy aggressors. Unfortunately, powerful North Vietnamese twin drives overran artillery Fire Support Base Kate, which covered Bu Prang, and cut off Duc Lap before the South Vietnamese 23d Division could maneuver forward. Aware of the dire circumstances at each threatened camp, the Special Forces group commander dispatched more mobile reaction forces into the fray. This prompt reinforcement saved Bu Prang and Duc Lap from complete destruction, although enemy artillery pulverized most compound facilities. On December 27 the South Vietnamese concluded the campaign by declaring victory in breaking the enemy sieges.

In early 1970 the Special Forces received its expected directions to discontinue the entire Civilian Irregular Defense Group program and ''stand down'' in conducting offensive operations. The 5th Special Forces Group controlled 38 native irregular camps at the beginning of June. The timetable issued by Military Assistance Command, Vietnam, dictated that all remaining camps would be converted to South Vietnamese Army control between the months of August and December 1970. The actual magnitude of continuing combat in 1970, however, precluded any disengagement from the battlefield until March of the following year.

On April 9, 1970, the northernmost Special Forces camp of Mai Loc was raided by enemy sappers, who caused widespread structural damage and killed numerous defenders before being driven out by regular Army reinforcements. The attack underscored the extreme peril that native camps faced near the Demilitarized Zone, and conversion plans for Mai Loc were dropped. The camp was closed down in late August. Shortly after the attack on Mai Loc, the enemy besieged Camp Thuong Duc. The compound was continually bombarded with mortars and rockets for more than 60 days. During one seven-day period in October, the camp garrison fought three pitched battles.

The Central Highlands was also dominated by siege warfare during early 1970. Camp Dak Seang was besieged by North Vietnamese Army infantry troops commencing on April 1, 1970. They launched several determined assaults that temporarily breached the camp's defensive lines. Special Forces Mobile Strike Force and Vietnamese ranger troops were sent in to reinforce the deteriorating situation, and they prevented the enemy from eradicating the camp. However, the ensuing siege lasted until May 8.

On April 12, while the battle for Dak Seang was still raging, the enemy pounded nearby Camp Dak Pek with a devastating pre-dawn mortar barrage. This surprise onslaught was followed by a major ground attack that partially overran the compound. Dak Pek was almost completely destroyed in the battle, but the enemy suffered grievous casualties in trying to overrun the site. The allied summer incursion into Cambodia created a lull in further enemy offensive activity. Special Forces highland detachments became engaged in handling the influx of displaced natives from the Cambodian frontier zone.

The Special Forces frontier camps in III Corps Tactical Zone were subjected to heavy barrages during the first part of 1970. The Special Forces was finally able to take the offensive when it participated in the general allied invasion of Cambodia during May and June. Several irregular strike force battalions composed of Cambodian mercenaries were employed in the vanguard of the main northern assault, while other regular camp companies drove into the Parrot's Beak area west of Saigon. Sizeable stockpiles of enemy weapons and materiel were seized in the dense Cambodian jungle, adding to the tremendous war booty previously seized by Major Ola L. Mize's native raiders in the Viet Cong stronghold of War Zone D near Rang Rang.

During 1970 the most violent Viet Cong attacks on Mekong region camps occurred early in the year. In January and March the enemy close-assaulted the hillside compound of Camp Ba Xoai but were handily defeated by the spirited defense of the Cambodian Khmer Kampuchea Kron garrison. Later Special Forces activity in the Mekong Delta became centered around actions to clear the Seven Mountains (see previous chapter). The overall success of those operations—coupled with the allied Cambodian invasion—enabled most Mekong Delta camps to enjoy a long respite from Viet Cong retaliation. Special Forces airboat and sampan sweeps added to this security by continuing to clear the canal waterways and marshes until the final Special Forces withdrawal orders were received.

The 5th Special Forces Group experienced severe frustration in transitioning its Civilian Irregular Defense Group program to the Vietnamese army ranger command. The American phasedown meant fewer Special Forces personnel, but administrative, operational, and logistical burdens increased with the transfer process. There was little cooperation between the highland natives and their traditional lowland Vietnamese adversaries. Montagnards were suspicious of Vietnamese intentions and remained skeptical about their fate, despite intensive Special Forces indoctrination and motivation efforts. For their part, the Vietnamese authorities displayed little interest in acquiring legions of primitive tribesmen.

Special Forces emphasis was heightened in the civic action arena, although many of these projects were handicapped by the unwillingness of the Saigon government to aid Montagnards and other tribal minorities. Setbacks were encountered whenever civil assistance commodities were misdirected or failed to reach remote areas in a timely manner. Despite these problems, Special Forces accomplished many construction tasks that included the building and repairing of hundreds of dwellings, bridges, schools, hospitals, and dispensaries throughout the country. The Special Forces also used close personal assistance and self-help methods to elevate agriculture, animal husbandry, and community living standards among the peasants. Special Forces turned over its medical and dental treatment programs to native CIDG political warfare team medics. This massive humanitarian effort improved rural conditions in Vietnam and served as a favorable testimony to Special Forces enterprise, even though much work was later destroyed or allowed to disintegrate following the war's unsatisfactory conclusion.

The Special Forces goal in Vietnam had always been to organize native villages to resist area insurgents, pacify the surrounding region, and then turn these areas over to central government control. This mission was fully accomplished by the end of 1970. The last 37 camp garrisons were converted into Vietnamese Army border ranger compounds, and the civilian irregular garrisons became light infantry battalions. In nearly all areas of Special Forces occupation, the local Viet Cong insurgency was either eliminated or subdued to the point of noneffectiveness. The villages were now involved in a conventional war between North and South Vietnamese armies, and these regular units were not engaged in unconventional special warfare.

In March 1971 the 5th Special Forces Group departed Vietnam, having earned the most salutary battle record of versatile operational performance in modern U.S. history. Much of this credit goes to the military professionalism exhibited by the Special Forces officers and sergeants. The combat deeds performed by loyal indigenous fighters must also be recognized. Their shared valor enabled Special Forces to demonstrate its organizational flexibility and military capabilities. The Vietnam-era Special Forces campaign record far exceeded all Pentagon expectations for its relatively small special warfare unit.

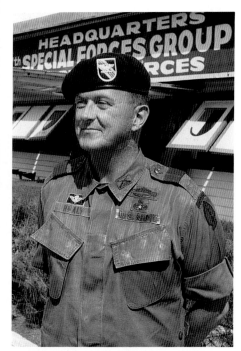

Top left: By 1969 the Special Forces was engaged throughout Vietnam with 17 B-Detachments and 63 field A-Detachments. CIDG efforts remained concentrated on sweeping known enemy operational base and war zone areas and hindering cross-border infiltration. Many field operations were conducted routinely with larger conventional Army units. Here a CIDG member of the 3d Mobile Strike Force Command shows the Red and White Scarf of Honor to Pvt. Danny Wasson of the 25th Infantry Division during 1969 sweeping operations north of Cu Chi. *(25th Inf Div PIO)* **Top middle:** A Special Forces sergeant directs a CIDG reinforcing column into battle during relief operations in the Straight Edge Woods near Tay Ninh on July

28, 1969. *(Author's Collection)* **Center left:** MACV commander Gen. Creighton W. Abrams presents the nation's highest unit award—the Presidential Unit Citation—to the 5th Special Forces Group on October 8, 1969. *(Clifford Roe/USA)* **Center right:** Col. Michael D. ''Iron Mike'' Healy, an outstanding officer with both solid conventional and excellent Special Forces credentials, took command of the 5th Special Forces Group at the end of August 1969. *(5th SFG PIO)* **Bottom:** Special Forces paramilitary troops conduct a helicopter combat assault into the Renegade Woods, a VC stronghold within War Zone C during mid-1969. *(Author's Collection)*

Top: Camp Cai Cai was located less than two miles from Cambodia. Enemy forces often raided the outpost from their Cambodian sanctuary, but Special Forces units were restricted by rules of engagement from crossing the border in pursuit. Any attempts to counter enemy forces operating out of Cambodia drew sharp U.S. criticism for ''provoking'' international incidents with a ''neutral'' country. *(Author's Collection)* **Center:** On January 8, 1969, Special Forces finally received permission to call in air strikes against the ''Little Triangle'' of Cambodia, where the NVA/VC staged attacks against Camp Cai Cai. The tougher American stance resulted in meetings with Cambodian officials within the Little Triangle on January 9-10, 1969. The Cambodian captain (center, hand pointing down) promised to cooperate with Capt. Leo Lynch, A-431 commander (far right). Interpreter Doan Duc Tuan stands between them. *(Author's Collection)* **Bottom:** This view from the Vietnamese side of the border canal shows fortified bunkers of the Little Triangle after they were hit by U.S. air strikes. *(Author's Collection)*

Top: Camp Ben Het depended on aerial support for its survival when besieged by two North Vietnamese Army regiments from May 5 to June 29, 1969. Running a gauntlet of enemy automatic-weapons fire, an Air Force F-4 Phantom swoops low over Ben Het to napalm NVA sappers attempting to breach the Special Forces camp's perimeter. During the battle the enemy advanced trenches and tunnels out of the jungle through Ben Het's outer wire, but they were stopped from overrunning the camp. *(Paul Harrington)*

Bottom: Smoke bombs explode at treetop level near the perimeter of Camp Ben Het as Air Force A-1 Skyraiders from the 633d Special Operations Squadron create a protective smoke screen for cargo aircraft parachuting supplies to the beleaguered Special Forces compound. *(Ron Smith)*

Top: Air Force A-1 Skyraiders plant a smoke screen around Camp Ben Het for transport aircraft air-dropping munitions during May 1969. *(USAF)* **Center:** Supplies parachuted from Air Force C-7A Caribou aircraft float safely to the Special Forces at Camp Ben Het. *(USAF)* **Bottom left:** Special Forces parachute rigger Sp5 John Shaw, his green beret stuffed in right pocket, shouts ''Let's Go!'' after his Air Force C-7 Caribou makes a low-level cargo drop over besieged Camp Ben Het, seen behind him, during May 1969. *(USAF)* **Bottom right:** The slow airspeed of cargo aircraft enabled them to deliver supplies over small drop zones, but it also subjected them to intense enemy ground fire. Highly coordinated tactical air support is demonstrated as a C-7 Caribou parachutes ammunition to Ben Het behind a smoke screen laid by Skyraiders. *(Paul Harrington)*

Top left: The gutted remains of a demolished North Vietnamese PT-76 tank, exploded by mines, anti-tank fire, and its own burning internal ammunition, rests outside Camp Ben Het on March 4, 1969. *(Jerry Kringel)* **Top right:** Camp Ben Het was attacked by a tank-supported NVA battalion on the night of March 3, 1969. Two of the Russian-built PT-76 tanks struck a mine field on the approach road and were finished off by U.S. Army tanks from the 1st Battalion, 69th Armor, stationed temporarily in the Special Forces compound. *(DOD)* **Bottom left:** Third Mobile Strike Force Command intelligence Sgt. First Class Roy Chelnut catches up with the news during a break from patrolling operations around Ben Het. *(Gilley/USA)* **Bottom right:** Detachment A-244 senior weapons Sgt. First Class Richard Grier and his native irregulars survey a heavy machine gun torn from an exploding enemy PT-76 tank in the background that had attempted a nocturnal attack on Camp Ben Het just hours earlier. *(Jerry Kringel)*

Top: Camp Dak To was besieged by the NVA 28th and 66th Regiments at the same time as the battle of Ben Het from May 5 to June 29, 1969. Enemy fire downed this helicopter over the wire perimeter as it attempted to leave the camp with several wounded defenders. *(Author's Collection)* **Center:** On May 11 enemy sappers conducted a major assault on Dak To and managed to penetrate the wire obstacles before being repulsed. This dramatic photograph was taken during this action. *(Author's Collection)* **Bottom left:** The shrapnel-riddled gatepost to Camp Bu Prang still stands at the conclusion of the North Vietnamese siege conducted October 28 to December 16, 1969. During this battle the camp was successfully defended by Detachment A-236 under command of Capt. William L. Palmer, although several outlying fire support bases were overrun by enemy troops. *(Gary Clark)* **Bottom right:** A Special Forces sergeant at Camp Bu Prang checks the field of fire atop a light machine gun bunker, looking toward the Cambodian border two miles away. *(USA)*

Top: Camp Bu Prang Detachment A-236 operations Master Sgt. Walter A. Talkington (extreme right foreground), one of the Special Forces members who built new Bu Prang more than two years earlier, transmits the password as he leads his Montagnard company back to camp after destroying an enemy weapons platoon. *(USA)* **Center left:** Camp Bu Prang enjoyed excellent relations with the nearby villagers, and they routinely delivered rice to highland hamlets like Bu Tam Rang before the battle. *(USA)* **Bottom left:** One of the key allied positions in the defense of Camp Bu Prang was Fire Support Base Kate, surrounded October 29-31 by North Vietnamese regulars. In a daring escape, Capt. William L. Albracht led his troops through enemy lines to reach safety. *(Author's Collection)* **Bottom right:** The ammunition bunker at Camp Bu Prang explodes after taking a direct hit by enemy rockets on the morning of November 18, 1969. The blast and resulting fire destroyed the compound's artillery stockpile, burned down the rice house, and crippled communications to relief forces trying to reach the isolated Special Forces compound. *(Author's Collection)*

Top: Camp Duc Lap was located nine miles east of the Cambodian border in the mountainous jungle terrain of Quang Duc Province. Camp garrison Detachment A-239 was surrounded by the 28th NVA Regiment from late October through most of December 1969. *(Author's Collection)* **Bottom left:** Detachment A-236 medical Sgt. Fritz A. Mertz assembles body bags lowered by helicopter that contain the remains of CIDG troops killed on a scouting mission outside Camp Bu Prang. The military effectiveness of Bu Prang and Duc Lap in blocking enemy penetration of South Vietnam caused the NVA to shift an entire division from the tri-border area in a major attempt to destroy both camps. *(Hector Robertin/USA)* **Bottom right:** Camp Duc Lap was shelled and probed continually during the enemy siege, but it received its three heaviest barrages on November 17 and December 1 and 2. The 3d NVA Division finally retreated from the area on December 20, 1969. This enemy sapper was killed before he could reach the camp gate. *(John Borgman)*

Top left: The North Vietnamese Army, which conducted numerous infantry attacks against Camp Dak Seang in April 1970, managed to reach the western wall before being repulsed by helicopter gunships and defensive artillery fire. Staff Sgt. Danny L. Little (center) was one of several irreplaceable Special Forces veterans killed during the battle. He is seen here just outside the camp a few weeks before the siege. *(Stephen Putthoff)* **Top right:** Camp Dak Seang, defended by Detachment A-245, was located between several rugged mountain ranges in a heavily forested region ten kilometers from the Laotian border. An NVA regiment besieged this Special Forces camp from April 2 to May 8, 1970. *(Author's Collection)* **Center left:** 5th Mobile Strike Force troopers arrive to reinforce Dak Seang during the battle. *(5th SFG PIO)* **Bottom:** Camp Dak Pek, located astride a major NVA infiltration route into Kontum Province, was besieged from April 12 to May 9, 1970. The campsite occupied seven hills in the northern fringes of the mountainous, bamboo-covered Dak Poko Valley. *(Lynn Dievendorf)*

Top left: Detachment A-242 personnel check the stake and mine fields on the fortified hillside of Camp Dak Pek. *(Frank Sullivan/USA)* **Center right:** NVA rockets explode beside a helicopter evacuating casualties from Dak Pek during the 1970 siege. The camp was an important MACV-SOG launch site for cross-border raids into Laos, and Special Forces was ordered to defend it at all costs. *(Army News Features)* **Bottom:** Camp Dak Pek was divided into eight separate defensive areas, each surrounded by an elaborate trench system with bunkers and foxholes. On April 12, 1970, NVA assault troops captured three hills within the camp complex but multiple air strikes and Special Forces-led counterattacks finally broke the siege and cleared the enemy from the camp. *(Author's Collection)*

Top: Special Forces-led commandos of MACV-SOG Command and Control North provided the basis for the Special Mission Service that became operational in January 1972 and staged cross-border operations into Laos from Da Nang and Kontum. Here, Lt. Kenneth R. Bowra, wearing captured North Vietnamese ammunition pouches, poses with his Bru Montagnards in February. Most of these men are armed with CAR-15 submachine guns, but Man Loi (front row, third from left) carries an XM203 experimental grenade launcher. *(Kenneth Bowra)*

Bottom: The Special Mission Service, part of the Vietnamese Strategic Technical Directorate, fielded reconnaissance teams such as RT Cobra, which performed intelligence collection, interdiction operations, and other specialized commando tasks in Laos, Cambodia, and North Vietnam. *(Kenneth Bowra)*

Top left: The primary Special Forces target in Laos and Cambodia was the Ho Chi Minh Trail, a logistical artery that served as the key line of communications connecting North Vietnam with its battlefronts in Cambodia, Laos, and South Vietnam. Cross-border raiding detachments such as this team were launched from Nakhon Phanom and Ubon, Thailand, against Laotian infiltration routes used by the North Vietnamese Army. *(Dan McKinney)* **Top right:** The NVA north-south supply network—the Ho Chi Minh Trail—contained repair facilities, rest centers, hospitals, and ammunition depots that were often defended by female guards to avoid siphoning manpower from combat units. *(Author's Collection)* **Bottom:** The Ho Chi Minh Trail existed as a variable assortment of jungle pathways that were well camouflaged against aerial detection. This raised section of the trail network was discovered by reconnaissance elements from the 46th Special Forces Company operating in Laos. *(Author's Collection)*

Top left: President Richard M. Nixon and his top military advisors decided to eradicate the North Vietnamese supply bases in Cambodia by calling for an invasion during May-June 1970. In the foreground (left to right) sit Henry A. Kissinger, Gen. Creighton W. Abrams, Deputy Defense Secretary David Packard, and Adm. Thomas H. Moorer. In the background (left to right) sit Adm. John S. McCain, Defense Secretary Melvin R. Laird, President Nixon, and Joint Chiefs of Staff chairman Gen. Earle G. Wheeler. *(Army News Features)* **Top right:** The 3d Mobile Strike Force Command receives orders as it drives deeper through enemy jungle. *(Lee Mize)* **Center left:** Cambodian refugees watch the Special Forces advance in Cambodia. The Mobile Strike Force Commands were used during the offensive to safeguard unit flanks and spearhead several major drives in conjunction with other allied operations. *(DOD)* **Center right:** CIDG riflemen await the signal for coordinated attack given through their radios. *(Lee Mize)* **Bottom right:** A refugee center set up for displaced Cambodians was furnished with fresh vegetables and guards by the Cambodian CIDG troops of the 3d Mobile Strike Force Command. *(5th SFG PIO)*

Top left: LLDB 3d Military Region commander Col. Chuan and II Field Force Vietnam Lt. Gen. Julian J. Ewell survey communist weapons captured by the 3d Mobile Strike Force Command under the direction of Maj. Ola Lee Mize on right. *(5th SFG PIO)* **Top right:** An enemy storage site discovered by Special Forces-led contingents. *(Lee Mize)* **Center left:** More enemy weapons are displayed after the 3d Mobile Strike Force Command discovered one of the largest enemy caches of the war. *(5th SFG PIO)* **Center right:** 1st Cavalry Division Brig. Gen. Elvy B. Roberts stands beside victorious Special Forces troops of the 3d Mobile Strike Force Command led by Maj. Mize. *(Lee Mize)* **Bottom:** A CIDG soldier on the offensive inside Cambodia during June 1970. *(Army News Features)*

Top: Camp Ba Xoai's Special Forces-led Cambodian and Vietnamese garrison defeated repeated enemy attacks during January and March 1970. The camp's spirited defense led the U.S. high command to believe that Special Forces could safely accelerate the conversion of its native camps to full Vietnamese control. *(Author's Collection)* **Bottom left:** On January 14, 1970, a reinforced Viet Cong battalion charged Camp Ba Xoai's perimeter following a blistering rocket and mortar barrage that destroyed many hillside defensive positions. *(Author's Collection)* **Bottom right:** During the January ground attack on Ba Xoai, the camp defenders bravely defied enemy fire by staying on top of their bunkers and delivering more accurate return fire. Nevertheless, the camp suffered extensive damage, including the loss of the generator power bunker, mortar pits, searchlight bunker, the primary communications bunker, and the Special Forces team house. *(Author's Collection)*

Top left: Camp Mai Loc was located five miles south of the Demilitarized Zone and was the northernmost Special Forces camp in South Vietnam when it was attacked on April 9-10, 1970. North Vietnamese Army sappers took advantage of a gap in the western perimeter wire, shown here, that the CIDG defenders kept open for convenient access between the camp compound and neighboring villages. *(Author's Collection)* **Top right:** The bunker at Camp Mai Loc where Detachment A-101 Master Sgt. Gale Stopher Jr. was killed on April 10, 1970. *(Author's Collection)* **Bottom:** The successful NVA raid on Camp Mai Loc penetrated the camp interior and caused extensive damage to the tactical operations center and other vital facilities. The camp was closed later that year on August 27, when Detachment A-101 was deactivated as part of the Special Forces withdrawal from Vietnam. *(Author's Collection)*

Top left: Detachment A-101 defenders call in an air strike from their perimeter at Camp Thuong Duc as NVA troops attempt to cross the river west of camp. On the afternoon of May 20, elements of the 1st Mobile Strike Force Command were engaged in heavy fighting in this area. *(Richard McDonald)* **Top right:** Camp Thuong Duc was besieged by the 312th NVA Division and 141st NVA Regiment from late April through early June 1970. Enemy plans to launch a series of attacks against allied installations across Military Region I during May, in concert with the second phase of the NVA Spring-Summer campaign, were disrupted by the successful defense of this outpost. *(Author's Collection)* **Bottom:** (Left to right) Detachment A-109 Sgt. First Class Hall, Sgt. First Class Crandford, and Lt. Richard A. McDonald adjust a jeep-mounted 106mm recoilless-rifle sight at Camp Thuong Duc. These valuable weapons gave Special Forces camps a higher degree of mobile defensive firepower. *(Richard McDonald)*

Top left: Without much MACV concern about the fate of native tribes or their camps once Special Forces departed, the phaseout of the CIDG program was ordered by Gen. Abrams at the end of August 1969 and accelerated in compliance with Vietnamization directives during 1970. Special Forces made every attempt to upgrade defensive quality during the withdrawal period. Here, Staff Sgt. Alvin J. Rouly instructs a grenadier of the 3d Mobile Strike Force Command in the use of the M-79 grenade launcher. *(Robert Lafoon/USA)* **Top right:** Camp Trang Sup, opened in February 1963 and used for training purposes, represented one of Special Forces' longest-occupied camps when it was transferred to the South Vietnamese border ranger program at the end of November 1970. Budgetary constraints and a pressurized timetable inhibited a smooth transition of the CIDG program from Special Forces to South Vietnamese control. *(Author's Collection)* **Bottom:** Camp Tra Bong was nearly destroyed in early September 1970, one week after being turned over by Special Forces to the South Vietnamese border ranger program. The CIDG defense garrison, newly redesignated as the 61st ARVN Ranger Battalion, was unable to communicate properly without Special Forces guidance and failed to secure timely artillery or aerial support from their MACV advisors. *(Author's Collection)*

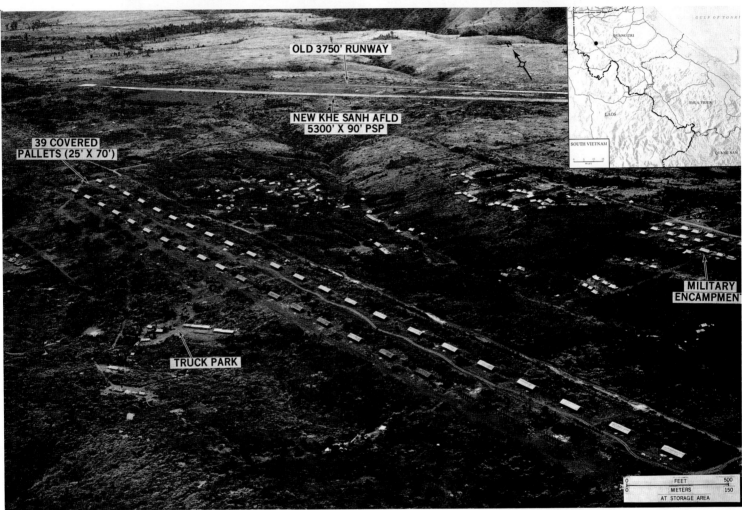

OLD 3750' RUNWAY

NEW KHE SANH AFLD
5300' X 90' PSP

39 COVERED
PALLETS (25' X 70')

MILITARY
ENCAMPMEN

TRUCK PARK

FEET	500
METERS	150
AT STORAGE AREA	

Top left: MACV Gen. Abrams—seen here at left with Col. Mike Healy in the center—began to share many of the 5th Special Forces Group commander's concerns about the survivability of the Montagnards and other ethnic minorities in the absence of Special Forces assistance. By 1970, however, Gen. Abrams was forced to abide by strict scheduling for Special Forces withdrawal from Vietnam, in accordance with higher national directives. *(5th SFG PIO)* **Top right:** When the 5th Special Forces Group executed its final withdrawal from the South Vietnamese border it had fought so long to protect, it left behind the wreckage of many battlefields, typified by this scene at Kham Duc photographed during August 1970. *(Niskanen/USA)* **Bottom:** The North Vietnamese Army was quick to follow up the general Special Forces withdrawal. This major NVA base complex was situated at the old Special Forces Khe Sanh outpost first established on July 8, 1962. It was photographed exactly ten years later, during mid-1972, by reconnaissance aircraft surveying enemy-held territory. *(DOD)*

Top: Perhaps the greatest Special Forces achievement during the Vietnam conflict was the success of its civic-action efforts, exemplified by the upgraded agricultural methods being employed in this field photographed near a Special Forces camp in 1970. Unfortunately, the conclusion of the Second Indochina War five years later resulted in the triumph of a reactionary communist regime that destroyed these progressive innovations and reduced Vietnam to catastrophic impoverishment. *(USIS)* **Bottom left:** The uncertain future of the native hill tribes in war-ravaged Vietnam was mirrored by Lt. Nim and Nay Go—faithful Montagnard medics since 1965—as they watch the last Special Forces commandos leave their outpost in the Central Highlands during September 1971. The abandonment of the Montagnards, fiercely protested by Special Forces, would constitute one of the most tragic episodes of the conflict. *(Mike Dwyer)* **Bottom right:** Special Forces Sgt. Stephen C. Tenorio of Guam renders the final inspection of Vietnamese mobile strike-force troops at Cao Lanh in the Mekong Delta. *(James Ensign/USA)*

Members of 5th Special Forces Group Detachment A-502 proudly wear the group flash on their green berets in this last picture taken before team disbandment at Nha Trang on February 1, 1970. *(Author's Collection)*

5TH SPECIAL FORCES GROUP DEPARTS

Top right and bottom right: The honor guard of the 5th Special Forces Group (Airborne) departs Nha Trang to return the colors to Fort Bragg, North Carolina, on the first day of March 1971, concluding a decade of Special Forces service in the Republic of Vietnam. *(5th SFG PIO)*

A 46th Special Forces Company sergeant shows Vietnam-bound Royal Thai infantrymen how to zero their M16 rifles by adjusting elevation and windage (front and rear sights) during combat preparatory courses at Chonburi, Thailand, in January 1968. The Special Forces was responsible for training the wartime national armies of Laos, Cambodia, and Thailand, as well as retraining several South Vietnamese divisions late in the war. *(Thomas Seddon Jr./USA)*

SPECIAL FORCES MISSIONS THROUGHOUT SOUTHEAST ASIA

SPECIAL FORCES MISSIONS THROUGHOUT SOUTHEAST ASIA

While the 5th Special Forces Group was engaged in South Vietnam, other Special Forces detachments were being sent routinely to assist nation-building and counter-guerrilla programs in Thailand. The 1st Special Forces Group on Okinawa was involved in unconventional warfare maneuvers and training exercises in Thailand before the Vietnam conflict escalated into a major war, and it continued in this capacity throughout the conflict. By 1966, however, wartime Vietnam demands and the increasing level of specialized support needed by Thailand had outstripped group resources. During April 1966 the U.S. Joint Chiefs of Staff raised Company D of the 1st Special Forces Group as a new unit at Fort Bragg and trained it exclusively for Thai operations. This reinforced company arrived in that country during October and took over the bulk of Thai-related Special Forces assignments, being attached to the U.S. Army Support, Thailand, command on January 1, 1967.

The primary Special Forces mission in Thailand involved establishing a combined training base at Lopburi, the ancient capital of Thailand located 93 miles north of Bangkok. From this headquarters, the Special Forces assisted the Royal Thai armed forces in improving their counterinsurgency capabilities against subversive bandit elements and communist guerrillas threatening remote regions of the country. This was a far different program than the native village defense projects instituted in Vietnam. The Thai assignment was more traditionally tailored to Special Forces methodology and ideally suited to an advanced society like Thailand, where the government enjoyed genuine popular support.

The two-fold secondary Special Forces task involved advising the Royal Thai Army Special Warfare Center at Lopburi and distributing U.S. military aid to Thai special warfare units. The Thais expressed an enthusiastic desire to maintain control of training with their own cadre staff. The Special Forces welcomed this cooperative attitude, which contrasted starkly with Viet-namese reluctance to teach demanding military subjects. American and Thai cadre personnel participated jointly in conducting realistic battle instruction for both Thai police and army units, and certain phases were taught entirely by Thai experts.

The Special Forces company was also given classified instructions to maintain unit readiness for potential unilateral unconventional warfare operations and other duties assigned by higher authorities. Most of these involved secret plans to conduct guerrilla operations in case contingency Laotian invasion plans were approved by the president. The Special Forces prepared for such eventualities by undertaking periodic cross-border patrols, usually of a reconnaissance nature, into Laos. Raids were also conducted in Laos in conjunction with Thai police aerial reinforcement units, or with MACV-SOG teams using Thai airfields as launching platforms for Laotian ground strikes. In later years the Thai-based Special Forces became heavily engaged in training, equipping, and sending CIA-funded Thai infantry and artillery battalions onto the Laotian battlefront.

The seemingly detached nature of Thai duty from the "real" Southeast Asian war was suddenly erased with the pronouncement that Royal Thai forces would be sent to help fight in Vietnam. In March 1967 the Special Forces began the 20-week training program for the first expeditionary Thai regiment, the "Queen's Cobras," at a multitude of stations. Infantry instruction was conducted at Chonburi, artillery training was given at Kokethiem, mechanized warfare was taught at Saraburi, and engineer specialization was conducted at Ratburi. The company's selection for this wide range of conventional military instruction was a high-command tribute to the recognized expertise of the professional Special Forces officers and sergeants.

On April 15, 1967, the company accomplishments were further rewarded when Company D was renamed as the independent 46th Special Forces Company. The retention of a company-level title was deceptive to some extent, because the unit was organized and functioned as a small independent group. For example, the command was augmented to the point that it included nearly 600 assigned personnel by the time of Tet-68, compared to just more than 700 troopers with the 1st Special Forces Group in Okinawa at the same time. An unconfirmed statement about the choice of its unusual numerical selection—made at the time of redesignation—claimed that 46 was chosen to signify the fact it would work on "either side" (i.e, Cambodia and Laos) of the 5th Special Forces Group in Vietnam. Whether or not this wartime report had any basis in fact, the 46th was destined to do just that.

One of the reasons for the large relative size of the Special Forces company was the need to create an expanded command and signal operations center. Special Forces subordinate detachments were posted to scattered locations to give some coverage in depth over the vast Thailand countryside, and control arrangements were stretched to link up the various elements. Many Thai outposts gained an enviable reputation for operating in splendid isolation, and nowhere was a detachment commander more authoritative than in the Thai wilderness.

By September 1967 the 46th Special Forces Company contained three B-Detachment field training sites near Sakon Nakhon, Pak Chong, and Ban Kachong. The numerous training projects reflected its extensive scope of activities. In addition to Vietnam preparation, other Royal Thai rifle companies were given five-week counterinsurgency instruction for combat inside Thailand. Special Forces personnel accompanied and advised companies that were assigned to the Communist Suppression Operations Center on combatant anti-partisan operations in the northeastern region and in the Khra peninsula.

Other Special Forces counterinsurgency training covered company, leadership, base security, and specialist courses. A counter-sabotage course for Thai railway security forces was also conducted. Police paramilitary training courses were established at the border patrol police training center and all regional complexes. Additional training courses were given to police medical and provincial police teams. At the Royal Thai Special Warfare Center itself, the Special Forces taught special warfare proficiency, ranger patrolling, scuba diving, basic parachutist technique, and High Altitude-Low Opening airborne infiltration courses. To protect the numerous U.S. Air Force installations in Thailand, Special Forces regularly trained Air Force quick-reaction forces, as well as the Thai security guards.

At the end of March 1972, the 46th Special Forces Company was given the cover designation of U.S. Army Special Forces, Thailand. In actuality, the unit became the 3d Battalion of the 1st Special Forces Group, but this fact remained classified because of political sensitivity regarding the use of Okinawa as a U.S. "springboard" for Southeast Asian commitments. After two more years of operations, in which Cambodian Special Forces training became an important adjunct of Special Forces activities in Thailand, the battalion was returned to Fort Bragg, North Carolina, and inactivated.

The Special Forces connection to Cambodian military operations began in May 1970, when the 5th Special Forces Group began training Cambodian recruits for a new allied Cambodian government army (the *Forces Armées Nationales Khmeres*, or FANK) at established facilities inside Vietnam. The Special Forces was given responsibility for this training because of its previous experience with Cambodian ethnic minorities in the Civilian Irregular Defense Group program. By October the FANK program had mushroomed into the creation of an entirely new national army. Special Forces was directed to train 30 battalions from the ground up—starting with weapons issuance and continuing through practical combat field exercises—and send the units back to fight in Cambodia when deemed battle ready.

In March 1971 this Special Forces training effort was reclassified under the U.S. Army Individual Training Group. The work was difficult and dangerous, and it always suffered from the historical antagonism existing between Vietnamese and Cambodian factions. By the conclusion of the Cambodian mission in February 1973, 86 Cambodian battalions were trained by Special Forces in Vietnam. Direct Special Forces assistance and advisory operations were undertaken inside Cambodia itself with personnel serving the Military Equipment Delivery Team, Cambodia. Special Forces troops remained in Cambodia until the fall of Phnom Penh and were instrumental in preventing an earlier collapse of the main front. Special Forces troops parachuted ammunition deliveries and rations to beleaguered forts, escorted Mekong River convoys, and supported Khmer units engaged in defending key locations.

Special Forces troops remained in Vietnam after the departure of the 5th Special Forces Group and continued to conduct cross-border raids and provide strategic reconnaissance. These members of the Special Mission Force and Strategic Technical Directorate Liaison Service performed herculean service in the wake of several major North Vietnamese offensives against South Vietnam. The Special Forces teams provided forward ranger elements that scouted in front of the lead South Vietnamese units and coordinated air strikes. This service enabled the South Vietnamese Army to recover portions of Pleiku Province and recapture Quang Tri in 1972. Based on their success in training regular Cambodian formations, Special Forces troops in South Vietnam retrained many components of shattered South Vietnamese divisions. Special Forces commando task forces were also flown into Thailand and Vietnam to execute missions of high national priority, such as the attempted rescue of U.S. prisoners held at Son Tay.

All Special Forces organizations were withdrawn from eastern Asia before the 1975 fall of Saigon. The 1st Special Forces Group on Okinawa left the island and was inactivated at Fort Bragg at the end of June 1974. With the exception of a few individual Special Forces personnel assigned to the Army staffs in Phnom Penh and Saigon and perhaps a few individuals who voluntarily returned to assist tribal brothers resist capture, Special Forces was not officially present at the bitter conclusion of the war. Thus, the Special Forces groups, companies, and detachments that fought the war were mercifully spared the agony of witnessing the final defeat of Cambodia, Laos, and Vietnam.

Ironically, the guerrilla insurgents and special warfare countermeasures that pervaded the early Indochina conflict were absent from the 1975 battlefield. The communist tanks smashing through the palatial capital gates were not part of any insurgency movement but armored behemoths at the forefront of a North Vietnamese regular army waging a purely conventional, blitzkrieg-style campaign of open conquest. The population's ''hearts and minds'' that Special Forces struggled so hard to win over to the allied cause, sadly no longer mattered.

Top and bottom: The large number of U.S. prisoners held in facilities scattered throughout North Vietnam hastened planning by the Joint Chiefs of Staff for a rescue operation conducted by Special Forces. Joint Contingency Task Force Ivory Coast was activated in November 1971 under the command of Brig. Gen. Donald D. Blackburn to conduct a raid that would retrieve the inmates from the Son Tay prisoner-of-war camp near Hanoi, North Vietnam. *(DOD)*

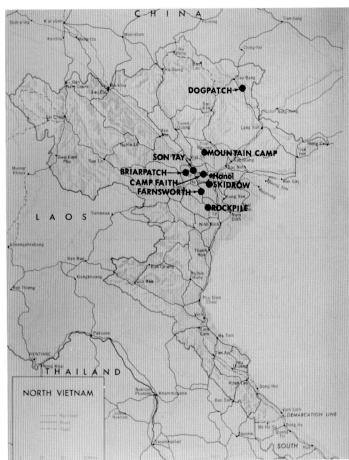

344

Top: The Son Tay raid was a precision commando operation conducted by highly trained Special Forces commandos on November 21, 1971. Although the prisoners were removed from Son Tay just prior to the raid, considerable gallantry was demonstrated in landing and seizing the prison compound despite the presence of large enemy troop concentrations. Four days later, President Richard M. Nixon (left) decorated ground commander Col. Arthur D. "Bull" Simons standing to his side, as well as Special Forces Sgt. First Class Tyrone J. Adderly (center), Air Force Technical Sgt. LeRoy M. Wright (on crutches), and overall raid commander Brig. Gen. LeRoy J. Manor (far left). *(DOD)* **Center left:** A low-level aerial reconnaissance photograph of the Son Tay prisoner-of-war facility. *(DOD)* **Center right:** A model of the Son Tay prison compound shows the inner courtyard at lower center, where Air Force Lt. Col. Herbert E. Zehnder landed his rescue helicopter containing Capt. Richard J. Meadows' Special Forces assault group. *(DOD)* **Bottom:** Secretary of Defense Melvin R. Laird presents awards to Son Tay raiders at Fort Bragg, North Carolina. *(USAJFK Ctr Museum)*

Top left: During August 1971 Task Force Advisory Elements 1, 2, and 3 were formed from Command and Control North, Central, and South of MACV-SOG. Staff Sgt. Jensen of Task Force Advisory Element 1 prepares to take off in a chase ship rigged with an extraction ladder. *(Jensen)* **Top right:** The emblem of Task Force Advisory Element 1 was a close variation of its predecessor MACV-SOG Command and Control North symbol. *(Jensen)* **Center left:** The North Vietnamese Nguyen Hue spring 1972 offensive forced MACV to redirect the Special Mission Service teams from cross-border strikes to Vietnamese Military Region 1 ranger duty, providing air-ground coordination for South Vietnamese airborne and marine forces that recaptured Quang Tri during September 1972. *(John Mulhall/DOD)* **Center right:** Following Quang Tri, the Special Mission Service commandos served as standard infantry until heavy casualties forced their disbandment in mid-November 1972. *(Jensen)* **Bottom:** Special Mission Service recon troops attached to the 81st ARVN Airborne Battalion during heavy fighting west of Hue during 1972. *(Author's Collection)*

Top: On April 23, 1972, the North Vietnamese Army commenced a general offensive in the western Central Highlands that reached the outskirts of Kontum city and threatened Pleiku. In response, Military Region 2 commander Col. Michael D. Healy deployed the Special Forces-led teams of the Special Mission Service Liaison Service to perform as ranger elements for the 22d and 23d ARVN Divisions. *(RVN Info Office)* **Bottom:** Special Forces liaison service teams served as ranger infantry, coordinated B-52 bombing strikes, and spearheaded the South Vietnamese counteroffensive southwest of Pleiku that succeeded in recapturing Duc Co, shown here, from enemy forces. *(DOD)*

Top: Special Forces efforts in Thailand during the Vietnam conflict were concentrated on advising the Royal Thai Army Special Warfare Center, improving the proficiency of Royal Thai Army and police counterinsurgency organizations, preparing Thai military forces scheduled for Vietnam assignments, and conducting special missions in Laos and Cambodia. This Special Forces-led patrol advances through a Thai northeastern border village controlled by the communist insurgents during 1967. *(Army News Features)* **Bottom left:** Thai Special Warfare Center students learn how to use explosive charges under Special Forces supervision at Lopburi. *(Author's Collection)* **Bottom right:** 46th Special Forces Company Capt. Bruce W. Koch briefs students boarding a Thai C-47 during a Jumpmaster Course at Lopburi in August 1967. *(USA)*

Top left: Sgt. First Class Floyd Marshall supervises a Thai commando student learning how to employ the M-18AI claymore mine during a demolitions class at Camp Erawan on January 31, 1968. *(Thomas Larsen/USA)* **Top right:** Special Forces Sgt. Charles Mancebo, a radio operator in Detachment B-410, prepares to parachute with a reconnaissance team of the Thai Communist Suppression Operations Command during counterinsurgency operations near Sakon Nakhon in January 1968. *(USA)* **Center left:** A Detachment B-410 sergeant from the 46th Special Forces Company dispenses radio batteries to Thai troops engaged in a major counterinsurgency sweep through the Phu Phan mountains of northeastern Thailand during November 1967. *(Thomas Larsen/USA)* **Center right:** The underwater operations detachment of the 46th Special Forces Company instructs students in self-contained underwater breathing apparatus during a Scuba course at Camp Vayama on the Gulf of Thailand. *(Phillip Smith/USA)* **Bottom:** Lt. Larry Lincoln of the 46th Special Forces Company engages in crossbow target practice at Ban Kam Perm, Thailand, on November 18, 1967. *(USA)*

Top right: The 46th Special Forces Company performed a wide range of civil-assistance, education, and medical programs throughout Thailand that not only solidified Thai-U.S. relations, but ensured a legacy of goodwill between Special Forces and Thai villagers. *(Author's Collection)* **Center left:** Medicine is prescribed under the supervision of Sgt. Richard Wise during a routine village health check in Thailand. *(USA)* **Bottom left:** Thai wildlife preserved by the 46th Special Forces Company. *(Thomas Gaskin)* **Bottom right:** Teams from the 1st Special Forces Group on Okinawa represented the first Special Forces deployed to Thailand. The 46th Special Forces Company was created from assets of the Group's Company D during April 1967. Later, in a secret wartime redesignation, the company became the 3d Battalion of the 1st Special Forces Group. *(Donald Valentine)*

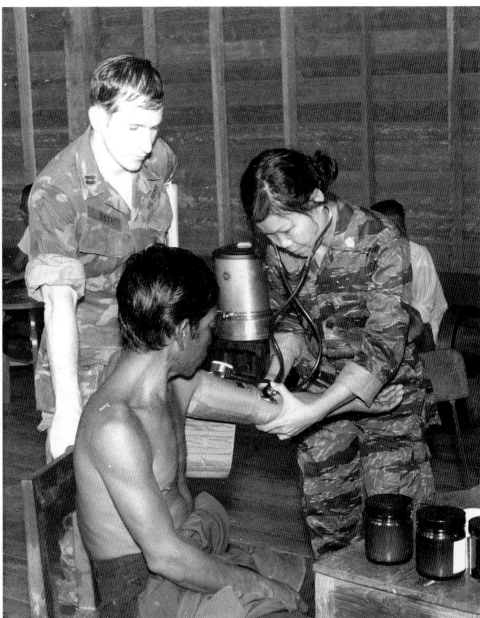

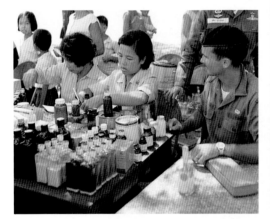

Top left: Another important facet of 46th Special Forces Company operations involved the training, preparation, and advising of Thai expeditionary forces sent to Vietnam from March 1967 through March 1972. These infantrymen from the Royal Thai Volunteer Force ''Queen's Cobras'' learn helicopter assault techniques from Special Forces instructors at Nong Takoo, Thailand. *(Thomas Larsen/USA)* **Top right:** Thai infantrymen at Chonburi learn to use the M-79 grenade launcher during Project Folder Mark training for regiments of the Thai Black Panther Expeditionary Division scheduled for Vietnam duty. *(Author's Collection)* **Center left:** A combat patrol of the Thai Expeditionary Division conducts a sweep along a jungle trail near Bear Cat, east of Saigon, during 1969. Several 46th Special Forces Company advisors accompanied these forces onto Vietnam battlefields during the war. *(DOD)* **Center right:** 46th Special Forces Company Lt. Col Kollat reenlists Sgt. Fender on the famous Bridge over the River Kwae at Kanchanaburi, Thailand, on July 15, 1967. The personnel are part of Task Force Slick engaged in training the Queen's Cobras that would deploy to Vietnam that September. *(John Borgman)* **Bottom:** Vehicular machine gun skills being taught to Thai armored cavalrymen by Detachment B-430 at Saraburi, Thailand. *(Author's Collection)*

Top: Some Special Forces advisors were temporarily attached to Project 404 "Army Attache Augmentation," a clandestine umbrella organization for Laotian activities. This joint U.S.-Thai commando patrol rehearses prior to reconnoitering enemy-held areas of Laos late in the war. *(Author's Collection)*
Center: The SR (Special Requirements) Project fielded Thai artillery inside Laos, often with Special Forces advisory support. This view shows the SR Project headquarters at Moung Sai, Laos, during April 1968. *(Author's Collection)* **Bottom left:** Special Forces continued to assist Deputy Chief, Joint U.S. Military Advisory Group, Thailand, in secretly aiding the Royal Laotian government armed forces (including neutralists and paramilitary units), but the Laotian war remained a frustrating seesaw-like struggle. This Lao battalion—being regrouped under Special Forces supervision at Pranburi, Thailand, during early 1966—helped to recapture the strategic Nam Bac valley on August 7, only to be decimated in the February 1968 loss at the same locality. *(Author's Collection)* **Bottom right:** This Special Forces-advised 75mm mountain pack howitzer crew, posted near Attopeu on the southern Laotian front, used roofing material as both "native house" camouflage and partial screening against torrential monsoon storms. *(Author's Collection)*

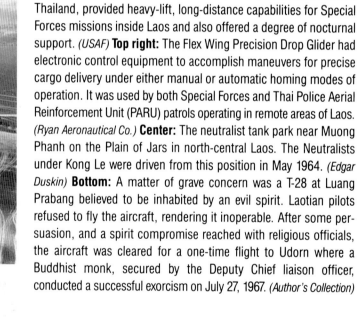

Top left: Late in the war, Air Force Sikorsky HH-53 rescue and recovery helicopters stationed at Udorn and Nakhon Phanom, Thailand, provided heavy-lift, long-distance capabilities for Special Forces missions inside Laos and also offered a degree of nocturnal support. *(USAF)* **Top right:** The Flex Wing Precision Drop Glider had electronic control equipment to accomplish maneuvers for precise cargo delivery under either manual or automatic homing modes of operation. It was used by both Special Forces and Thai Police Aerial Reinforcement Unit (PARU) patrols operating in remote areas of Laos. *(Ryan Aeronautical Co.)* **Center:** The neutralist tank park near Muong Phanh on the Plain of Jars in north-central Laos. The Neutralists under Kong Le were driven from this position in May 1964. *(Edgar Duskin)* **Bottom:** A matter of grave concern was a T-28 at Luang Prabang believed to be inhabited by an evil spirit. Laotian pilots refused to fly the aircraft, rendering it inoperable. After some persuasion, and a spirit compromise reached with religious officials, the aircraft was cleared for a one-time flight to Udorn where a Buddhist monk, secured by the Deputy Chief liaison officer, conducted a successful exorcism on July 27, 1967. *(Author's Collection)*

Top left: Special Forces deployed Detachment B-36 with the Cambodian contingents of the 3d Mobile Strike Force Command into Cambodia during the May 1970 invasion. As a result of the success of this initial component, which remained in Cambodia to form the Palace Guard for the new government, MACV directed Special Forces to create the U.S. Army Vietnam Individual Training Group (UITG) to train battalions of the Republique Khmer at bases in South Vietnam. This company of Cambodian soldiers, among the earliest arrivals from their country at South Vietnam's Lam Son Training Center, marches from the firing range to a classroom area. *(RVN Photo Service)* **Top right:** Long Hai was the headquarters of Detachment B-36 and became the primary training center of the UITG effort in January 1971, when the Special Forces was directed to train 30 additional Cambodian battalions. *(Author's Collection)* **Center:** The expansion of the UITG program added new training bases, such as Phuoc Tuy, shown here, created in September 1971 to accommodate more Cambodian training cycles. *(Author's Collection)* **Bottom:** The Special Forces team that trained the Cambodian Marine Fusilier Battalion poses at Long Hai in August 1972. When the Cambodian training operations were completed in late February 1973, a total of 85 battalions had been prepared for battlefield employment by Special Forces instructors. *(Jeff Russell)*

Top: The U.S. Army Vietnam Individual Training Group (UITG) was redesignated as the *Forces Armée Nationale Khmer* (FANK) Training Command in May 1972. Chi Lang Training Center, shown here, was the most difficult base because of its proximity to North Vietnamese ground attacks. *(Author's Collection)* **Center:** Chi Lang National Training Center on November 2, 1971, showing the reinforced bunker at right. *(Author's Collection)* **Bottom left:** Chi Lang National Training Center headquarters, reinforced by sandbag and sand-filled barrel protection against rocket and mortar shelling. *(Author's Collection)* **Bottom right:** Special Forces FANK Command trained Cambodian soldiers, many of whom arrived at training centers without any gear prior to receiving their weapons, in tactics ranging from the squad to the combined-battalion level. The same program also had responsibility for retraining several South Vietnamese formations. *(Jeff Russell)*

Top: Thai and U.S. Special Forces were responsible for training many Cambodian units in Thailand during the final stages of the conflict. Here, Lt. Col George Marecek, commander of the 3d Battalion, 1st Special Forces Group (given the cover designation of U.S. Army Special Forces, Thailand), arrives at the Phnom Penh airport to inspect Khmer battlefront positions during February 1974. *(George Marecek)* **Center left and center right:** The Military Equipment Delivery Team, Cambodia, was created on January 30, 1971, to supervise military deliveries to Khmer field units and was relocated to Phnom Penh in October. This view shows ammunition being delivered by Special Forces personnel in defense of the Cambodian capital area. *(George Marecek)* **Bottom:** These Cambodian rangers received Special Forces training on the 106mm recoilless rifle at Lopburi, Thailand, in early 1974. *(George Marecek)*

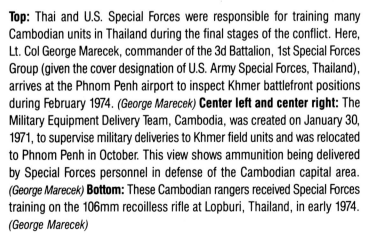

Top: Special Forces advisors who supported Khmer field units faced extremely hazardous duty, including the parachuting of ammunition into besieged forts and stabilizing front lines with whatever materiel they could deliver. Capt. Kenneth Bowra, a Special Forces advisor with the U.S. Military Equipment Delivery Team, Cambodia (MEDTC), is stationed along the front line in Cambodia. *(Kenneth Bowra)* **Center:** A Khmer M-113 armored personnel carrier on the Bassac River front, east of Phnom Penh, in February 1974. These Cambodian troops received training in Lopburi, Thailand, by U.S. and Thai Special Forces. *(George Marecek)* **Bottom:** The Bassac River sector south of Phnom Penh was held by Cambodian forces for months before the Khmer Rouge finally stormed the capital in April 1975. This photograph of enemy positions being hit by 60mm mortar fire directed by Special Forces troops was taken in December 1974 through binoculars lined up with a SOG-issued Pen ''EE'' Olympus camera. *(Kenneth Bowra)*

Top: The end of American involvement in the Second Indochina War was marked by the final troop withdrawals and the release of 590 U.S. prisoners held by the North Vietnamese during March 1973. From left, Sgt. First Class Carroll E. Flora and Staff Sgt. Nathan Henry are released at Hanoi's Gia Lam airport to waiting C-141 transport aircraft. *(Larry Wright/USA)* **Bottom:** The disengagement of U.S. forces from eastern Asia included the withdrawal of the 1st Special Forces Group from Okinawa in May 1974, ending all permanent Special Forces presence in that region. This final review of the group before disbandment was held on Okinawa, although the actual inactivation ceremony was conducted by a color guard at Fort Bragg at the end of June 1974. *(Author's Collection)*

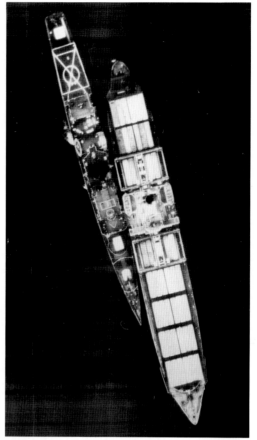

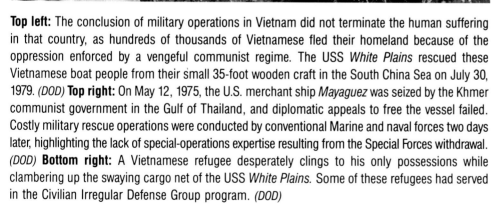

Top left: The conclusion of military operations in Vietnam did not terminate the human suffering in that country, as hundreds of thousands of Vietnamese fled their homeland because of the oppression enforced by a vengeful communist regime. The USS *White Plains* rescued these Vietnamese boat people from their small 35-foot wooden craft in the South China Sea on July 30, 1979. *(DOD)* **Top right:** On May 12, 1975, the U.S. merchant ship *Mayaguez* was seized by the Khmer communist government in the Gulf of Thailand, and diplomatic appeals to free the vessel failed. Costly military rescue operations were conducted by conventional Marine and naval forces two days later, highlighting the lack of special-operations expertise resulting from the Special Forces withdrawal. *(DOD)* **Bottom right:** A Vietnamese refugee desperately clings to his only possessions while clambering up the swaying cargo net of the USS *White Plains.* Some of these refugees had served in the Civilian Irregular Defense Group program. *(DOD)*

Top left and top right: Sgt.-Maj. Joe Lopez left Vietnam in November 1970 after being wounded by North Vietnamese troops during the battle of Camp Dak Seang on the Cambodian border. Among the many comrades he was forced to leave behind was Huang Le, his interpreter and bodyguard. They were finally reunited after Huang Le, imprisoned for almost five years after the war, escaped in a small fishing boat to the Philippines and reached the United States in 1980. Combat Special Forces veteran Lopez commented, ''I thought at last he's here, at last he's safe. We've gone from one extreme to another—from hell, fire fights in Vietnam to this, our life here in Arlington, which is really a bed of roses.'' *(James Bland/The Shorthorn)* **Bottom left:** ''Too Many Wars''—these Vietnamese children salute Special Forces using both French and American styles. *(Roger Pierson)* **Bottom right:** The last Special Forces Medal of Honor recipient of the Vietnam conflict was Roy P. Benavidez, shown being decorated by President Ronald Reagan in the Pentagon courtyard on February 24, 1981. He earned the medal as a staff sergeant for his gallantry on a helicopter evacuation mission that rescued several isolated patrol members trapped in heavy combat near Loc Ninh on May 2, 1968. *(DOD)*

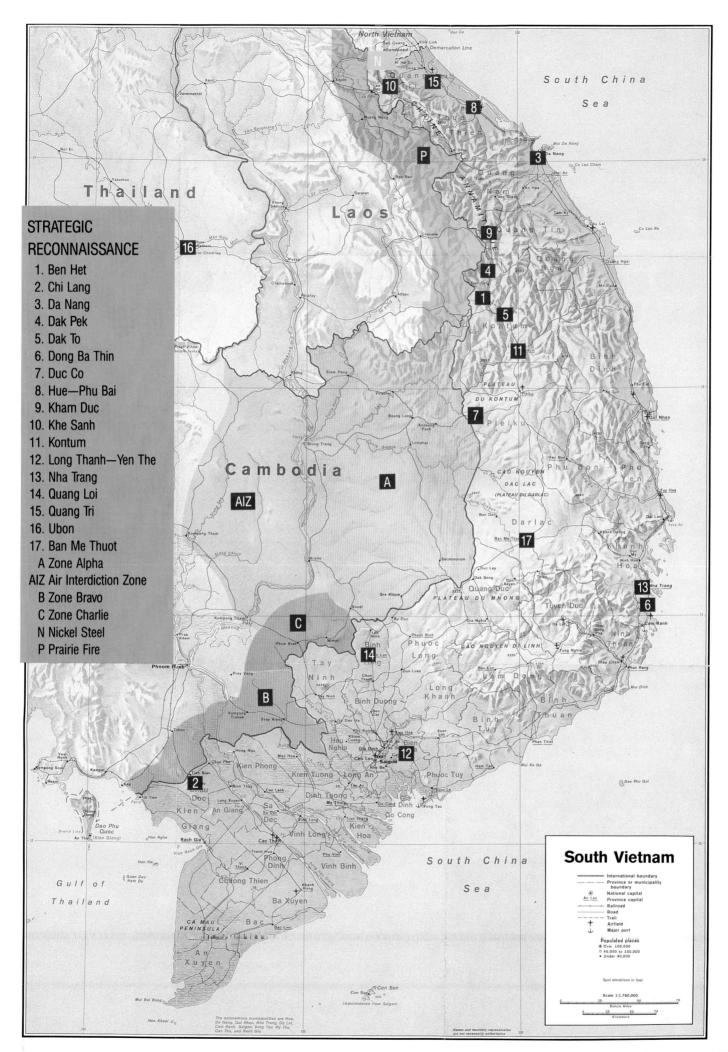

STRATEGIC
RECONNAISSANCE

1. Ben Het
2. Chi Lang
3. Da Nang
4. Dak Pek
5. Dak To
6. Dong Ba Thin
7. Duc Co
8. Hue—Phu Bai
9. Kham Duc
10. Khe Sanh
11. Kontum
12. Long Thanh—Yen The
13. Nha Trang
14. Quang Loi
15. Quang Tri
16. Ubon
17. Ban Me Thuot
A Zone Alpha
AIZ Air Interdiction Zone
B Zone Bravo
C Zone Charlie
N Nickel Steel
P Prairie Fire

South Vietnam

International boundary
Province or municipality boundary
National capital
An Loc Province capital
Railroad
Road
Trail
Airfield
Major port

Populated places
Over 100,000
40,000 to 100,000
Under 40,000

Spot elevations in feet

Scale 1:1,760,000

Statute Miles

Kilometers

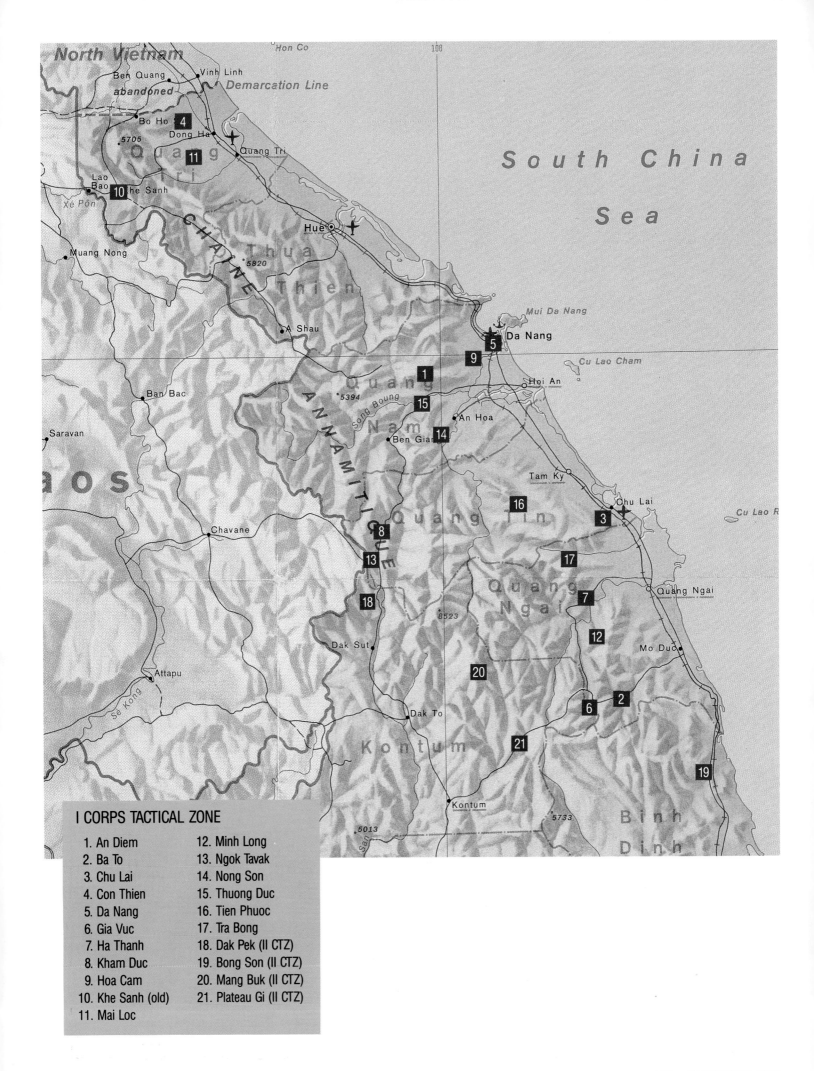

I CORPS TACTICAL ZONE

1. An Diem
2. Ba To
3. Chu Lai
4. Con Thien
5. Da Nang
6. Gia Vuc
7. Ha Thanh
8. Kham Duc
9. Hoa Cam
10. Khe Sanh (old)
11. Mai Loc
12. Minh Long
13. Ngok Tavak
14. Nong Son
15. Thuong Duc
16. Tien Phuoc
17. Tra Bong
18. Dak Pek (II CTZ)
19. Bong Son (II CTZ)
20. Mang Buk (II CTZ)
21. Plateau Gi (II CTZ)

MAP—I CORPS TACTICAL ZONE

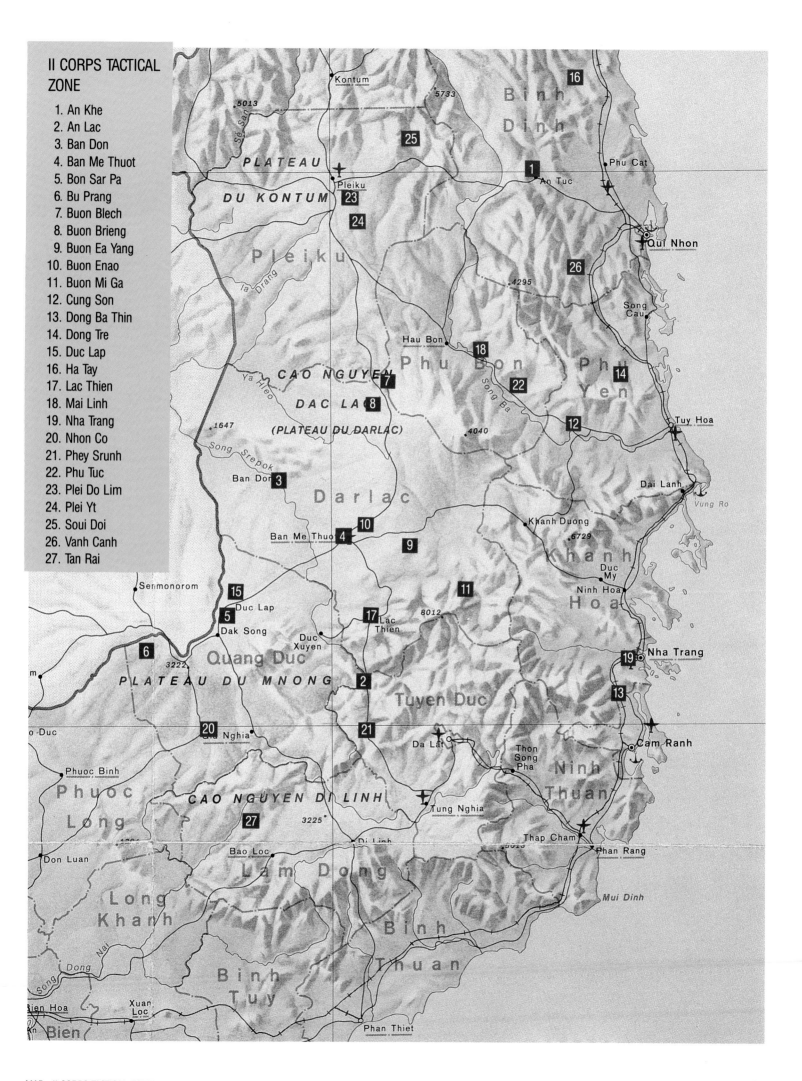

II CORPS TACTICAL ZONE

1. An Khe
2. An Lac
3. Ban Don
4. Ban Me Thuot
5. Bon Sar Pa
6. Bu Prang
7. Buon Blech
8. Buon Brieng
9. Buon Ea Yang
10. Buon Enao
11. Buon Mi Ga
12. Cung Son
13. Dong Ba Thin
14. Dong Tre
15. Duc Lap
16. Ha Tay
17. Lac Thien
18. Mai Linh
19. Nha Trang
20. Nhon Co
21. Phey Srunh
22. Phu Tuc
23. Plei Do Lim
24. Plei Yt
25. Soui Doi
26. Vanh Canh
27. Tan Rai

MAP—II CORPS TACTICAL ZONE

363

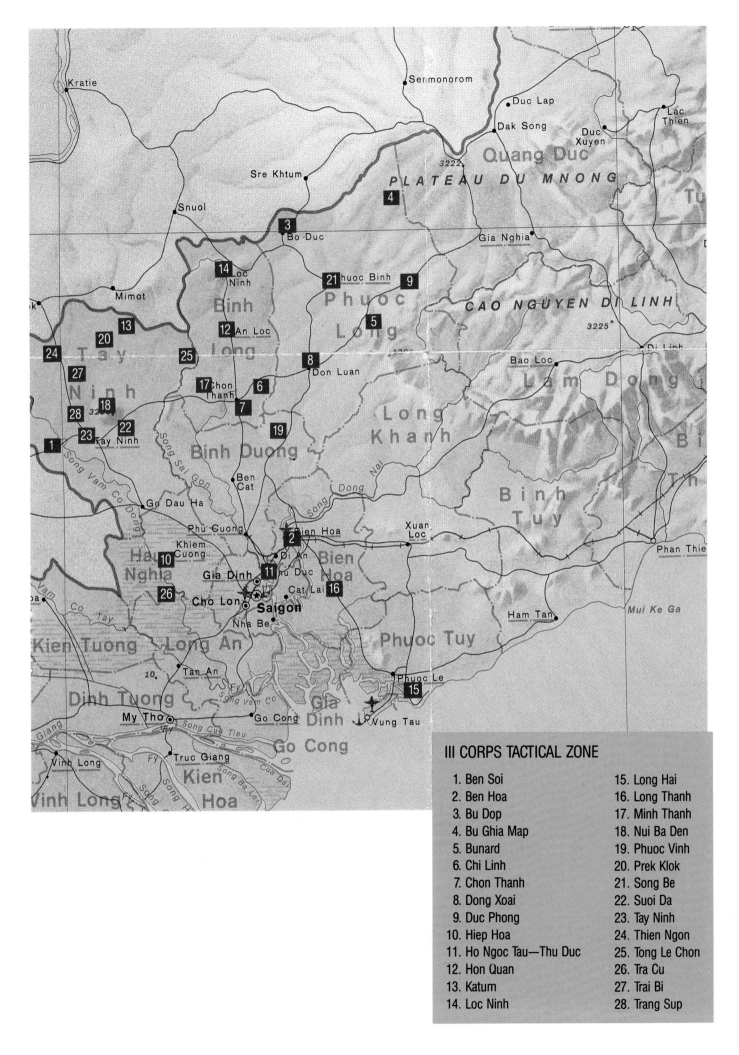

III CORPS TACTICAL ZONE

1. Ben Soi
2. Ben Hoa
3. Bu Dop
4. Bu Ghia Map
5. Bunard
6. Chi Linh
7. Chon Thanh
8. Dong Xoai
9. Duc Phong
10. Hiep Hoa
11. Ho Ngoc Tau—Thu Duc
12. Hon Quan
13. Katum
14. Loc Ninh
15. Long Hai
16. Long Thanh
17. Minh Thanh
18. Nui Ba Den
19. Phuoc Vinh
20. Prek Klok
21. Song Be
22. Suoi Da
23. Tay Ninh
24. Thien Ngon
25. Tong Le Chon
26. Tra Cu
27. Trai Bi
28. Trang Sup

MAP—III CORPS TACTICAL ZONE

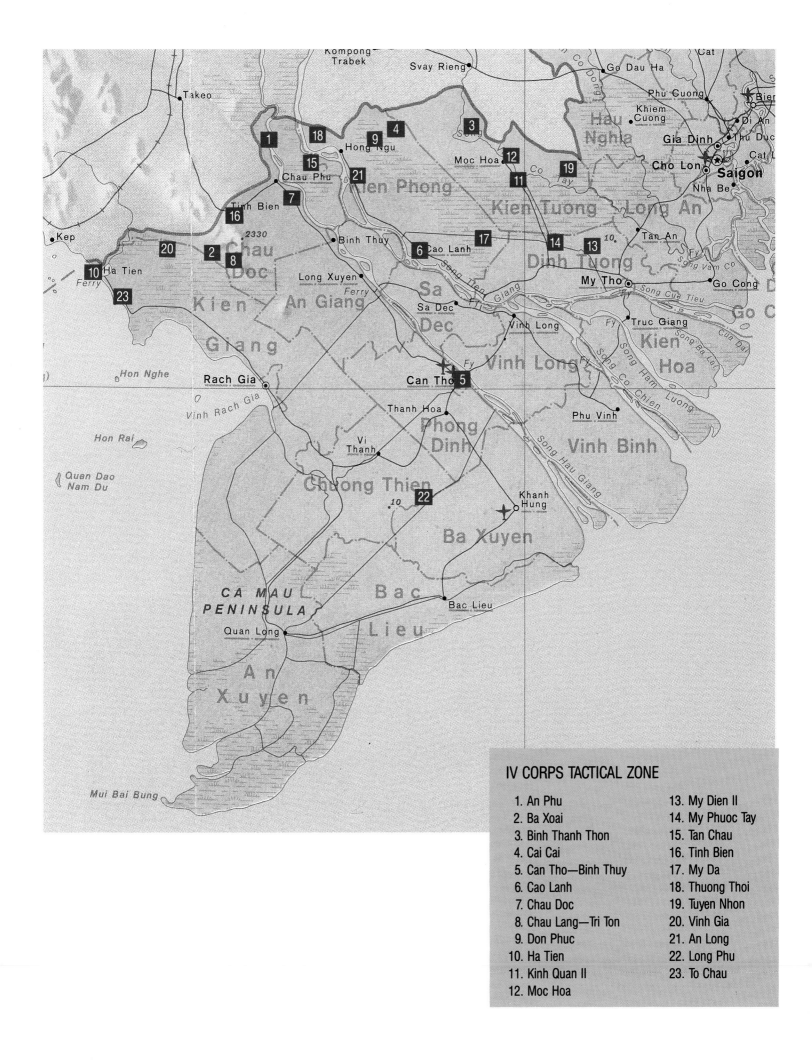

IV CORPS TACTICAL ZONE

1. An Phu	13. My Dien II
2. Ba Xoai	14. My Phuoc Tay
3. Binh Thanh Thon	15. Tan Chau
4. Cai Cai	16. Tinh Bien
5. Can Tho—Binh Thuy	17. My Da
6. Cao Lanh	18. Thuong Thoi
7. Chau Doc	19. Tuyen Nhon
8. Chau Lang—Tri Ton	20. Vinh Gia
9. Don Phuc	21. An Long
10. Ha Tien	22. Long Phu
11. Kinh Quan II	23. To Chau
12. Moc Hoa	

MAP—IV CORPS TACTICAL ZONE

365

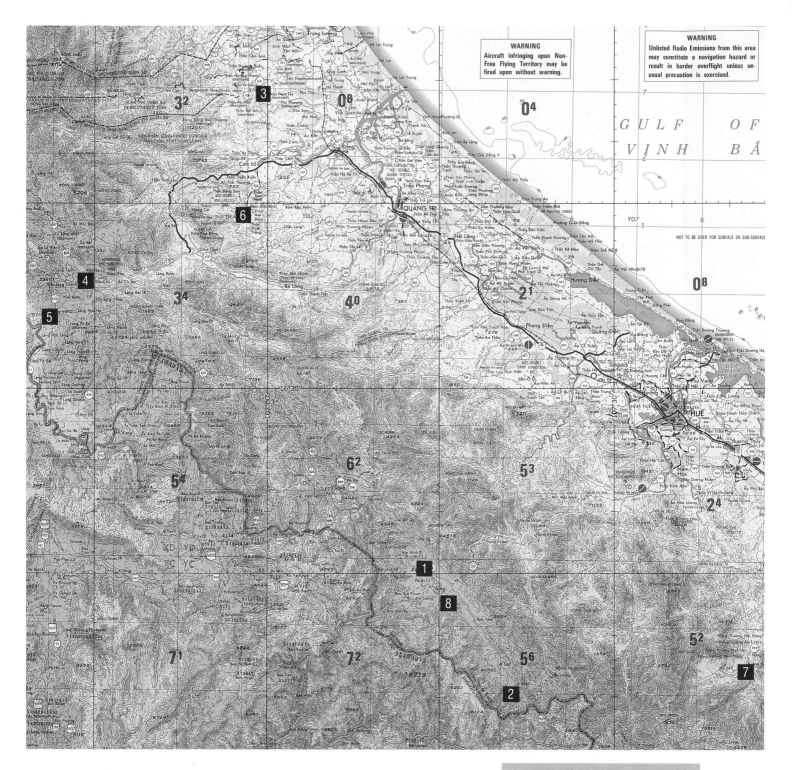

WARNING
Aircraft infringing upon Non-
Free Flying Territory may be
fired upon without warning.

WARNING
Unlisted Radio Emissions from this area
may constitute a navigation hazard or
result in border overflight unless unusual precaution is exercised.

GULF   OF
VINH   BĂ

NOT TO BE USED FOR SURFACE OR SUB-SURFACE

NORTHERN SOUTH VIETNAM

1. A Luoi
2. A Shau
3. Con Thien
4. Khe Sanh
5. Lang Vei
6. Mai Loc
7. Nam Dong
8. Ta Bat

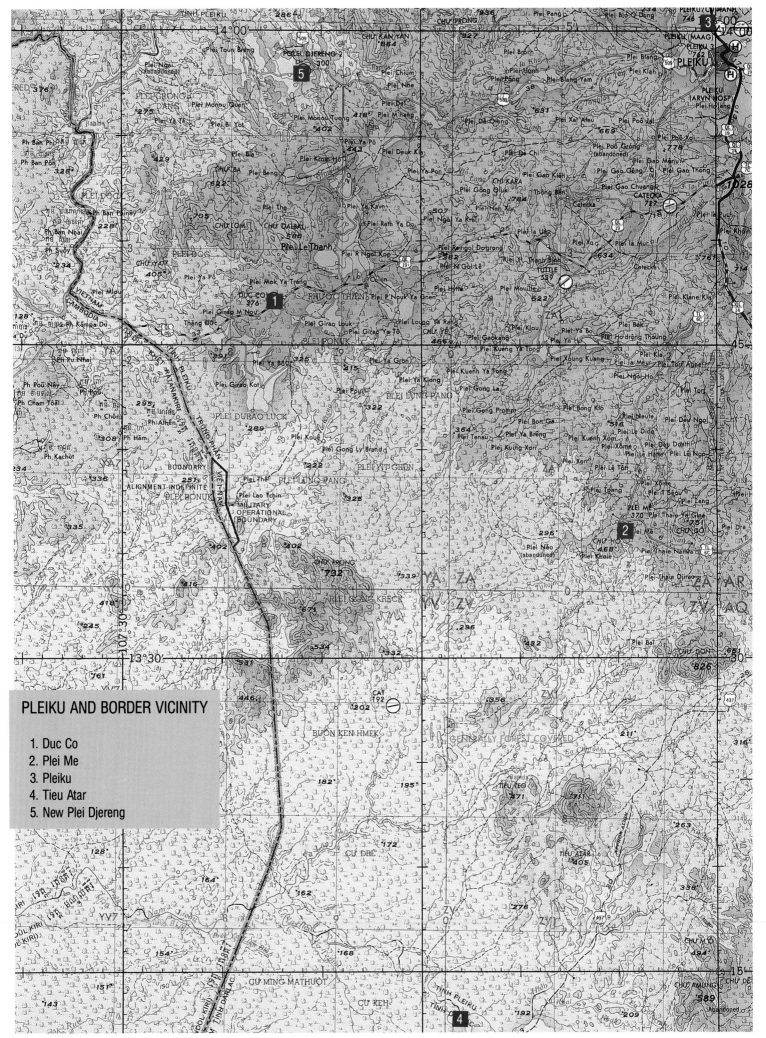

PLEIKU AND BORDER VICINITY

1. Duc Co
2. Plei Me
3. Pleiku
4. Tieu Atar
5. New Plei Djereng

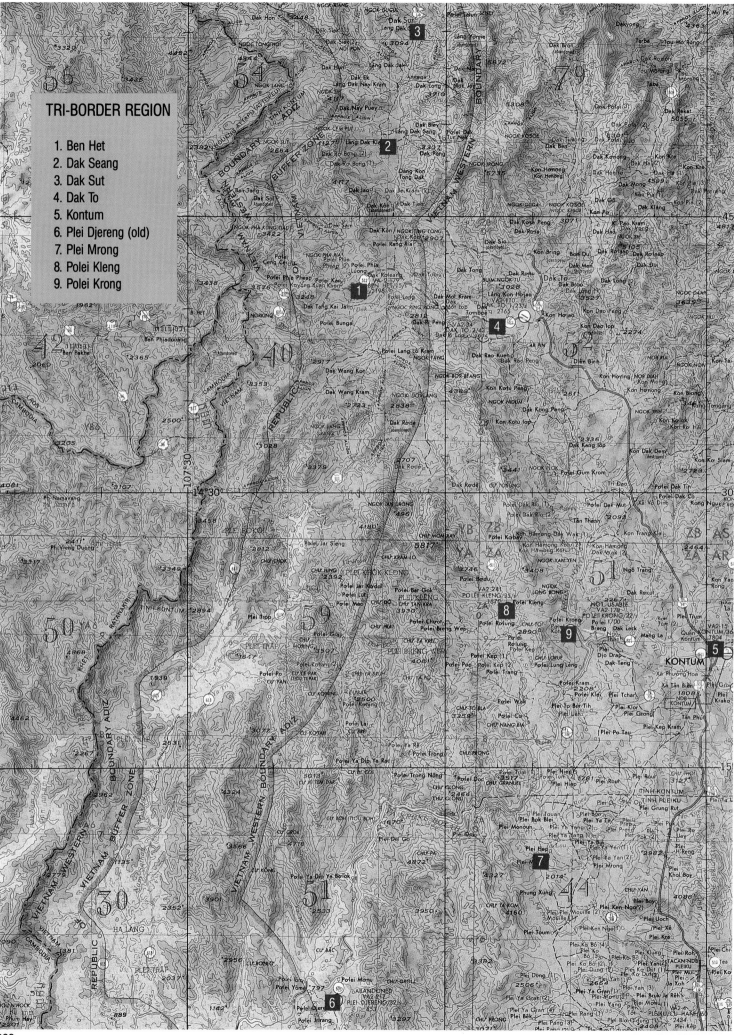

TRI-BORDER REGION

1. Ben Het
2. Dak Seang
3. Dak Sut
4. Dak To
5. Kontum
6. Plei Djereng (old)
7. Plei Mrong
8. Polei Kleng
9. Polei Krong

368

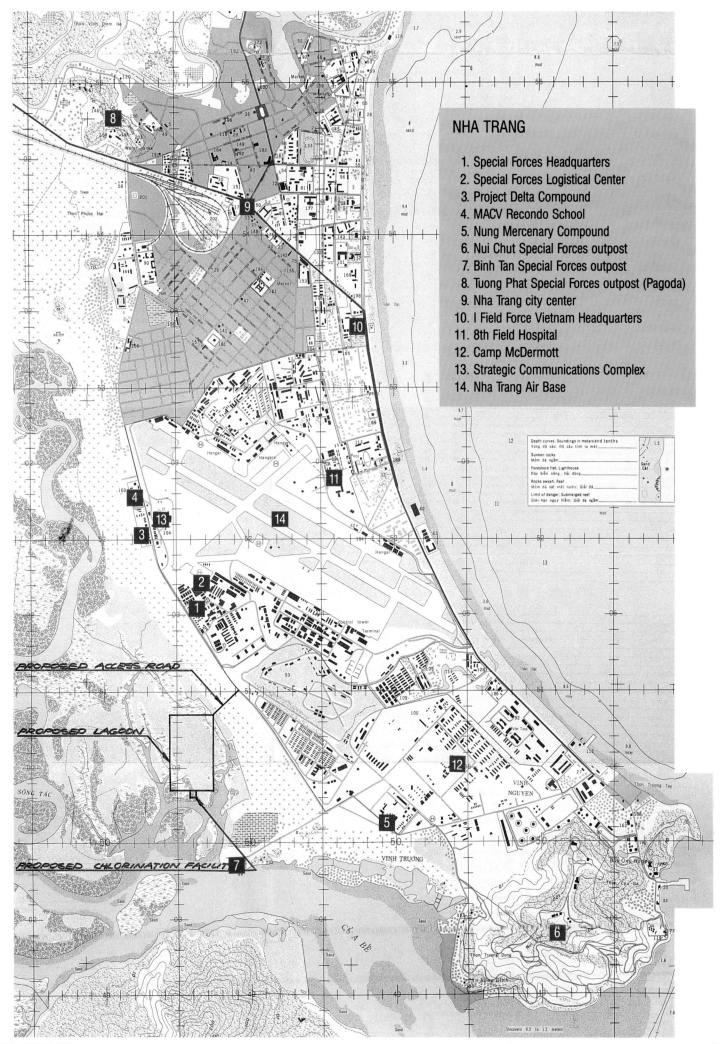

NHA TRANG

1. Special Forces Headquarters
2. Special Forces Logistical Center
3. Project Delta Compound
4. MACV Recondo School
5. Nung Mercenary Compound
6. Nui Chut Special Forces outpost
7. Binh Tan Special Forces outpost
8. Tuong Phat Special Forces outpost (Pagoda)
9. Nha Trang city center
10. I Field Force Vietnam Headquarters
11. 8th Field Hospital
12. Camp McDermott
13. Strategic Communications Complex
14. Nha Trang Air Base

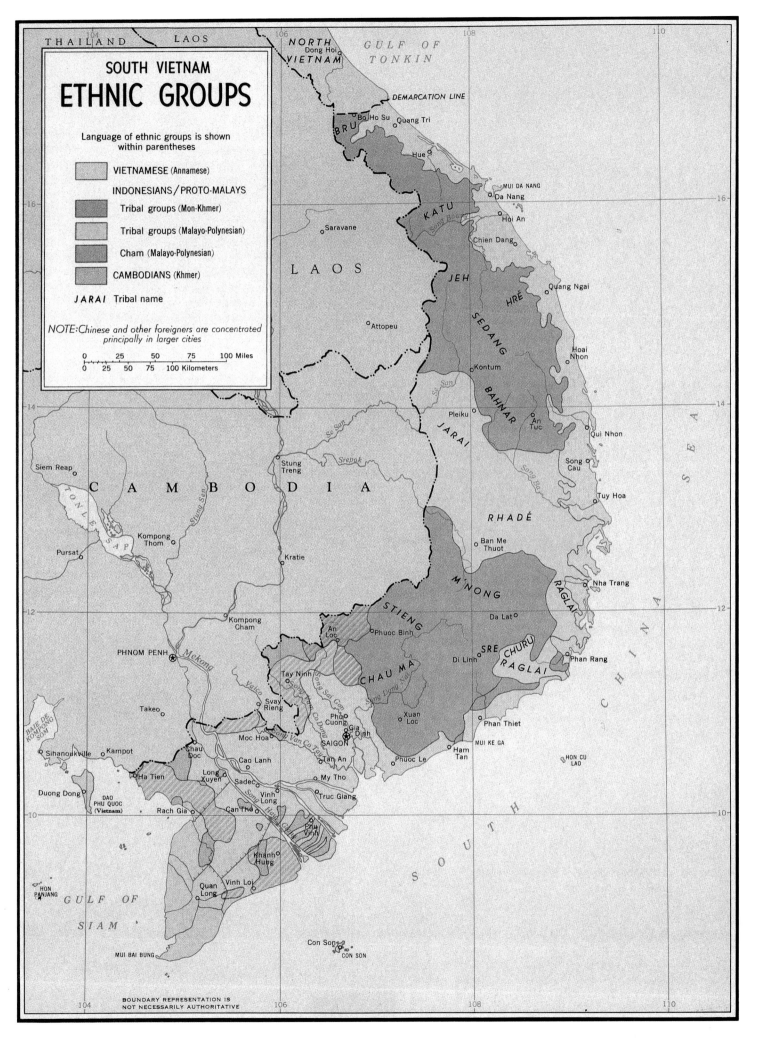

SOUTH VIETNAM
ETHNIC GROUPS

Language of ethnic groups is shown
within parentheses

VIETNAMESE (Annamese)

INDONESIANS/PROTO-MALAYS

Tribal groups (Mon-Khmer)

Tribal groups (Malayo-Polynesian)

Cham (Malayo-Polynesian)

CAMBODIANS (Khmer)

JARAI   Tribal name

NOTE: Chinese and other foreigners are concentrated
principally in larger cities

0   25   50   75   100 Miles
0 25 50 75 100 Kilometers

THAILAND   LAOS

NORTH VIETNAM

Dong Hoi

GULF OF
TONKIN

DEMARCATION LINE

BRU   Bo Ho Su   Quang Tri

Hue

KATU   MUI DA NANG

Da Nang

Hoi An

Song Bung   Chien Dang

JEH

HRÉ   Quang Ngai

SEDANG

Saravane

LAOS

Attopeu

Hoai
Nhon

Kontum

BAHNAR

Se San   Pleiku   An
Tuc

Qui Nhon

JARAI   Song Ba   Song
Cau

Se San

Stung
Treng   Srepok

Tuy Hoa

Siem Reap

CAMBODIA

RHADÉ

Kompong
Thom

Ban Me
Thuot

Pursat

Kratie

M'NONG   RAGLAI   Nha Trang

Kompong
Cham

Da Lat

STIENG

An
Loc   Phuoc Binh   SRE   CHURU

PHNOM PENH   Mekong   Di Linh   RAGLAI

Tay Ninh   CHAU MA   Phan Rang

Song Dong Nai

Takeo   Svay
Rieng   Song Sai Gon   Xuan
Loc

Phu
Cuong   Gia
Dinh   Phan Thiet

Moc Hoa   SAIGON   MUI KE GA

Kampot   Chau
Doc   Tan An   Ham
Tan   HON CU
LAO

Sihanoukville   Cao Lanh   Phuoc Le

Ha Tien   Long
Xuyen   My Tho

Sadec   Vinh
Long   Truc Giang

Duong Dong   DAO
PHU QUOC
(Vietnam)   Rach Gia   Can Tho

Phu
Vinh

Khanh
Hung

Quan
Long   Vinh Loi

HON
PANJANG

GULF OF

SIAM

MUI BAI BUNG

Con Son

CON SON

SOUTH

CHINA

SEA

BAIE DE
KOMPONG
SOM

TONLE SAP

BOUNDARY REPRESENTATION IS
NOT NECESSARILY AUTHORITATIVE

MAP—MAJOR ETHNIC GROUPS OF SOUTH VIETNAM

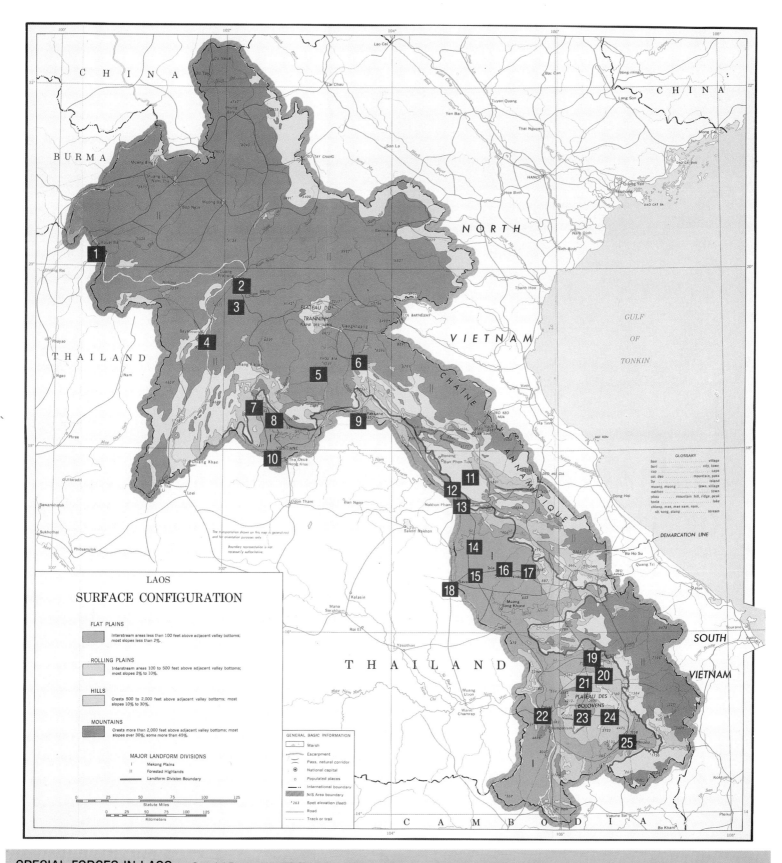

SPECIAL FORCES IN LAOS Special Forces WHITE STAR Program Unit Positions upon Declaration of Laotian Neutrality, 23 July 1962

1. FTT 2 Ban Houei Sai
2. DET-BB; FTT 10, 24; ATT 1 Luang Prabang
3. FTT 22, 23 Kiou Cha Cham
4. FTT 1, 39 Sayaboury
5. FTT 3, 14, 19, 33, 40, 41 Site 20
6. FTT 9 Ban Man
7. FTT 30; ATT 4 Phonghong
8. FTT 47 Ban Keun
9. FTT 8, 11, 37; ATT 5 Paksane

10. WSMTT Team Control; FTT 36 Vientiane vicinity
11. FTT 46 Relocating on front
12. FTT 5 Relocating on front
13. FTT 20 Thakhek
14. FTT 13, 15 Xieng Sone
15. FTT 21, 27, 28, 43 Seno
16. FTT 7, 38 Dong Hene
17. FTT 26; ATT 3 Muong Phalane
18. DET-BC; ATT 6 Savannakhet

19. FTT 4, 6, 12, 17, 31, 44 Saravane
20. FTT 25 Relocating on front
21. FTT 16 Ban Thateng
22. DET-DD, ATT 2, Prov FTT 2 Pakse/Moung Kau
23. FTT 29, 34, 35, 45 Pak Song
24. FTT 18, 42 Ban Houei Kong
25. FTT 32 Attopeu

NOI GƯƠNG TRẦN HƯNG-ĐẠO

TOÀN DÂN ĐOÀN KẾT
CHỐNG CỘNG CỨU NƯỚC

8-926 (4)

MỪNG NĂM MỚI - MỪNG HÒA BÌNH

DÂN TỘC
DÂN HÒA
DÂN TIẾN

THÁNG HAI 1969
NĂM MẬU THÂN - KỶ DẬU

Special Forces psychological operations in Vietnam concentrated on three primary themes: appeal to Vietnamese patriotic sentiment, familial bonding, and communal pride. **Top left**: Vietnamese patriotic appeal poster, printed in July 1968, of General Tran Hung Dao, who defeated three Mongol invasions of Kublai Khan in the thirteenth century. (*Author's Collection*) **Top right**: Vietnamese February 1969 calender poster, printed in December 1968, focused on wife and children awaiting the return of their loved ones. (*Author's Collection*) **Bottom**: Communal poster entitled "How to Build a New Spirit," printed in July 1968, depicted Vietnamese Special Forces defending, improving, and safeguarding democratic practices in a rural village. (*Author's Collection*)

MỘT MỤC TIÊU CỦA ẤP ĐỜI MỚI LÀ:
XÂY DỰNG MỘT TINH THẦN MỚI

TOÀN-DÂN THAM-GIA BẦU-CỬ

ĐOÀN KẾT ĐỂ TẠO SỨC MẠNH CỘNG ĐỒNG, CỞI MỞ ĐỂ THÔNG CẢM, ĐỀ CAO NHÂN NGHĨA LỄ TRÍ TÍN, PHÁT HUY VĂN HÓA DÂN TỘC ĐỂ BẢO VỆ TINH HOA GIỐNG NÒI, HỌC HỎI ĐỂ TẠO TIẾN BỘ VỀ KHOA HỌC VÀ Ý THỨC TRÁCH NHIỆM ĐỂ XỬ DỤNG XỨNG ĐÁNG QUYỀN CÔNG DÂN.

SELECTED READINGS

Berry, John S. *Those Gallant Men*. Novato, CA: Presidio, 1984.
Account of the 5th SFG double-agent murder case.

Bows, Ray A. *Vietnam Military Lore, 1959-1973*. Hanover, MA:
Bows & Sons Publishing, 1988. Includes several accounts of
individual Special Forces heroism.

Clarke, Jeffrey J. *Advice and Support: The Final Years, 1965-1973*.
Washington: Army Center of Military History, 1988. A solid
Special Forces summary is part of this very strong history.

Donahue, James C. *No Greater Love*. Canton, OH: Daring
Books, 1988. Campaign memoir of the Mobile Guerrilla Force
in Vietnam.

Kelly, Col. Francis J. *U.S. Army Special Forces, 1961-1971*.
Washington: Dept. of the Army, 1973. Official Army study.

Morris, Jim. *War Story*. New York: Dell, 1979. Notable recol-
lection of a Special Forces officer in Vietnam.

Rottman, Gordon L. *U.S. Army Special Forces, 1952-84*.
London: Osprey. Well-researched uniform reference.

Sherman, Stephen. *The Green Beret Magazine*. Vols. I-V
(1966-1970). Houston, TX: Radix Associates (2314 Cheshire
Lane). Fine-quality reprints of *The Green Beret Magazine*,
orginally published by the 5th Special Forces Group Information Office.

Simpson, Col. Charles M. *Inside the Green Berets*. Novato,
CA: Presidio, 1983. Special Forces officer memoir.

Stanton, Shelby L. *Green Berets at War: U.S. Army Special
Forces in Southeast Asia, 1956-1975*. Novato, CA: Presidio,
1985. Narrative history of Special Forces wartime activities.

Stanton, Shelby L. *Vietnam Order of Battle*. Millwood, NY:
Kraus Reprints, 1986. Detailed overview of Special Forces and
Army organization in Vietnam.

INDEX

(*NOTE:* For special catagories, check under Special Forces heading below.)

EXPLANATORY NOTES

Maps: The map section divides Vietnam into geographical areas. To avoid duplication, the Corps Tactical Zone maps do not include Special Forces camps that appear on maps detailing certain sectors within the zones. Additionally, the maps are specifically tailored to illustrate camps mentioned in the text and do not show all Special Forces camps existing in Vietnam.

Narrative: Readers desiring more information on events in this book are encouraged to consult the author's narrative history, *Green Berets at War,* for further background, campaign data, and battlefield details of the Special Forces in Vietnam.

In special tribute to Col. Charles William Norton Jr., who spent 37 years in widespread conventional and special-warfare assignments that included World War II, Korea, and Vietnam service. His career progression—from private through master sergeant to colonel—encompassed 23 years spent on active Special Forces duty, including command of the 7th Special Forces Group. His dedication to the active and veteran Special Forces community provides an outstanding example of professional military leadership.

ACKNOWLEDGMENTS

Foremost appreciation is expressed to the late Col. George C. Morton and his family, who rendered immense support to this project and made it possible. I thank my publisher, Ross Howell, and the excellent Howell Press staff, especially book designer Marilyn F. Appleby and editor Kathleen D. Valenzi, for their hard work and dedicated professionalism in making this book a reality.

My deepest appreciation also extends to the capable review and staff assistance provided by the U.S. Army Office of the Chief of Military History; U.S. Army Military History Institute; Office of the Secretary of Defense Historical Branch; Suitland Reference Branch of the National Archives; Department of Defense Public Affairs Office; Defense Audio-Visual Agency; U.S. Army John F. Kennedy Special Warfare Center; U.S. Army Command and General Staff College; and the 1st Special Operations Command Public Information Office.

A special debt of gratitude is given for the wisdom and knowledgeable assistance of Ms. Roxanne Merrit at the John F. Kennedy Special Warfare Museum, Fort Bragg, North Carolina. Robert A. Buerlein of the American Historical Foundation provided valuable pictures of Special Forces combat knives. Adam Dintenfass and Ray Bows shared rare photographs from their Special Forces collections. Many other people also helped the book, including Linda O'Neil of the JFK Center; Christopher Funk on behalf of George Funk; Gail Hosking Gilberg on behalf of Charles E. Hosking Jr.; Eleanor Bott Gregory on behalf of Russell P. Bott; and John J. King on behalf of Paul C. King Jr.

The following Special Forces and military veterans kindly offered expertise and personal photographs from their own participation in the Vietnam conflict: Jack Abraham; U.S. Adolph; Robert Albracht; William Albracht; Allen L. Baker; Kenneth K. Barclay; Bill Beasley; Robert J. Bechtoldt; Mark Berent; Gen. Donald D. Blackburn; John D. Blair IV; Stephen C. Boone; John E. Borgman; Ken Bowra; Ray Bows; Richard Boylan; Donald E. Bradshaw; Bill Brooks; Isaac Camacho; Paul F. Campbell; Allen B. Clark Jr.; Gary B. Clark; Lee Clayman; John R. Colby; William P. Couse; Larry Cox; William T. Craig; Scott Crerar; Charles B. Darnell; Jimmy Dean; Troy Dillinder; John Dixon; James C. Donahue; Louis T. Dorogi; Michael D. Eiland; John F. Erskine; William Ewald; Fred Fiedler; Sully H. Fontaine; Gerald W. Foy; Dr. Thomas A. Gaskin; Robert J. Graham; Donald A. Greene; Carl A. Hargus; Ray Harris; Gen. Michael D. Healy; Stephen C. Hembree; Jack G. Henderson; Robert L. Henderson; Homer C. House; Robert H. Huckabee; Charlie M. Inot; Ernest A. Jensen; Jeffrey L. Junkins; Francis J. Kelly; John P. Kendra; John W. Korsbeck; John W. Kruse; Howard R. Linscott; Joe Lopez; William T. Lueders; Richard A. Manson; Richard A. McDonald; Lewis Merletti; Jim Morris; J. Stryker Meyer; Ola L. Mize; Tom Myerchin; Charles William Norton Jr.; Will Ovsak; Rod Paschall; James M. Perry; Roger B. Pierson; John Plaster; William L. Posey; Dr. Stephen L. Putthoff; Ken Quackenbush; Seth Robertson; Leo Roppo; Gilbert Rubio Jr.; Jeffrey L. Russell; Clayton S. Scott; Clifford Shelley; David E. Shephered Jr.; Clyde J. Sincere Jr.; Gen. John Singlaub; Dr. Samuel J. Skemp; Lynden R. Steele; Howard Stevens; Joseph Talan; Billy Thompson; Vic Underwood; Rolf W. Utegaard; Donald E. Valentine; Nicholas Walsh; Gary Webb; Scott J. Whitting; Jason T. Woodworth; Alan Woods; Scott Worsham; and Gen. William P. Yarborough.

The author is working on future volumes on the military and would welcome photographs or clarifications from veterans. Please address submissions to Howell Press. All material will be promptly returned, and contributors will receive full credit as desired if their material is used.